e-RESEARCH

e-RESEARCH

Methods, Strategies, and Issues

TERRY ANDERSON
University of Calgary

HEATHER KANUKA
Athabasca University

Boston New York San Francisco
Mexico City Montreal Toronto London Madrid Munich Paris
Hong Kong Singapore Tokyo Cape Town Sydney

Series Editor: *Arnis E. Burvikovs*
Editorial Assistant: *Christine Lyons*
Editorial-Production Administrator: *Joe Sweeney*
Editorial-Production Service: *Colophon*
Composition Buyer: *Linda Cox*
Manufacturing Buyer: *JoAnne Sweeney*
Cover Administrator: *Kristina Mose-Libon*
Text Composition: *Publishers' Design and Production Services, Inc.*

For related titles and support materials, visit our online catalog at www.ablongman.com.

ISBN: 0-205-34382-1

CIP Data on file at the Library of Congress.

Printed in the United States of America

10 9 8 7 6 5 4 3 2 RRD-IN 08 07 06 05 04 03

This book is dedicated to e-researchers everywhere and especially to struggling graduate students with hopes that it provides at least one good idea that will make their task more productive, relevant, and easier. As well, we thank our ever-suffering spouses for their ongoing love, support, and encouragement.

CONTENTS

CHAPTER EIGHT
Focus Groups 102

CHAPTER NINE
Net-Based Consensus Techniques 120

PREFACE

There are two fundamental equalizers in life—the Internet and education.
John Chambers, CEO, Cisco Systems Inc., 1999

E-Research: Methods, Strategies, and Issues is a guide and reference for both experienced and novice researchers. It assumes researchers have an interest in expanding their research skills by using the Internet in one of two ways. First, researchers may wish to study behavior that happens on the Net, such as activity that takes place in online schools or in virtual communities. Second, *e-Research* will be helpful for researchers whose interest and focus is activity that does not take place on the Net, but who wish to use the Net to improve the efficacy of the data collection, literature review, analysis, or dissemination phases of the research process. The increasingly wide variety of activity that can and does take place on the Net, coupled with the migration to and creation of research tools for the Net, creates conditions in which competent professionals and student researchers find the Net an indispensable aid to quality research activity and results.

BOOK ORGANIZATION

We write this text as practicing academic researchers. We have structured the chapters based on a model of academic research that we commonly use with senior undergraduate, masters, or doctoral projects and/or theses. We trust that the model will be familiar to many readers. Chapter 1 begins with an overview of the Internet, its applications and the effect of the Net on the processes and products of academic research. Chapter 2, "What Is the Net?" overviews the Internet as a technology and describes ways to find information on the Net using various tools and search engines effectively and efficiently. Chapter 3, "Designing e-Research," helps researchers define their problems and choose the type of research paradigm they will use to investigate the problem. Chapter 4 addresses the process of conducting a literature review online—finding out what others have discovered about both the problem and the proposed methodology. Ethics and the moral issues related to e-research are the focus of Chapter 5. Since research is ever more commonly undertaken by groups made up of researchers from various locations worldwide, we discuss ways in which the Net can be used to support multidisciplinary and distributed work teams in Chapter 6. Chapters 7 to 12 discuss ways in which qualitative and quantitative research is conducted on the Net and includes interviews, focus groups, consensus techniques, surveys, and content analysis. Research has little impact unless the results are disseminated; as such, Chapter 13 covers ways in which the Net can be used as an efficient means of disseminating research results. Finally, Chapter 14 concludes with a brief peek into the e-crystal ball to glimpse the future of the Net.

E-Research need not be read sequentially; rather, you are invited to proceed directly to the section that most immediately meets your research needs. We hope the book both informs and entertains you, and that it provides a valuable aid as you undertake important research projects. We welcome your comments or suggestions on any components of this text.

We would like to thank the following reviewers: Andrew S. Gibbons, Utah State University; Greg Kearsley; Barba Patton, University of Houston—Victoria; and Thomas C. Reeves, The University of Georgia.

ACCOMPANYING WEB SITE

We have created a supplementary Web site to this test that can be found at www.e-research.ca. On this site you will find chapter summaries and links to the sites, resources, and online papers referenced in the book. You will also find updates and additional links that we discovered after the book went to press. We also provide reviews and suggestions for ways in which the text may be integrated into university and college level courses. Finally, you will find feedback forums for your suggestions, comments, and questions. We hope you will explore this site and provide your suggestions for improving subsequent editions of *e-Research*.

CHAPTER ONE

INTRODUCTION

Our Age of Anxiety is, in great part, the result of trying to do today's jobs with yesterday's tools.
Marshall McLuhan

"The Net changes everything," the famous quote from Oracle Corporation, in a sense both understates and overstates the premise that guides e-research. The birth of the Internet (the Net), the first cost-effective, globally interactive communication medium, opened the door to modes of intercourse, transaction, and data gathering and dissemination that are as profound as any other invention in the history of humankind. The Net creates a new global context in which many fundamental aspects of our social, educational, commercial, and even spiritual existence is challenged, reshaped, and expanded.

This new context which operates at micro levels, impacts the means, applications, and frequency of our communications with family, friends, and coworkers. It also operates at macro levels, facilitating global commerce, restructuring the workplace (including educational systems), and fundamentally shifting political systems. Living in a wired world both allows and forces us to rethink pre-Net conceptions of time, place, access, affordability, interactivity, and decision making. However, as journalist Jeff Bradley (2000) noted, "As a rallying cry, 'the Net changes everything' conveys all of the potential promise and peril of entering uncharted territory. But, as an operating philosophy, it leaves much to be desired."

E-Research is both a conceptual guide to the creation of an "operating philosophy" for research using the Net and a practical guide for educational researchers. Making the most effective use of the Net challenges researchers to develop and practice their knowledge of research philosophy, ethics, and basic methodologies. Philosophically, the Net-enhanced researcher acquires an attitude of curiosity, a critical but accepting attitude towards technological tools, and a willingness to look at the world through new technological and communication lenses. The e-researcher realizes that a Net-based focus provides a new frame through which to study the world and the creatures that live in it. E-research does not preclude nor does it make obsolete the older methods and techniques of research. Rather, it adds new arrows to the researcher's quiver. E-research operates under different economic, security, and ethical constraints than other investigative techniques, thus both restricting and opening the door to augmentation or even substitution of traditional research techniques. E-research also challenges the researcher's technical skills. Although it is not necessary to gain the skills of a network engineer, a computer programmer, or a systems analyst to effectively use Net tools, it is important to understand the basic operational features of the Net. Such an understanding allows e-researchers to be critical consumers of new tools and provides a background on which particular and relevant new knowledge can be acquired and built. Aiding the reader to understand, appreciate, and control the underlying economics, operating techniques, and ethical considerations of e-research is the primary goal of this book.

WHAT IS RESEARCH?

Research is a natural human process that each of us engage in from earliest childhood to advanced age. As children, our research focuses on understanding and manipulating our environment, usually aided by toys and parents and later by friends and teachers. As adults, our research needs diverge to unique interests—often related to our occupation but also covering our family concerns and leisure activities.

The *Cambridge International Dictionary of English* defines research as a "detailed study of a subject, especially in order to discover (new) information or reach a (new) understanding." Note that the "newness" included in the dictionary definition can apply on an individual or a societal level. Discovering something new for an individual, even if it is knowledge or information known to others, is a valid research endeavor even if it does not warrant distribution in learned journals.

As adults, the methods we employ in carrying out our research change over time as well. Through formal schooling we acquire the literacy skills that permit us to learn from the work of others. We also learn to conduct active tests by which our ideas are confirmed, refuted, and refined. We acquire the skills of reflection and intuition by which all parts of our mind and our experience are directed towards solutions to our research problems. We learn to apply our research in real-life situations to solve problems or further our practical understandings. Finally, and perhaps most importantly, we learn to communicate our ideas. Through communication our ideas are further developed and honed. From all of these processes we learn that good research, rather than providing simple answers, leads us to further questions and opportunities to increase our knowledge.

Thus, research has many characteristics and qualities and operates in many different contexts. One of the most important of these qualities is quality itself. How do we know that the research we engage in as ordinary citizens, students, or professionals is of high quality? To answer this question, we must first realize that perceptions of quality are themselves normative—determined by the community within which the research is distributed, applied, and evaluated. In the 1970s most researchers clung doggedly to the belief that an unbiased scientific methodology guided and judged all our quality research. The scientific method purported to provide a set of principles and techniques with underlying assumptions of control, operational definition, validity, and reliability that, if followed diligently, provided measures and guarantees of quality. However the scientific method began to be questioned by many researchers in the 1980s and 1990s. It was argued that there is sufficient evidence that all forms of knowledge are socially constructed and thus depend, at least to some degree, on consensual agreement for their veracity. This agreement is socially and culturally defined, and thus our conception of quality relies on common understandings of context, tools, and language to be judged as quality. The divergence of opinion between quantitative research (the scientific paradigm) and qualitative research (the interpretive paradigm) practices continues today. Research paradigms are discussed further in Chapter 3.

Despite the differences in perception and the ontology of research, there are a few characteristics that define quality in research. First, quality research is important research. It addresses real concerns of importance to you, your colleagues, and to a wider social context. Second, quality research is adroitly focused on solutions to an important problem. It follows, then, that it addresses questions that are answerable. It constantly surprises us to carefully read the research questions drafted by beginning researchers, only to discover on close reading that answering the question is either logically, philosophically, or ethically impossible! Third, quality research is systematic. By this we mean that quality research involves more than "hit and miss" probes into a bewildering environment. Through careful planning, attention to detail, and reflection, the research process develops or adopts a structured approach that attempts to reveal as much as possible about the variables of context that affect the objects of our investigation. Fourth, quality research is transparent. From the extreme replication imperatives of the science laboratory, to the thick descriptions of the ethnographic researcher, quality research attempts to make the process of research as visible as possible so that it can be understood, if not replicated, by the interested observer. Fifth, quality research is made available to the public. Despite the growing practice of hiding research results to protect their commercial value, it is important that research be made visible, primarily so it can be validated within a social context. Research also needs to be made visible in order to contribute to the human condition. In an increasingly commercial world it sounds naive to be promoting free distribution of research results—yet we are reminded of Isaac Newton's famous quote, "If I saw further, it is because I stood on the shoulders of giants." We will not benefit from the view from others' shoulders if the results of their research are hidden behind commercial or political barriers. Fortunately, the Net provides new platforms for making research visible, and is even underlying the popular (if multiply attributed) insight that "information wants to be free" (Clarke, 2000).

The use of the Net in itself adds little intrinsic value to enhancing the quality of research. However, like any useful tool in the hands of a skilled practitioner, the Net can provide opportunities and techniques that enhance many components of our research practice. In this book we attempt to illustrate through instruction, hints, our experiences, and examples the means by which the Net can be used to improve research practice. This book also discusses some of the perils of conducting Net-based research. While the Net provides many new opportunities to improve our research practices, it also introduces new problems and challenges.

WHAT DOES THE *e* IN e-RESEARCH MEAN?

We often joke that adding the letter *e* in front of every noun we use is an unfortunate distinction of the early years of this Internet technology era. We struggled with the stigma of trendiness that will mark and date a text referring to *e-research*. In fact we fear a visit from the "Society for the Preservation of the Other 25 Letters" when they see the effusive use of the *e* prefix used in this book! However, we think the term captures some of the excitement, breadth, and diversity offered by an ever-increasing and sometimes bewildering set of new Net-based tools and techniques. Only a few years ago *e* (as in *e*mail) meant a tool that was primarily text-based, operated on a relatively insecure communications link, and provided a wide variation in performance and quality of service. In education, e-applications focused on the lowest common denominators so that students and faculty could access contents with even the slowest and most dated of hardware. Convergence of audio, video, and multimedia channels to a Net-based platform, which is continuing to fall in price and rise in power has resulted in an explosion of applications in almost every domain. This has also resulted in a change of our connotations of the Net or the *e* word. Generally, the *e* prefix means that the activity or noun modified takes place on a high-speed, digital network that is available "anytime/anywhere." Today that network is the Internet.

WHAT EDUCATIONAL RESEARCH ACTIVITIES DOES e-RESEARCH ENCOMPASS?

The Net now supports a wide variety of communication modes and information processing tools. As such, it is becoming easier to define the subset of behaviors that cannot be researched on the Net as opposed to those that can be the subject of research. Not withstanding the dangers of missing novel ways of using the Net, we list below some of the most obvious manifestations of e-research.

- Distribution and retrieval of text-based surveys.
- Open-ended or structured text-based interviews conducted via email or computer-mediated conferencing.
- Focus groups using real-time Net-based video or audio conferencing.
- Analysis of Web logs and other tracking tools for measurement and synthesis of online activities.
- Net-based telephone interviews.
- Analysis of text transcripts of learning or social activities.
- Analysis of social behavior in virtual reality environments.
- Online assessment and/or evaluation of performance or knowledge.

We expect that the increasing power and ubiquity of the Net coupled with its imaginative use by researchers will result in continuing expansions and variations of the scope of research practiced around the globe.

THE SPECIAL TASK OF e-RESEARCH

The networked world is awash in volumes of data. E-research helps us to convert this data into information and present and disseminate this information in ways that allow it to be transformed into knowledge and wisdom by the researchers, their sponsors, educators, and the general public. The quantity of information produced, coupled with the speed in which it can be accessed, filtered, sorted, and combined creates endless opportunity. However, this abundance forces e-researchers to be more selective and critical of the veracity of the data they gather. In addition, it is becoming increasingly apparent that we can no longer, if we ever could, gather all relevant data. Instead we must make judicious decisions about which type and what quantity of data is most helpful in answering our research questions.

E-research is more than a set of new research techniques. The quantum physicist studying subatomic particles realizes that the very act of viewing these tiniest of particles disturbs and changes the objects. The e-researcher is a component of the Net. E-researchers provide and create tools for analysis and conceptual understanding of human behavior as it develops on the networks. In some cases the e-researcher is the outside evaluator, in other contexts the practitioner e-researcher is both a participant and researcher of the environment in which the research occurs. E-researchers are also usually members of other Net communities, thus they bring their experience and insights into the way online individuals and groups communicate and operate. They act as Net-savvy artisans of a network culture. Informally, they interact with peers, family, and coworkers—investing their time in the development of new skills and in the process gaining "Net efficacy."

E-research takes its place alongside e-commerce and e-learning as alternative ways to act, understand, and create knowledge in a networked society. New tools require new skills, but also allow creativity and an ability to manipulate the world in different ways. These new tools span both the physical and temporal barriers. We are accustomed to conceiving of technology spanning geography—after all, humans have had nearly 150 years since the telegraph first allowed us to communicate in real time over geographic distance. The Net easily meets this challenge. But equally, the Net spans temporal distance. Users are now able to benefit from asynchronous interaction through the tools of email and voicemail, or the capture and time shifting of audio or visual presentation. New tools such as asynchronous voice conferencing and "video capture" (an advanced form of picture mail) promise to allow full multimedia interaction in asynchronous formats.

Asynchronous communication has also been with us for a long time. From St. Paul's letters to the early Christian church to the friendships that have grown and flourished via pen pal letters—asynchronicity has provided a uniquely reflective means by which humans communicate and by which we are communicating with you at this very moment. However, asynchronicity has long been confounded with text literacy. Now we realize that text-based communication, supported either asynchronously or in real time (as practiced in ICQ—an online instant messaging program, MOOs—Mud Object Oriented, MUDs—Multi-User Dungeons, Palaces, and other Net-based chat systems), is but one form of communication. In an advanced, Net-based context, voice, sound, and video become as easily formatted, stored, and retrieved as text. Already, early versions of asynchronous voice conferencing (for example, see www.wimba.com) and asynchronous "virtual people speaking your email" animations of voice messaging (i.e., http://www.lifefx.com) are becoming available in addition to synchronous audio and video conferencing.

Because the Net so aptly supports both synchronous and asynchronous communication, it should be no surprise that e-research utilizes this capability to provide a wide variety of research methods and tool capacities. Research applications can be customized to take advantage of either synchronous or asynchronous formats—or both. For example, online focus groups allow the researcher to gather groups of subjects from widely disbursed geographic locations. These groups can be conducted synchronously using voice or text formats so that instant feedback is provided to both researchers and participants, and the immediate presence can be used to build common understandings and ideas. Alternatively they can be conducted asynchronously, permitting reflective interactions that are not dominated by the participants who think and communicate most quickly.

E-research also utilizes the distributed data and information processing capacity of the Net. Stand-alone data processing applications (including statistics programs, registration systems, and programs that monitor network activity) are all becoming "Net-enabled" and thereby can be applied to locations and times that are noncontingent with the behavior or process being studied. Thus, e-researchers are able to use research tools, monitor activity, and collect data without traveling long distances or coordinating local time schedules.

E-research permits the exploration of new fields of knowledge. As more social and economic interaction takes place on the networks, new fields of human endeavor are created. Researchers can now study the ways in which students learn online or how online education and civic groups make decisions and conduct business. These new human activities grow in economic and political importance daily. These fields of study are not readily accessible to researchers who cannot access or who lack the skills to proficiently use the Net. Thus, this text is a guide that can be used for both instruction and motivation to acquire and effectively use the new tools and techniques of networked research.

If, as Benedikt (1991) argues, cyberspace "has a geography, a physics, a nature and a rule, of human law" (p. 123), then obviously it is an environment that can provide insight into human behavior and nature, through examination of the cultural and sociological constructs that humans create within this context. Thus, cyberspace as an evolving and extremely intricate human context attracts the researcher. It is unclear how many of the research tools that have been developed, tested, and normed in real communities will be as useful in virtual contexts. Likely, existing tools will need to be modified to maximize their usefulness in this new milieu. Moreover, it is certain that creative minds will develop new tools uniquely designed for producing both knowledge and wisdom in the virtual context. Thus, e-research is concerned both with the application and adoption of tools from the real world and the invention, refinement, and calibration of a new genre of tools.

We are convinced that a networked society is not a fad and that we are at the beginning of a new era in human collective activity. This era is not marked by elimination of the value or unique functionality of face-to-face and place-bound interaction. Rather, it represents the growth of parallel and alternative forms of many types of human interaction and discourse. These parallel forms are not inherently better, nor worse, than pre-Net forms of interaction and education. However, network-enhanced interaction better fulfills some human needs at certain points in time by providing access, convenience, utility, speed, and cost-effectiveness. These attributes result in the eager exploration of cyberspace by many citizens, thereby creating a new human context that selectively, and individually, forms a merged environment of networked and face-to-face environments. We know little of this merged context—either at a macro level or at the individual interaction level. Thus, e-research is critically important in providing a means to first understand and then to create a networked social and economic context that assists individual human beings and their collective organizations to live productively, joyfully, and securely on our planet.

SCOPE OF e-RESEARCH

As we researched this book, it became apparent that the network was becoming an integral component of many activities that had been undertaken previously using non-networked tools. It also became obvious that new forms of behavior and community were being established in which the existence and support of the network were necessary for the behavior to exist. Thus, the scope and extent of e-research is expanding at unprecedented levels. What we needed was a conceptual rubric to help us differentiate those forms of behavior and research activities that we were to examine in this book from those that we were to leave to other authors. Table 1.1 may be useful for the reader in understanding where this book fits in the larger arena of research and network writings. The shaded cells are the focus of this book—activities in the unshaded cells are adequately covered in earlier, more traditional research and methods texts. Table 1.1 illustrates that e-research works at two quite distinct levels: first as a new medium to undertake research tasks that were previously done using alternate media or without mediated tools at all and second as a tool that allows us to investigate activity that itself would not be possible without the Net.

RESEARCH ATTRIBUTES OF e-RESEARCH

Studying the applications and communities that have formed in virtual space is a researchers' dream world due to the data collection that is often integral and automatically gathered during online activity. The major activity of many communities is

TABLE 1.1 Scope of e-Research—Possible Research Activities.

	ACTIVITY ON THE NET—"CYBERSPACE"	ACTIVITY NOT ON THE NET—"REAL WORLD"
RESEARCH ACTIVITY ON THE NET	Analysis of Web server and application logs, data mining for exploration, description or quasi-experimental research Online surveys, interviews, and focus groups with subjects using the Net Online ethnographies and participant research with virtual community members	Email, Web surveys, and online focus groups focusing on offline activities, experiences, beliefs, and attitudes WebCams and other sensors recording offline behavior
RESEARCH ACTIVITY NOT ON THE NET	Face-to-face interviews, telephone surveys, and mail surveys of Net participants Quasi-experimental or experimental lab simulations of Net activities "Think aloud" or other observations of subjects engaged in Net-based activities	Pre-Net research, such as mail, telephone, or face-to-face surveys; Delphi studies; or focus groups Experimental or quasi-experimental non-Net-based research Ethnographic study of non-networked components of society

verbal discourse and the transcript of this interaction is routinely captured and stored on the Net as text files. These files can readily be imported into text analysis tools, thus eliminating cost, time, and transcription. Second, the Net is renowned for the continuous tracking of most types of online activity, such as the sequence of participant activities at a site or the amount of use of an online resource. As such, it is capable of collecting valuable data that provide a unique window into human activity on the Net.

The Net also provides a unique context in which to study innovations in the social sciences and particularly in education. Modern learning theory stresses the value of multiple perspectives, of working with peers on collaborative and cooperative tasks, of searching and constructing information artifacts, and of exploring and learning in multicultural communities. The Net provides new and cost-effective possibilities for each of these contexts. Many of the techniques being developed for online learning are finding application in the classroom—and vice versa. As we learn the unique educational capacity of both online and real-time classrooms, we will design learning exercises and activities that maximize each environment.

QUALITIES OF THE e-RESEARCHER

This book is designed to help researchers become proficient e-researchers. It does so, not by describing step-by-step details or how to operate Net-based software (there are many books and other learning resources that address this task). Neither is it a book focused on developing generic or specific research skills—again there are specialized texts dealing with all of the methods and tools of good research practice. Rather, this book focuses on describing and illustrating, in clear and simple language, the variety of ways in which researchers may use the Internet to enhance their professional practice. We also provide suggested activities and links to related Internet sites. This combination of conceptual overview of network programs, practices, and operating processes, coupled with suggestions for hands-on activity, is designed to quickly increase the readers' self-efficacy in regard to both the skills of research and the capacity to effectively use networked resources.

Figure 1.1 illustrates the e-research skills that exist at the intersection of networking skills and research skills. The processes on the right of the diagram detail the course of research in any domain. We do not believe the function of each component of the research process is fundamentally different in either e-research or traditional research. The Internet skills listed on the left of the model are the prerequisite skills and capacity needed to be a competent network user. The e-researcher needs to develop these skills and will do so in the process of undertaking and completing an e-research project. Like other complex skills, there is no single minimal level of competency needed, but increasing skills at all levels results in more effective and efficient

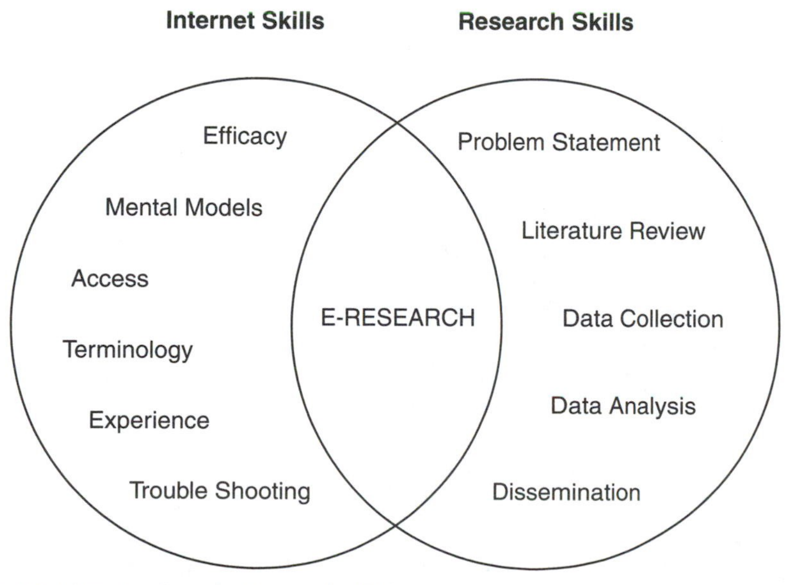

FIGURE 1.1 Set of e-Research Skills

use. In addition, it can be assumed that these skills will change and evolve as the network and its tools evolve.

As Figure 1.1 also illustrates, our listing of Internet skills begins with "Internet efficacy." Efficacy has long been associated with competence and accomplishment. Internet efficacy means the confidence and willingness to learn to use new tools and to become competent at applying these tools to authentic problems. Bandura's (1977) pioneering work illustrates the importance of having the confidence to learn new skills and acquire new attitudes. A major source in creating the digital divide (those with technological skills and access to network technologies and those without) lies beyond economic and class attributes, and includes the self-confidence necessary to attempt to use new networking tools. The effective e-researcher has to have the confidence and willingness to experiment with and learn to use network tools—even those that are unfamiliar and, at least initially, are perceived as highly complex and perhaps intimidating. Eastin and LaRose (2000) developed an eight-item scale to reliably assess (and in a sense behaviorally define a measurement for) Internet self-efficacy. This scale includes items such as "I feel comfortable describing network technology, software, searching for information and learning Internet applications." They determined that it was not Internet skill alone that determined competency, but rather a strong sense of Internet efficacy that allowed users to effectively adapt to the requirements of working in this transitory environment.

Mental models of how the Internet works and the way that various organizations and resources function and communicate on the network are also needed to be an effective e-researcher. Mental models are usually graphical but can be abstract renderings or pictures of the way in which ideas, processes, or practices are organized and related to each other. They help us to predict, anticipate, and manipulate artifacts and structures around us. Construction of accurate mental models of the Internet and the way in which practitioners use it is necessary for the development of Internet skills and competencies. For example, it is necessary to have access to a mental model of asynchronous decision making and robotic control before one can even imagine how a group of people could plant and harvest a "virtual garden" as was done in the TeleGarden project in 1996 (see http://www.usc.edu/dept/garden/). Readers interested in exploring Internet mental models will probably enjoy Mark Stefik's 1996 book, *Internet Dreams: Archetypes, Myths, and Metaphors.*

Access is perhaps the most obvious prerequisite of skillful Internet use. However, access is more complicated than what might be initially apparent. There are different types of access, some related to the speed with which Internet resources can be used and others related to the capacity of the computer to render and display complex graphic images. Our own experiences convince us that the speed with which images appear is directly related to both satisfaction and persistence. In addition, use of many multimedia resources, especially those requiring extensive video, are restricted to those with both high bandwidth connection and equipment new and powerful enough to render the images in real time. Access is also available to researchers differentially in regard to both time and space. Those whose access to the Internet is restricted to home or office, or whose other personal commitments do not allow evening or weekend access, will likely not be as effective in their e-research projects as those whose access is available "anytime/anywhere." Access is also restricted for those who have a variety of physical or mental disabilities. Much necessary e-research is needed to examine and develop prosthetics that allow all people to access and benefit from the Net.

Mastery of appropriate terminology is important in any field and especially so when the field is expanding and new terms are routinely introduced. There are many useful terminology reference sites and glossaries that can be linked to as needed (see especially Jenkins, 2000). However, a new e-researcher may find that reviewing online tutorials such as those found at the WebTeacher site at http://www.webteacher.org/ or reading through a generic introductory text such as Wing, Whitehead, and Maran's *Internet and World Wide Web Simplified* (1999) can be most useful in acquiring basic terminology and functionality detail.

Eastin and Larose (2000) found that "prior Internet experience was the strongest predictor of Internet self-efficacy. Up to two years' experience may be required to achieve sufficient self-efficacy." While we would agree that time on task is an important component of Internet self-efficacy and effective use of the Internet, we do not think that two years of use is a prerequisite to doing effective e-research. However, we all know colleagues, friends, and family members who acquire Internet skills and related Internet self-efficacy at vastly different speeds. Some of us, for example, seem to have a learning style or motivation preference that makes us predisposed to enjoy the challenges associated with the types of learning experiences found on the networks. Alternatively, others of us find learning these skills to be an arduous task. Our advice to the beginning e-researcher is to expect to spend time, some of which will involve exploration down blind alleys. The investment in time most often results in serendipitous returns—much of which will have application in later networking tasks.

Network skills come from systematic efforts that reflect the use of the technology. Some of us find that our skills are improved rapidly through enrollment in face-to-face or online courses. Others of us develop our skills through self-study and even random exploration. Whatever way you learn best, you can be assured that, over time, you will see a sharp increase in your networking and research skills as you undertake and complete e-research projects.

Finally, troubleshooting on the Internet is a particularly useful skill as many Net technologies are not fully developed or optimized for inexperienced users. As your self-efficacy as an e-researcher increases you will find both the opportunity and the need to develop trouble-shooting skills related to both Internet hardware and software. Our only advice is to use your research skills in these practical applications, searching, studying, and finding assistance from a variety of online and localized resources. It follows that you can be helpful and acquire a great deal of knowledge by collaborating with and assisting others struggling with networked tools.

When you expand your Internet skills and Internet self-efficacy, and combine it with your existing knowledge and skills as a researcher, you will be able to do effective e-research. We hope this text serves as a source of information that will turn into knowledge as you apply the information to personally relevant contexts. This knowledge bridges the tools and culture of the network and the established tradition of academic or commercial research. Increasing your e-research skills will increase your capacity to apply them in novel and effective ways. There are far too many perplexing questions and important, unsolved problems crying for solutions in both the networked and non-networked worlds of education. We hope this text helps us in at least a small way to contribute to their solution.

PERILS OF e-RESEARCH

We are not immune to the occasionally well-argued and always vitriolic critics of new technology applications in research and education (for example, Neil Postman and David Noble). However, most of us who use the Net do not hold an extreme view of technological determinism. Rather, our moderate view of technological determinism acknowledges how we both use, and are used by, technology. The Net, like all technology, is capable of amplifying and extending the best and the worst of human nature—including that enacted in the practice of educational research. Indeed, it is easier now to conduct shoddy research, to more quickly and broadly disseminate incorrect or misleading results, to more readily exploit the trust of research subjects, to more easily plagiarize the work of others, and to rely on breadth rather than depth of coverage on most any scholarly topic.

As in other times of rapid change, the ethical, moral, and legal checks to such behavior often lag behind the capacity of the unscrupulous or uncaring to profit from their application. Therefore e-researchers are cautioned always to reflect before acting, to seek the counsel of others within and outside their own community, and to be scrupulously honest and open when explaining and documenting their activities. Doubtlessly, we will make mistakes as we pursue new knowledge using new techniques. However, this is no reason to abandon our effort. Progress in both humanity and in scientific research has always advanced unevenly, making false starts and reaching dead ends. E-research offers no panacea—it guarantees neither efficacy nor quality of result. Yet, we are convinced that the promise exceeds the peril. We write this book with the hope that researchers will adopt e-research techniques and tools with the ever-present critical edge that defines all effective research.

ON NAMING THE NET

Throughout the creation of this text we have struggled with the task of consistently naming the network environment that is the context in which our research takes place. Often we use the term *online* to refer to networked behavior, however we are becoming increasingly aware that wireless networking removes even the line from online activity! The more technical term *Internet* may be more accurate, but as networking progresses beyond the original Transmission Control Protocol/Internet Protocol (TCP/IP) set of standards that defined the original Internet, this word too seems too confining. We rigorously reject the term *virtual* with its connotations of unreality, since we are convinced that online behavior and the interactions and feelings that it invokes are very real to most participants. For similar reasons we do not use the term *cyberspace*, because we believe it belongs more appropriately within the slightly futuristic writings of its inventor, William Gibson, and less so in the more mundane world of network-based education development and delivery. Likewise, we do not aggrandize the notion of partnership between networked technology and human beings to indulge in the language of cyborgs or cybernetics—even though we remain open to the notion of the continuous development of some quite astounding technical aids to human processes, many of which will be neurologically linked directly to our bodies. Although much of the context of networking focuses on communication among network users, we also do not use the term *computer mediated communication*. The Net provides access to data, virtual environments, textbooks, and many other nonhuman reference sources. Describing the use of these resources as communications seems too anthropomorphic for our liking. Thus, we are left with a shortage of precise and well-understood terminology. We have settled on the use of the adjective *networked* and the noun *Net* (with a capital) to describe this context. *Net* seems to reflect the technical nature of the environment, but also carries with it the context of human interconnectedness that is critical to educational applications of the Internet.

Our discussion of terminology underscores the multiple functions of the Net. At one level the Net is merely a technology, one that is based on digital transmission, routing, error checking, and sending and receiving of data in many formats. These transmissions may be private and exclusive to as few as two participants or as wide as broadcasts to millions. At the same time, the Net is a rich social environment or context in which many aspects of human life, from schooling, to commerce, to sex, are supported. The Net is also a sociological and psychological filter, in which ideas are formatted and in many ways de-contextualized into text or audiovisual constructs. The Net is also a business in which fortunes are made and lost. Finally the Net is a repository, providing means and tools to store and retrieve a host of cultural, academic, commercial, and technical data.

We have experienced even greater difficulty describing non-networked activity, which we often like to contrast to activity mediated via the network. Describing non-networked research as "real" as opposed to "virtual" certainly does not work. Describing all aspects of life that are not mediated on a network as "offline" activity also seems somewhat condescending and technocentric. We are also not comfortable with the somewhat derogatory reference to humans as "wetware," "meatware," or "liveware." Thus, when we are discussing non-networked activity or contexts we usually refer to them as "face-to-face" or "traditional" and in their educational sense as "classroom" or "campus-based."

AN e-RESEARCH EXAMPLE

In the winter of 2001, Liam Rourke and I (Terry Anderson) developed a research proposal to investigate the capacity and impact of peer moderators in the computer-mediated-communications delivered graduate course that I was teaching. From our own teaching, we were aware of the excessive time commitments involved in teaching online and of the literature on peer teaching effectiveness. We had developed a tool to assess "teaching presence" (Anderson, Rourke, Garrison, & Archer, 2001) that we wanted to apply in a real-life context. We used the Net to scour the ERIC database and Google (a search engine) to search for related terms like *peer moderators* and *peer teaching*, and we ordered texts not available in our university library using online interlibrary loan request forms. We created a research plan and shared it with a colleague for critical review. We then downloaded and completed the research ethics forms from our faculty Web page and, of course, submitted them electronically. Upon approval of the project, we drafted a letter of introduction to students, in which we informed them of the intent of the research and the proposed activities. We emailed this letter and opened a forum on a conferencing system for discussion of the research process. In some cases, a follow-up email was required, but eventually all eighteen students gave their consent to participate. We then developed a short Net-based survey on the elements of teaching presence. These results were triangulated with information from a transcript analysis. During the six weeks of the experiment, we emailed each of the students reminding them of the day they were to complete the weekly online questionnaire. After the course completed, we conducted semi-structured telephone interviews with a sample of the students, applied our transcript analysis instrument with two independent coders, and reflected on our own experiences of the course. From these data sources, we drafted and revised a paper and emailed it to the students for comments (as a member check). After a final revision, we submitted the paper to the *Journal of Interactive Media in Education* (http://www.jime.ac.uk)—a non-blind, peer-reviewed, online journal. The article was reviewed by three reviewers and after some minor edits and improvements, it was accepted for publication by the editor. In addition, we posted the paper along with additional output from our research group on our own Web dissemination site at http://www.atl.ualberta.ca.

Was this an e-research example? Certainly the context and the site of investigation were based on the Net. We used the Net extensively to support data collection and administration of the project. For example, we conducted our literature review almost exclusively on the Net, used a conference to archive ongoing discussion with students, used email to obtain informed consent and to communicate, developed and administered a Web-based survey, and used the Web in a number of ways for dissemination of results. However, we weren't dogmatically committed to the Net. We used the telephone for interviews, as not all students had IP (Internet Protocol)-based telephony.

In this example, the Web was used in two common applications of e-research. First, it enabled and made more efficient the process of research practice as a means to research and disseminate the results. Second, the Net allowed us to investigate an educational activity taking place on the Net. Rapid communications with subjects throughout the course of the research as well as investigation of interaction through transcript analysis shaped the kind and nature of the research process.

SUMMARY

The primary goal of this book is to help the reader understand, appreciate, and control the underlying economics, operating techniques, and ethical considerations of e-research. Research has many characteristics and qualities and operates in many different contexts. One of the most important of these qualities is quality itself. Quality research addresses important problems and is honed to find solutions to those problems. It is systematic, transparent, and available to the public. The Net provides us with new tools for quality research as well as the exploration of new fields of knowledge. But the e-researcher must also have a set of research skills necessary to conduct quality e-research. These skills are twofold: Internet skills (self-efficacy, mental models, access, terminology, experience, and trouble shooting) and research skills (problem statement, literature review, data collection, data analysis, and dissemination).

REFERENCES

Anderson, T., Rourke, L., Garrison, R., & Archer, W. (2001). Assessing teaching presence in computer conference transcripts. *Journal of Distance Education, 15*(1), 7–23.

Bandura, A. (1977). Self-efficacy: Toward a unifying theory of behavioral change. *Psychological Review, 84*, 191–215.

Benedikt, M. (1991). Cyberspace: Some proposals. In M. Benedikt (Ed.), *Cyberspace: First steps* (pp. 119–224). Cambridge, MA: MIT Press.

Bradley, J. (2000, January). Online business still needs the basics. *Washington CEO*, [Online]. Available: http://www.washingtonceo.com/archive/jan00/0100-E-Com.html.

Clarke, R. (2000). *Information wants to be free*. [Online]. Available: http://www.anu.edu.au/people/Roger.Clarke/II/IWtbF.html.

Eastin M., & LaRose, R. (2000). Internet self-efficacy and the psychology of the digital divide. *Journal of Computer Mediated Communications, 6*(1). [Online]. Available: http://www.ascusc.org/jcmc/vol6/issue1/eastin.html.

Jenkins, S. (2000). *Internet glossary*. [Online]. Available: http://www.unisa.edu.au/itsuhelpdesk/faqs/glossary.htm.

Stefik, M. (1996). *Internet dreams: Archetypes, myths, and metaphors*. Cambridge, MA: MIT Press.

Wing, K., Whitehead, P., & Maran, R. (1999). *Internet and World Wide Web Simplified* (3rd ed.). New York: Wiley.

CHAPTER TWO

WHAT IS THE NET?

A mind stretched to a new idea never returns to its original dimensions.
Oliver Wendell Holmes

The Internet is one of the most complex machines ever developed. Describing and understanding the Internet at all levels of operation has been, and continues to be, the focus of Ph.D. theses of librarians, computer scientists, and electrical engineers. It is not necessary for e-researchers to understand the Net on this kind of detailed level of complexity, but we believe that e-researchers should be knowledgeable enough to discuss their needs and use of the Net with both technicians and potential research subjects. To help gain this larger conceptual understanding and functional vocabulary, this chapter covers the operation of the Net from an end user's perspective. Besides an understanding of its operations, we think it is important that researchers understand how to search the Net for information critical to the research process. Thus, we also focus on the techniques and strategies for efficient and effective Net searches.

WHAT IS THE NET?

As with many high-tech developments, the Internet has both a military and an academic association (Underwired, 1997). The Internet had a rather modest and unassuming origin in 1969, during the Cold War, when the American think tank RAND Corporation and the United States Pentagon joined to design an indestructible information resource (Diamond & Bates, 1995). During this time, the telephone was the primary communication system in use by the military. However, a problem with the telephone was its dependence on switching stations that could be targeted during an attack. The challenge, then, was to design a communication system that could quickly reroute digital traffic around failed nodes to ensure successful communication after a nuclear war. A strategic solution was possible, in theory, through the construction of a datagram network called a *catenet* and the use of dynamic routing protocols that could constantly and automatically adjust the flow of traffic through the catenet. Essentially, the network was assumed to be unreliable at all times and was designed to transcend its own unreliability. All the nodes in the network were equal in status to all other nodes; each node had its own authority to originate, pass, and receive messages. Nowadays, messages are divided into packets, and each packet has its own unique address. Every packet begins at a specified source node and ends at another specified destination node. Every packet winds its way through the network on an individual basis. The particular route that each packet takes is not important, only the final destination. Basically, each packet bounces from node to node in the general direction of its destination until it ends up in the proper place (Sterling, 1993). With this kind of communication, if a part of the network is destroyed, messages are automatically routed around the damaged node, resulting in only marginal delays, rather than incapacity of the Net. This rather unorganized kind of delivery system might seem inefficient, but it is remarkably sustainable and dependable as a communication system (Diamond & Bates, 1995).

RAND Corporation, Massachusetts Institute of Technology (MIT), and the University of California in Los Angeles (UCLA) studied this decentralized, indestructible, packet-switching network during the 1960s. In 1968, the National Physical Laboratory in Great Britain set up the first test network based on these principles (Sterling, 1993), and shortly thereafter, the American Pentagon's Advanced Research Project Agency (ARPA) funded a more ambitious project. The switches on the network were high-speed, but were still in need of a good, stable network. In the fall of 1969, a high-speed network was installed at UCLA and the first long-distance packet-switched network was in operation. By December 1969, there were four nodes on the network, which was named ARPANET, after the American Pentagon sponsor. The four computers on this network could transfer data on dedicated high-speed transmission lines and could even be programmed remotely from other nodes. Scientists and researchers could easily share information by long distance. In 1971, there were fifteen nodes in ARPANET; by 1972, there were thirty-seven nodes (Diamond & Bates, 1995).

In 1972–1973 an interesting use of the ARPANET was observed. The main traffic on ARPANET was no longer long-distance computing between scientists collaborating on research projects. Rather, the main traffic was moving from research collaboration and trade notes to "gossip and schmooze" (Sterling, 1993). It was not long after this that a "graduate student hacker attitude took over" (Diamond & Bates, 1995) and the invention of the mailing list transpired. The mailing list was an ARPANET broadcasting technique where one message could be sent to large numbers of network subscribers. One of the first and largest mailing lists was "SF-LOVERS" for science fiction fans (Sterling). In spite of the disapproval of the ARPANET computer administrators of this kind of *non-work*-related activity, it not only continued but grew "as if some grim fallout shelter had burst open and a full-scale Mardi Gras parade had come out" (Sterling in Diamond & Bates). By the 1980s, Transmission Control Protocol and Internet Protocol (TCP/IP), the software protocol used for packaging and addressing messages, was being used by other networks to link to ARPANET, including the National Science Foundation (NSFnet) and Usenet (a pre-ARPANET protocol developed in 1979 to facilitate sharing of news items via UNIX networks). It was originally called the ARPA-Internet but was eventually shortened to the Internet

(Diamond & Bates, 1995). As it progressed, ARPANET divided into two networks: military communications on MILNET and computer researchers on ARPANET.

In June 1990 ARPANET was decommissioned—"a happy victim of its own overwhelming success" (Sterling, 1993). Significantly, almost all of the current networks use the TCP/IP suite of protocols. Vince Cerf, a pioneer on the use and development of the Internet for decades, and who also had a tee-shirt made that said "IP on everything," told ComputerWorld in 1994, "I take great pride in the fact that the Internet has been able to migrate itself on top of every communications capability invented in the past twenty years . . . I think that's not a bad achievement" (Diamond & Bates, 1995).

The Internet has evolved into an unstructured network of millions of computers throughout the world. Today most of us access the Net through the use of a suite of programs known as the World Wide Web (WWW) that operate at the application level above TCP/IP. The original concept of the Web and the first server and Web browser software were developed in the early 1990s by an Englishman, Tim Berners-Lee. Modern Web browsers are computer-based graphical programs that allow the user to interface or *browse* through the Web. Browsers are menu-driven and icon-based software that provide a user-friendly tool for accessing the Web. Currently, the two most common Web browsers are Internet Explorer and Netscape Communicator; both function through a hyperlinked platform. The term *hyperlink* is generally used to describe the electronic representation of text and graphics that uses the random access capabilities of computers to overcome the sequential medium of print on paper (Marchionini, 1988). Hypertext has two key elements: nodes and links. The documents or units of information are called *nodes*; the electronic connections to and from the units of information are called *links*. Conklin (in Marchionini) points out that "links are the essence of hypertext since they facilitate jumping from node to node in non-linear fashion" (p. 8).

The original concept of hypertext can be traced to an American named Vannevar Bush. Bush described his vision for a device to help the human mind organize information in a landmark article called "As We May Think" in the July 1945 issue of the *Atlantic Monthly* (December, 1994). This device, the memex machine, would allow scientists to systematize and access their related information through an individualized associative structure instead of the traditional catalogue and index cards (Jackson, 1997). In Bush's vision, the memex machine would be a tool for the organization of information for scientists. Had the memex machine been built, it would have had an interconnected structure that would permit scientists to coordinate and organize their increasing information.

In 1967, Ted Nelson developed a vision of hypertext similar to that of Bush's. Unlike Bush's vision, however, Nelson envisioned a machine that would be more of a tool for the expression and development of ideas than an organizational tool for scientists (Jackson, 1997; Nelson, 1967). Nelson's vision included linking information from a variety of media such as text, images, and sound. Nelson (in Jackson) also saw:

> [H]ypertext as removing the confines of linearity imposed on ideas by existing media. In hyper-textual expression, ideas may branch in several directions, and paths through

> these ideas are followed and created by the reader who also becomes author. A hypertext document, therefore, cannot be recreated on a conventional page of linear text.

In 1989, Berners-Lee, who was very familiar with Nelson's vision of hypertext, circulated a proposal that led to the development of the World Wide Web at CERN (the European Laboratory for Particle Physics). Berners-Lee's vision for hypertext saw a way to manage large amounts of information as follows:

> In providing a system for manipulating this sort of information, the hope would be to allow a pool of information to develop which could grow and evolve with the organization and the projects it describes. For this to be possible, the method of storage must not place its own restraints on the information. This is why a "Web" of notes with links (like references) between them is far more useful than a fixed hierarchical system. When describing a complex system, many people resort to diagrams with circles and arrows. Circles and arrows leave one free to describe the interrelationships between things in a way that tables, for example, do not. The system we need is like a diagram of circles and arrows, where circles and arrows can stand for anything. . . .The system must allow any sort of information to be entered. Another person must be able to find the information, sometimes without knowing what he [/she] is looking for. (Berners-Lee, 1989)

In October 1990, Berners-Lee and Cailliau submitted a more detailed proposal to CERN for a "World Wide Web" hypertext project. A hypertext system, they proposed, would enable the linking of related data in physically separate locations. In simpler terms, hypertext allows for associations (links) between chunks of information (nodes). The subsequent system, referred to as a *Web* (hence the name World Wide Web), was built to provide help manuals for users of the CERN computer systems. These basic elements, in combination with hypertext's other characteristics, allow for the production of extensive, flexible documents, especially when combined with multimedia (also referred to as *hypermedia*).

Besides being described as the most complicated network, the Internet has also been described as the largest network ever constructed by human beings. This description magnifies the extent and persuasiveness of the communication capacity of the Net, but fails to give us a sense of what exactly the Internet is. Essentially, the Net's usefulness is built on two fundamental concepts. The first is an adherence to a single standard for communications between machines that are linked to the Internet. This standard, known by its technical name of Transportation Control Protocol/Internet Protocol (TCP/IP), is the Lingua Franca of all Net traffic.

The TCP standards of the Internet protocol define how information is transferred between hosts on the Internet. They detail how the information is broken into discrete packets, how these packets are transmitted, how the results are error-checked and retransmitted if errors are detected, and how the packets are reassembled at their final destination. As mentioned, this process takes place very quickly and is surprisingly robust, providing accurate transmission of error-free data. You can attest to this accuracy yourself if you consider how rarely you receive an email from a friend that has any transmission-induced errors—99.99 percent of the time those typos were created by your colleague, not as a result of its transmission across the Net.

The second part of the TCP/IP suite of standards, the IP, is charged with correctly addressing and routing each of the packets created by TCP to the correct destination. To do so, systems have been put in place to create a unique address or identifier for every machine that is connected to the Internet and to define a path or set of paths between any two machines. This is an amazing feat when you consider that the number of new machines connecting to the Net increased to approximately 91,000 per day in early 2001 (Internet Software Consortium at http://www.isc.org/ds/WWW-200101/index.html). In addition to creating and maintaining links between each host computer, the Net must be capable of routing messages between the large number of separate email users who may share accounts on a single host computer. Tens of thousands of additional email addresses and changes are made daily to the estimated 391,000,000 that were active in March 2001 (http://www.euromktg.com/globstats/). How does this work? Each unique address of every host machine is hierarchically numbered. You may be familiar with mnemonic Net addresses that look something like www.athabascau.ca, but to a machine connected to the Internet, these addresses are very quickly translated by a database program known as the Domain Name Server (DNS) into a series of ones and zeros, or (as they are sometimes expressed for humans) into hexadecimal numbers such as 134.1561.811. Each of these sets of numbers indicates a specific Internet domain. A domain is a set of addresses and associated Internet hosts that are controlled by a single organization. At the end of each address, at the root of the hierarchical system, lies the generic, top-level domain name, such as .edu (educational institution); .com (commercial entity); or a national domain such as .ca (Canada) or .us (United States). There is a single point or authority at which addresses are assigned and controlled in each top-level domain. Preceding the top-level domain in an Internet address is the second-level domain name such as athabascau, Microsoft, or UNESCO (domain names are case-insensitive). These second-level addresses are assigned a single registrar within these organizations. The address can be further divided to subgroups within the organization. Thus, each address has a unique identifier and destination, with a single source of reference where the address information is stored and searched.

The Domain Name System works as well as it does because no single site holds all the names and related addresses in its database. Rather, the database is distributed across the various domain registries. Each node on the tree (see Figure 2.1) represents a domain, and everything below a name is a site within its domain. When you request a connection to a Web site, your closest DNS server sees if it has recently resolved that address and, if so, retrieves the destination address and path from its records; if it has no knowledge of the site, it furthers your request for resolution to the next highest DNS in the hierarchy. This relaying continues, until you reach a DNS that has knowledge of your domain, and a path is returned to your computer. This may explain the occasional return of a "404 error—page cannot be displayed," even from a site that you are sure is in operation—it may be that the DNS server is temporarily disabled.

When a user creates and posts an email message or requests a Web site, a series of queries for address locations is initiated, and a path is created for each packet of the message between the origin and the destination. The packets may be routed through many nodes and in some cases take quite circuitous routes to reach their destination. However, the switching and the transmission happen very quickly, with response times measured in thousandths of seconds. The interested reader may wish to download the

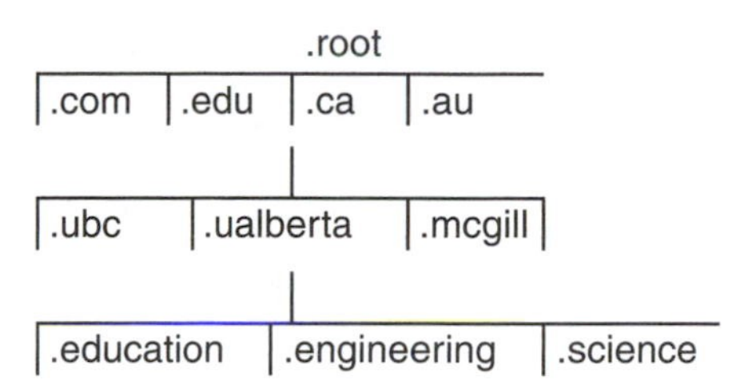

FIGURE 2.1 Illustration of the Hierarchical Domain Name Structure of the Internet

trial version of the network tracing program NeoTrace (http://www.neotrace.com) that illustrates the path data travels between your machine and any site you choose. The resultant time and path are displayed in table, graph, and map format and show the multiple hops that data takes to retrieve information for you via the Internet. For example, a recent trace between my computer in Edmonton, Alberta and a host in Australia, shows the data traveled west to Vancouver, then east to New York, before going "down-under," a circuitous route between twenty-two different routers that took a little more than two seconds.

While this information may seem to some readers to be tech-talk (aka tech-babble), we believe it is important to have a basic understanding of these operational and technical aspects of the Net. When e-researchers have a good understanding of the Net they can use it more effectively in the research process.

In addition to understanding the Internet in operational and technical ways, it is also important that e-researchers understand how to use the Internet's search tools. In academic terms, the original purpose of the Internet was to share information between scientists collaborating on research projects. Today this kind of information sharing on the Internet has created a vast repository of data. Searching through the morass of information that resides on the Internet can be an exciting and exhilarating experience, or a disappointing and frustrating one. Most of us who have used search engines have, at times, been left shaking our heads in confusion when the list of returned links is completely irrelevant to our search intent. Why does this happen? And how can we avoid it? Such errors stem from the inadequacies of human to computer communication—it simply does not yet work as well in practice as it does in theory. Specifically, information is not stored in structures that machines can easily and accurately navigate, and thereby machines are not able to identify and extract relevant and/or related information. There are, however, a few strategies that the e-researcher can use to avoid irrelevant information searches on the Net.

FINDING INFORMATION ON THE NET: SEARCH ENGINES AND SUBJECT GUIDES

Finding useful and accurate information on the Net requires a certain amount of skill, as well as access to a variety of research and retrieval engines. The first decision a searcher must make is to determine the nature of the inquiry. If, for example, you are looking for particular pieces of information that likely reside on only one particular machine, such as the entrance requirements for a specific graduate school, or the location of articles published in the *Journal of Distance Education*, then you would begin your search at a multipurpose *search engine* (such as Google or Alta Vista). If, however, you were interested in more general information, such as what schools offer graduate education programs or a broad source of information about distance education, then your most effective search tool would be a hierarchical *subject guide* (such as Yahoo!).

In hierarchical directories, or subject guides (such as Yahoo!), you would scroll down through hierarchical menus until you arrive at the site you are looking for. In simple operational terms, subject guides are organized around directories, which are created and populated by humans who have reviewed the listed sites and determined the particular subject headings under which they are most usefully classified. The benefit of subject guides over search engines is that the searcher does not have to wade through hundreds of documents to find relevant information. Directories provide the searcher with a straightforward, hierarchical means of information retrieval on the Web. However, this is precisely the reason that subject guides are not used with the frequency that search engines are. While subject guides can save the searcher much time by selecting only certain Web sites for each category, this also means that many sites are excluded. It is not possible for any group of people to accurately and continuously categorize and re-categorize all information available on the Net and accurately assign it to all possible relevant categories. As such, subject guides are not bias-free, because someone has made a decision about which resources will be included in the guide and under what categories.

On the other hand, search engines (such as Google, Alta Vista, Infoseek, HotBot, Excite, Lycos) use each word in the document and all meta tags contained in the page's introduction to create very large databases. These databases are developed and maintained automatically by software robots commonly known as *search bots*—or just *bots*. The search alphabetically links your request with the titles and phrases found on the Web sites and stored in the databases. In simple operational terms, search engines work with robots that index the contents of nearly every document on the publicly available Web. Then the contents are entered into databases on very large and fast search engines. When you enter a query at a search engine Web site, your input is checked against the search engine's keyword indices. The best matches are then returned to you as hits. Most search engines use search-term frequency as a primary way of determining the order in which the hits are organized, by listing first the document with the most uses of the keyword. If, for example, the word or one of the words in your query appears numerous times in a Web document, it is reasonable to assume that the document will likely turn up near the beginning of the search engine's list. Some search engines are designed to search for both the frequency and the positioning of keywords to determine relevancy, reasoning that if the keywords appear early in the document or in the headers, the document is more likely to be on target.

Finally, some of the better search engines use a technique (such as that developed by Google.com) that tracks which sites are actually visited from the hundreds that are returned as hits and places these "consumer choice" sites higher on the list with each subsequent search. Thus, these systems become more accurate and useful with use and are especially useful for finding often-searched sites and terms. The search bots constantly update the indexes, usually visiting popular sites every few weeks. It should also be noted that some search engines index every word on every page, while others index only part of the document, such as the title, headings, subheadings, hyperlinks to other sites, and the first twenty lines of text. Further, search engines that have full-text indexing systems claim to pick up every word in the text except commonly occurring stop words such as *a*, *an*, *the*, *is*, *and*, and *or*, and some search engines discriminate uppercase from lowercase, whereas others store all words without reference to capitalization.

At this point, it should be noted that the distinction between a search engine and a subject guide is becoming blurred, given that most search sites now offer both search options—as they try to provide everything to everyone as one-stop search portals. In spite of this new trend, the basic operational difference between search engines and subject guides remains. Specifically, search engines use robots to search for, and record, as many Web sites as possible. Whereas subject guides tend to wait for Web pages to be submitted by the author, which are then assessed and placed in the appropriate hierarchical subject category.

A search engine, rather than a subject guide, is usually used to find particular information on the Net. However, because search engines index almost every document on the Web, retrieving what you are looking for often results in an onerous activity of selecting from hundreds, thousands, or even millions of Web pages that are returned from search queries. Wading through these Web pages can consume a tremendous amount of time. To get relevant and useful results, it is important to make use of the search engine's advanced search features including quotation marks and Boolean operators. For example, typing the phrase *online research* into Alta Vista produces about 2,660,000 potential sites with either the word *research* or the word *online* mentioned in the documents. We can reduce this number substantially by refining the search to documents in which the words *online* and *research* are both found, by joining the two words with the Boolean operator *and.* For example, typing *online and research* now produces 138,000 successful hits—though, still not few enough to be useful. Fortunately, we can further refine the search by placing the words in quotation marks, thus instructing the search engine to select only pages where the word *online* precedes the word *research*. Now the search for *online research* produces only 62,000 hits but still too many Web sites to be useful. At this point we can continue adding *and* words to further reduce our search and hone in on pages that are particularly interesting. For example adding the words *and surveys* reduces the number of hits to 643; while the words *online research and focus group and education* produce a manageable 128 hits.

Relevancy ranking is critical for useful retrieval of information, and becomes more so as the number of Web documents grows. Most of us do not have the time to sort through the possible millions of hits to determine which Web documents are relevant and useful. Obviously, the more relevant and useful the results are, the more we are likely to value the search engine and, in turn, regard the Web as a useful information resource. In particular, when you are not getting the desired results from a search engine, you may have better luck using a subject guide, as subject guides provide the option to refine your search based on a particular topic. For example, searching for e-research within the field of higher education, a subject guide returns only pages about e-research in higher education, not e-research in elementary, middle school, business, or any other field. Searching within a hierarchical category of interest allows you to quickly narrow in on only the most relevant pages.

Overall, the best strategy for retrieving useful and relevant information is to use the same tactics that you would use in a library search. First, begin by analyzing your needs. What are you looking for? If the topic is very specific, search engines such as Google will likely result in hits that are relevant and useful. Alternatively, if you are looking for a broad topic, a subject guide such as Yahoo! would likely return the most successful results. Next, conceptualize your search question and then isolate the keywords in the question by eliminating words that are irrelevant.

You may find it useful to use a special purpose search tool that can most accurately meet your needs. Many search tools are designed with specific aims in mind and, as such, there is no *best* search tool. Rather, which search tool is best will depend on the kind of search you are doing. The following are a few examples of the different kinds of search tools available with specific aims.

- MedNet (http://www.mednets.com/) is devoted exclusively to medical information.
- Kids Search Tools (http://www.rcls.org/ksearch.htm) has been developed exclusively for children's searches, to be used by children.
- Search Engine Collosus (http://www.searchenginecolossus.com/) provides search engines focused on particular regions and countries.
- If you are not sure which search engine to use, or even what search engines are available, NoodleQuest (http://www.noodletools.com/noodlequest/) is a Web site with an automated Web form that will generate a list of appropriate search engines based on both your Internet skills and your search needs.
- Searchability (http://www.searchability.com/) and NeuvaNet (http://www.noodletools.com/noodlequest/) are Web sites that provide listings of specialty search engines with advice on how to choose the search engine most appropriate for your needs. For example, if you are looking for a few good hits fast, NeuvaNet recommends the use of Google (http://www.google.com/), Vivisimo (http://vivisimo.com/form?form=Advanced), and Ixquick (http://ixquick.com/).
- If you are looking for a general and broad academic subject and need to focus it, NeuvaNet recommends search guides such as:
  Encarta Online (http://www.encarta.msn.com/reference/)
  Encyclopaedia Britannica (http://www.britannica.com/)
  Northern Light (http://www.northernlight.com/search.html)
  Librarians' Index to the Internet (http://lii.org/), or Infomine (http://infomine.ucr.edu/)
- If you are looking for biographical information, try using Lives (http://amillionlives.com/), Biography.com (http://www.biography.com/search/), or Biographical Dictionary (http://www.s9.com/biography/).
- There is rapid progress being made in the cataloging and retrieval (through meta tag descriptors) of graphic images that you can use to enhance a research presentation. Two of the largest collections of graphic images and pictures are available at http://ditto.com/ and http://www.altavista.com/sites/search/simage.
- Sound and music files are also difficult to find due to problems in classification. Moodlogic (www.moodlogic.com) creates search applications that allow you to

listen to sound segments and use proprietary meta tag systems to selectively search through their large collections of songs and music.

- An excellent and always available starting point for spelling, translation, thesaurus, and encyclopedia references, and occasional relevant links is the program Atomica (http://www.atomica.ca). This free program, when installed on your machine, provides instant (ALT CLICK) access to any word in your browser, word processing document, or any other text program—very handy!
- Other services function by quickly submitting your single request to multiple search engines and displaying the results on a single (long!) screen. For example DogPile (www.dogpile.com) "fetches" the results of your search from sixteen different search engines.
- Finally, most search engines allow the user to turn on a "kiddie filter" to eliminate adult content hits, and some such as SurfSafely (http://www.surfsafely.com/) or Family Safe Startup Page (http://www.startup-page.com/) index only family-rated sites.

Once you have decided which search tool to use, refer to that system's online help section. Not all search engines work the same, nor do they have the same features and commands. Moreover, there is nearly always advice and tutorials available that can be extremely useful when refining your search. In the end, taking the time to read the online help documentation will save you time by achieving better search results. Also, keep in mind that rarely will you be satisfied with your first search results. Be prepared to try a variety of combinations of Boolean searches and synonyms for keywords. Finally, all search engines and subject guides have different methods of refining queries and/or retrieving information. The best way to learn them is to read the help files on the search engine sites, and don't be afraid to experiment!

TIPS FOR FINDING USEFUL AND RELEVANT INFORMATION

- Begin your search by analyzing your needs.
- Isolate your keywords.
- Select a search tool that matches your needs.
- Experiment with a variety of search engines and subject guides!
- Although our favorite search engines tend to change over time, we've found Google (http://www.google.com) to be the fastest, most effective, and least ad-cluttered site.

SUMMARY

The Net has evolved into an unstructured network of millions of computers throughout the world. Today most of us access the Net through the use of a suite of protocols known as the World Wide Web (WWW). Besides being described as the most complicated network, the Internet has also been described as the largest network ever constructed by human beings. As such, finding useful and accurate information on the Net requires a certain amount of skill as well as access to a variety of research and retrieval engines.

REFERENCES

December, J. (1994). Challenges for a webbed society. *Computer-Mediated Communication Magazine, 1*(8). [Online]. Available: http://www.december.com/cmc/mag/1994/nov/websoc.html.

Diamond, E., & Bates, S. (1995). The ancient history of the Internet. *American Heritage, 46*, 34–45.

Jackson, M. (1997). Assessing the structure of communication on the World Wide Web. *Journal of Computer Mediated Communication, 3*(1). [Online]. Available: http://www.ascusc.org/jcmc/vol3/issue1/jackson.html.

Marchionini, G. (1988). Hypermedia and learning: Freedom and chaos. *Educational Technology, 28*(11), 8–12.

Nelson, T. H. (1967). Getting it out of our system. In G. Schechter (Ed.), *Information retrieval: A critical review* (pp. 191–210). Washington, DC: Thompson.

Sterling, B. (1993). *A short history of the Internet by Bruce Sterling.* [Online]. Available: http://w3.aces.uiuc.edu/AIM/scale/nethistory.html.

Underwired. (1997). History of the Internet. [Online]. Available: http://www.underwired.com/report/uw.css.

CHAPTER THREE

DESIGNING e-RESEARCH

It is the theory that decides what can be observed.
Albert Einstein

Because the Net is a large, multipurpose, evolving tool, determining its best use in any research application is a challenging task. However, the Net is also famous for spurring innovation at "Internet speed," frequently leaving authors of paper books struggling to keep up. In this chapter we discuss what is perhaps the most important and challenging task of the e-researcher—to design research that asks meaningful and answerable questions and that coherently answers these questions in ways that match the personal worldview of the researcher, the sponsor of the research, and the subjects of investigation.

Considerable research is being conducted using the Internet as a data-gathering, analysis, and dissemination tool, even though the advantages and disadvantages of using the Internet for these purposes remain relatively unexplored. Often, those using the Net do so with little guidance with respect to what kind of research data is most appropriately collected online. Based on work by early adopters of e-research, it would appear that when the researcher has a good understanding of the Net (including its culture and technological limitations and advantages) that almost any kind of research could be effectively adapted. Further, when creatively approached and thoughtfully designed, research can be conducted and disseminated using the Net with a number of notable advantages, which are discussed in the last section of this chapter. This being said, there are circumstances under which the Net will be of little or no use to the research process. At one time, for example, the Net was only useful for observing activities that took place on it. Now, however, Net-based surveys, focus groups, interviews, and unobtrusive Web cameras (WebCams) allow researchers to observe and collect data about events that take place both on and off the Net.

Much of the research in the social sciences and education focuses on processes that cannot be seen and measured with external and quantifiable tools (e.g., the internal mental processes of learning). Since these processes are invisible, it takes the innovative skills of the researcher to develop both Net and non-Net techniques to understand them. Nonetheless, there are methods by which the Net seems to be particularly efficient and effective at collecting data—such as survey research (i.e., questionnaires, interviews, and focus groups). E-research is capable, for example, of reaching population samples that might otherwise be inaccessible due to time and cost restraints. E-research can overcome cultural boundaries, disability barriers, and, under certain circumstances, even language barriers. It also provides an unparalleled platform for anonymity to those experiencing social, legal, and/or emotional constraints and who are unable or unwilling to participate in other kinds of data collection methods.

Yet, while the Net offers a number of benefits, it also has a number of notable problems. Furthermore, it is likely that we are not yet fully aware of its limitations—or advantages. As the Internet is a relatively new tool in the research process, the problems that are emerging are not yet clearly understood and defined. For example, it has been our experience that return rates for Web-based surveys tend to be lower than for paper-based surveys. But we cannot generalize and assume this tendency applies to Web-based surveys as a whole, because the amount of systematic research conducted to date is insufficient. Nor do we know how much lower the return rates are, or if return rates are specific to certain populations (such as gender, age, ethnicity, or education) or certain areas of investigation. Nor do we know definitively how the data compares to established data-collection methods with respect to reliability, validity, or trustworthiness. Perhaps e-research is such a unique genre for conducting research that it demands its own codes of practice. Thus, while the Net provides us with a platform for research and exciting possibilities to expand our data collection tools, it also presents new uncertainties. Many of these issues will be discussed in the chapters on each method and in the chapter on ethics.

DESIGNING e-RESEARCH

The following hypothetical example illustrates the problems that arise when the design of e-research is not well thought through—beginning with the critical formulation of the research question.

THEO'S THESIS: WHEN GOOD e-RESEARCH GOES BAD

As a mature learner and long-time distance education student, Theo felt well prepared to embark on the research component of his graduate studies. The problem he intended to explore was one that had fascinated him as a distance learner: online control issues. While a student at a dedicated distance delivery institute, he had been perplexed at how some instructors could immediately gain a presence and take charge of discussions, while others seemed unable—or unwilling—to structure the course and make their presence felt.

Having two research courses under his belt and having read much related literature, Theo felt he was ready to state his research question:

Should distance educators limit learner control?

Theo wanted to get diverse opinions from distance educators throughout the country and decided that the most effective means (in terms of time and cost) was through an online open-ended interview. Theo emailed a number of distance educators and found ten who agreed to participate. However, when the question was presented, a number of participants were not sure what he meant, others responded to areas he was not interested in, and a few did not respond at all. As Theo discovered, online communication can be a challenge. With the remaining participants, Theo asked probing questions, and in the end, as he expected, the data revealed that distance education students prefer structured courses.

During Theo's defense, however, it became evident that committee members had concerns with his study. His outcome was not congruous to the research question (structured courses versus learner control). The committee expressed a concern with what kind of distance education environment his research results were applicable to. For example, were results intended for self-directed distance learning (e.g., correspondence study) or for cohort-based distance learning that uses computer mediated conferencing (CMC) discussion groups? And would learner control in CMC discussion groups be the same as in discussion groups that use Net-based video or audio conferencing? Moreover, is it that the learners prefer structured courses or that the instructors perceive that their learners prefer structured courses? The committee determined that the study did not contribute new knowledge to the learning process, nor could the outcomes be used in a meaningful way to improve practice in distance education.

As we can see from this example, there are many things that can go wrong with an e-research study. Many of the problems that Theo experienced could have been avoided with good research design, irrespective of whether the Net was used in the research process or not.

In its most basic sense, research design encompasses the procedures a researcher uses to study a question, a set of questions, or hypotheses. Designing e-research will in most ways mirror the design process for non-Net-based research. The purpose of developing a research design is to clearly articulate a solvable, important problem and to structure the research by illustrating how the major parts of the project (samples or study participants, measures, treatments or programs) address the objectives of the research. While some researchers understand research design to be the choice a researcher makes between quantitative and qualitative methodologies (e.g., Borg & Gall, 1989), others consider the design process much broader in scope and in methodologies (e.g., Creswell, 1994). While we acknowledge the diversity of research design, there is nevertheless a tendency for researchers to be uniform in their design format. Typically, research designs will include the following:

- A research methodology paradigm.
- The use of related and relevant literature.
- The purpose and/or objectives of the study.
- A problem statement, research questions, or hypotheses.
- An acknowledgement of limitations and a setting of delimitations.
- A statement of the significance of the study.
- A plan for data collection and analysis.

- A statement about how the study advances methods and procedures for data collection and analysis.

The purpose of this chapter is not to provide a detailed discussion of research design—there are excellent resources available (e.g., Creswell, 1994; McMillan & Schumacher, 2001). Designing an e-research study will not be much different from a non-Net research design, with the exception of how the study advances methods and procedures for data collection and analysis. At this point, we stress that it is particularly important for e-researchers not only to share the findings of the study, but also to explore how the use of the Net influences the research process and the procedure for data collection and analysis.

ASKING THE ANSWERABLE

As we can see in Theo's e-research, one of the most difficult tasks for any researcher, regardless of whether the Net is being used in the research process, is to decide on a problem in need of investigation. Typically, research focuses on understanding a phenomenon, testing a theory in a real-world context, explaining an observed event, or developing a solution to an existing problem. The focus of the investigation, referred to as the problem statement, is usually stated as a specific research question. The question will serve to clarify the problem statement (Creswell, 1994). If the e-researcher is exploring the use of the Net as the focus of the investigation, it is important that the question is asked in a researchable manner. Examine the following two examples.

> **Example 1.** Should researchers learn how to use the Internet for more efficient and effective survey research?
>
> **Example 2.** Is an online survey better than established survey methods?

Both of these questions are unanswerable. The difficulty in answering the first question is threefold. First, this question requires a value judgment, in that it asks whether something *should* or *should not* be done using the Net. The word *should* is a value term that implies notions of good and bad—it is essentially impossible to collect data with empirical referents. Second, it requires an absolute response. Rarely is there an event worthy of study that can be answered definitively with "yes" or "no." In particular, there are too many factors that can influence the effectiveness of the use of the Net for survey research. Typically, research on the use of the Net results in interventions that are shown to be effective in one setting, but do not translate to all, or even to many other, settings. For example, educational phenomena are multifaceted interactions that occur in a dynamic, uncertain, and unstable world and involve the most complex of subjects: human beings. Thus, meaningful research on the use of the Net typically involves a complex phenomenon that, at best, we can only hope to gain further knowledge of through rigorous and systematic investigation. Third, the question implies that the Internet does support "more efficient and effective survey research." This assumption is itself a research question that should not be taken as a given in the statement of a research problem.

The difficulty with the second question is twofold. As with the first question, it requires an absolute response. Even more problematic, however, is that it would be impossible to identify all the ways and to what populations established survey research is administered and to compare how these situations are administered on the Internet. As such, this research question is also unanswerable. Yet, with relatively minor changes in wording, both of these questions can become researchable. Examine the following questions.

> **Example 1.** How does the use of the Internet for research influence research effectiveness?
>
> **Example 2.** In what ways are online questionnaires more effective, as compared to paper-based questionnaires, for educational research?

While these questions are in need of further clarification either through subquestions (or hypotheses) that narrow the focus of the study or through definitions of key words in more precise terms (e.g., *influence* and *effectiveness*), the e-researcher can answer them, making the research doable. Good research questions are answerable and have clarity.

Good research questions that focus on the use of the Net are also significant—sometimes referred to as the *so what* factor. The answer to a research question about the Net should result in advancing our understanding, significantly improving practice, or expanding our knowledge of a phenomenon. It is all too easy for beginning researchers (or even experienced researchers who are new to the Internet) to become seduced by the technology itself, rather than the affects of it, producing results that have little relevance and/or significance (or the *so what* factor). The research question is a most critical component in avoiding the *so what* factor. Many researchers write and rewrite their question numerous times. Even in the early stages of data collection (e.g., the pilot study) researchers often gain additional insight to the problem under investigation and further clarify and revise the research question.

Finally, e-research questions should be structured and worded in language that is compatible with the focus of the study and the research method or paradigm. To determine the language most fitting, careful attention must be paid to the aims of the research and the validity of the selected method and tools. The research method that is most appropriate for the e-researcher will depend on the intent of the study.

As mentioned at the beginning of this chapter, the role of the Net in the research process is multifaceted, complex, and not yet well understood. The least understood aspect of the Net is how—or in fact, whether—it influences the research process. In the 1960s, Canadian media theorist Marshall McLuhan argued that the "medium is the message." This generated a seemingly unsolvable debate over the effect of technology on communication, in particular, whether or not technologies are neutral and if biases arise from the ways in which technology is used or through the technology itself.

There have been convincing arguments on both sides of this debate. For example, James Kulik and associates (see Kulik, Kulik, & Cohen, 1980; Kulik, 1984; Kulik, Kulik, & Schwab, 1986) conducted a series of meta-analyses dealing with the effects of computer technologies on educational outcomes. The conclusions of these studies were that technologies either had no significant effect or a positive effect on learner achievement. Responding to claims that technologies have a positive effect, Richard Clark summarized six decades of educational media research and concluded that technologies are "mere vehicles" (Clark, 1983, p. 445). Moreover, Clark observed that much of the literature that concludes that educational media has a positive effect, results from studies with deep methodological flaws that confound the way the media is used with the effect of the media itself. This now famous article by Richard Clark (in the *Review of Educational Research*) asserts the following: "[M]edia are *mere vehicles* that deliver instruction but do not influence student achievement any more than the truck that delivers our groceries causes changes in nutrition . . . only the content of the vehicle can influence achievement" (p. 445). The truck driver analogy that Clark uses to contextualize and bring relevance to the argument for the neutrality of technologies is held by a number of educational media researchers. In the same way, for example, Jonassen (1996) asserts that "carpenters use their tools to build things; the tools do not control the carpenter. Similarly, computers should be used as tools for helping learners build knowledge; they should not control the learner" (p. 4). While both Clark's and Jonassen's arguments sound solid in their rationale, social science media theorist Chandler (1996) reminds us that the influence of media is a complex phenomenon. Building on the assumption of the non-neutrality of technologies, Chandler postulates that media shape our experiences through their selectivity. In particular, he asserts that when we interact with media we act and are acted on, use and are used:

> [Media] facilitates, intensifies, amplifies, enhances, or extends certain kinds of use or experience whilst inhibiting, restricting or reducing other kinds . . . there are losses as well as gains. A medium closes some doors as well as opening others, excludes as well as includes, distorts as well as clarifies, conceals as well as reveals, denies as well as affirms, destroys as well as creates. The selectivity of media tends to suggest that some aspects of experience are important or relevant and that others are unimportant or irrelevant. Particular realties are thus made more or less accessible—more or less "real"—by different processes of mediation.

Chandler has identified the key features of technological impact that reshape many of our social structures as:

- *Selectivity*. Selectivity is the way a technology is formalized within its own system. The outcome of selectivity occurs when some aspects of our experiences are amplified through the use of communication technologies causing others, in turn, to be reduced.

- *Transparency*. Transparency occurs when we become so familiar with a technology that we do not recognize its influence and hence, the consequences of its use. This results in an inability to exercise our choices.

- *Transformation*. Transformation occurs when the use of technology becomes an end in itself. Specifically, when using a technology, we function within its structure.

- *Resonance*. Resonance refers to the significance or enduring effect attached to the use of one technology over another. How significant the resonance is depends on the media transformations, which, in turn, derive from the nature and use of a particular technology.

These features will filter the design of the e-research program, beginning with the selection of the research problem itself. E-researchers will likely focus on problems in which the use of the technology is integral to the innovation or problem under investigation. They will need to insure that the transparency of the components of the infrastructure and especially of the formal social system itself in which they operate are is not ignored in their focus on exiting Net-based innovations. E-researchers must also be cognizant of their often insidious motivation to act as a proponent or advocate, rather than as an observer focused on maintaining as much objectivity as possible. When we become transformed by the technology, we lose our capacity to examine it. Finally, each Net technology gains resonance in its application—supporting or undermining earlier modes of communication and information processing. The e-researcher is therefore challenged by these technological features to insure that he/she chronicles as accurately as possible the effect of the Net on the education or social system—rather than only its hidden effects on the individual researcher. All of these elements exist in dynamic interaction, and, as such, comprise an ecology of mediation. We encourage e-researchers to reflect on the elements that Chandler proposes throughout their e-research projects and to include them in the dissemination of findings. Doing so will help them understand the influence of the Net on the research process.

CHOOSING A RESEARCH PARADIGM

Ordinarily, educational research studies will state a purpose, pose a question, collect data on a specific population, and analyze the data, resulting in outcomes that make a contribution to the knowledge in the field. There are, however, different ways of arriving at the knowledge or methods of inquiry—most often termed *quantitative research* and *qualitative research*—including critical theory, historical and action research, literature reviews, and mixed method research (Reeves, 2000). Quantitative research has been referred to as experimental or empiricist research and is associated with the positivist or scientific paradigm. Qualitative research is sometimes referred to as naturalistic design, and is associated with the interpretive or constructivist approach or the post-positivist perspective. Research that uses critical theory typically involves the deconstruction of systems, the revelation of hidden agendas, and the documentation of various forms of disenfranchisement. A historical paradigm attempts to detail the objective reconstruction of historical events. A literature review involves a synthesis of existing research and often entails a meta-analysis or frequency count of reported outcomes. A mixed method, as the name implies, combines a number of methods such as qualitative and quantitative research—the results of which are analyzed together to triangulate or provide converging views from different perspectives on a problem. Action research involves a partnership between the researcher and those immersed in a situation; it focuses on solutions to real problems in daily life. In practice, all of these methods can be broadly classified under one of two educational paradigms—quantitative or qualitative. We will not attempt to recap the development or the often-heated arguments between proponents of these two paradigms. However, it is important to discuss their differences and to note, where applicable, how the Internet changes these methods of inquiry.

To understand the differences between the two most common approaches to research (quantitative and qualitative), the literature has divided the two paradigms on several dimensions (Glesne & Peshkin, 1992; Guba & Lincoln, 1988; McCracken, 1988). While these dimensions are often not fully applicable to actual research, as Patton (1988) notes, they highlight the contrasts of each paradigm. The most fundamental difference in each paradigm is the assumption about the nature of the problem. In particular, the method e-researchers choose often reveals what they value as knowledge and, perhaps more importantly, what their perspective of the nature of reality is. For example, quantitative methods are based on an assumption that the world is comprised of observable and measurable facts. With respect to e-research, this involves using the Internet as a data-gathering tool to find cause and effect through an objective, formal, and deductive design, which aims to be context and value free. E-researchers need to guard against their own biases by remaining as neutral and as independent as possible from their research. It is also important to achieve accuracy and reliability through established statistical validity and reliability practices (Borg & Gall, 1989; Fraenkel & Wallen, 2000). Quantitative researchers strive for transparency and objectivity, thus allowing their results to generalize to other places and people. Currently, many e-researchers using quantitative studies assume that the use of the Net for data collection is no different, with respect to reliability and validity, from more traditional forms of data collection. However, as we will see in the following discussion, this is not necessarily a correct assumption.

In contrast, qualitative methods assume multiple realities, which are subjective, value-laden, complex, and context-bound. Accuracy is achieved through credibility, transferability, confirmability, and dependability (Guba, 1981). What results is the discovery of patterns and the development of theories that expand our understanding through narratives that "exploit the power of form to inform" (Eisner, 1981, p. 7). The qualitative e-researcher interacts with the research using an in-depth inductive process and an emerging design that is identified during the research process. With respect to the Net, the qualitative e-researcher generally views it as more than simply a tool for data gathering. In particular, the e-researcher's and subject's assumptions and values in relation to the role of the Net will be part of the research process. Thus, the Net and the research results are indivisible, in that the e-researcher's biases and beliefs about the Net will influence the research process, and hence, should be reflected on and addressed throughout the study.

The different assumptions of each research approach will not only influence the methodological approach selected, but also the purpose of the research and the role of the e-researcher. Some researchers argue that integrating diverse approaches draws on the advantages of each method, providing different perspectives of our world (Eisner, 1981; Firestone, 1987; Glesne & Peshkin, 1992). For example, the types of methods most commonly associated with quantitative research are experimental studies and questionnaires; the types of methods most commonly associated with qualitative research are ethnographies, grounded theory investigations, case studies, interviews, and phenomenological studies (Creswell, 1994). While these methods are commonly associated with one paradigm, there are occasions when qualitative researchers will use questionnaires and quantitative researchers will use interviews (Glesne & Peshkin); this results in a mixed method study. Some research theorists argue that qualitative and quantitative approaches are incompatible (Lincoln & Guba, 1985; Schwandt, 1989). This position is based on the argument that each research paradigm rests on different assumptions about the nature of the world, requiring different instruments and procedures for investigation. Glesne and Peshkin further explain that most researchers have a tendency to adhere to the methodology that is most consistent with their socialized worldview:

> We are told that the research problem should define whether one chooses a qualitative approach or a quantitative one. This, however, is not how we believe research necessarily is done or even how it should be done. To the contrary, we are attracted to and shape the research problems that match our personal world view of seeing and understanding the world. (p. 9)

Thus, it is important for e-researchers to be self-aware to the extent that they can articulate their own personal worldview. If you are a beginning researcher, our advice is to read many different research studies that use a wide variety of methodologies. From this overview, certain approaches will strike you as more effective in addressing the questions and providing answers that are meaningful to you. This worldview should guide your selection of an appropriate question, paradigm, and methodology to use in your e-research study.

MATCHING THE LANGUAGE WITH THE METHOD

As mentioned in the previous section, an essential aspect of the problem statement and research question is the expression of the assumptions of the research paradigm through language that is consistent with the research method. When the Net is used in the research process, care should also be given to ensure that the language and method correspond.

In qualitative research, the research question is often presented in the form of a *grand tour* question, often followed by subquestions (Creswell, 1994). A grand tour question, according to Werner and Schoepfle (1987), is constructed through the use of nondirective wording, which ensures unlimited inquiry. For example, words that convey the language of an emerging design of qualitative research will include nondirectional language, such as *discover*, *explain*, *seek to understand*, *explore*, and *describe the experiences*. Generally, there is a single focus and a specific research situation, without reference to the literature or theory. This is not to say a review of the literature on related theories is not part of the process of conducting qualitative research; rather, as the intended outcome is often theory development, reference to a particular theory is typically not made in the problem statement or the e-research question.

Grand tour questions in e-research are generally—though not always—followed by five to twelve subquestions that narrow the focus of the study and describe the use of the Net in the research process, but still permit for an emerging research design (Creswell, 1994; Miles & Huberman, 1984). The following are examples of grand tour questions used in different research questions.

> **Example 1.** *Grounded theory, open coding*: What are the categories of discussion that emerge from Web-based threaded conferencing interactions between North American and European cultures?
>
> **Example 2.** *Phenomenology*: What is it like for children who are geographically isolated to participate in learning activities delivered over the Internet?
>
> **Example 3.** *Ethnography*: How is social presence established in Web-based learning activities?

Alternatively, in quantitative research, the research question is often presented with a narrow focus—sometimes as a statement rather than a question—followed by restating the purpose of the study (Creswell, 1994). Generally, these restatements are in the form of research questions (or objectives) if it is a survey project and hypotheses if it is an experimental project. Hypotheses are declarative statements that make a tentative proposition about relations between two or more variables; research questions are also about relationships, but are phrased as questions (Borg & Gall, 1989). Quantitative problem statements are typically constructed through the use of directive wording, which ensures the research propositions are testable. For example, words that convey the language of an experimental design will include directional language, such as *affect*, *influence*, *compare*, *determine*, *lead to*, *cause*, and *relate*. The research questions or hypotheses are usually derived from a theory that provides a framework for the study.

As one goal of quantitative research is to increase our understanding of cause and effect relationships, an effective way to seek such understanding is through the use of theory (Vierra, Pollock, & Golez, 1998). In a sense, theories are proposed explanations that researchers test for rejection or acceptance. However, as Vierra et al. note, rarely are theories rejected or accepted; rather, they are most often revised. Hence, researchers generally make reference to their work as theory building, which reflects the ongoing process of testing, revising, and retesting. In quantitative studies, researchers test theories through a deductive methodological process—often classified as either a causal comparative method or a descriptive study. The causal comparative method (often associated with grounded theory methodology) is primarily concerned with discovering causal relationships and involves a comparison between two or more groups in terms of a dependent variable or as a relationship of two or more independent and dependent variables. A descriptive study is primarily concerned with discovering "what is" and involves describing responses based on the independent or dependent variables. Observational and survey methods are frequently used to collect descriptive data (Borg & Gall, 1989) and will be covered in further detail in Chapter 10, which focuses on quantitative research.

The following are examples of descriptive and causal comparative questions.

Example 1. *Descriptive*: In what ways has the integration of the Internet into the high school curriculum changed students' self-directed learning skills?

Example 2. *Causal comparative*: Does the integration of the Internet into the high school curriculum lead to increased self-directed learning skills when compared with curriculum that does not integrate the Internet?

TIPS FOR WRITING GOOD RESEARCH QUESTIONS

- When developing your research question, make sure it does not require a value judgment.
- Avoid asking questions that can be answered in any absolute way (i.e., "yes" or "no") or seem to imply universality over large domains or fields of study.
- Match the language to the method of the study (quantitative versus qualitative).
- Pay attention to the wording of published research studies to identify the perspective, methodology, or research paradigm from the problem statement.
- Consider how the Net may influence responses to your research question.
- Be sure that the research question guides your use of the Net rather than letting the Net guide the research question.

SUMMARY

Qualitative and quantitative e-research methods offer different strengths and weaknesses that require alternate, but not necessarily mutually exclusive, research strategies. The choice an e-researcher makes between a qualitative or quantitative approach will essentially depend on the kind of research question being asked and their own worldviews of how knowledge is best generated. In the most basic sense, when the purpose of research is to generate theory, qualitative research is an appropriate strategy. Alternatively, when the purpose is to test theory, quantitative research is more appropriate. Regardless of the type of method used, the Net can be an efficient and effective tool in the research process. However, those adopting the Net as a research tool currently do so with little guidance, especially with respect to what kind of research data is most appropriately collected online. The remainder of this book provides guidance in using the Internet as a tool in the research process.

REFERENCES

Borg, W. R., & Gall, M. D. (1989). *Educational research. An introduction* (5th ed.). White Plains, NY: Longman.

Chandler, D. (1996). *Engagement with media: Shaping and being shaped.* [Online]. Available: http://users.aber.ac.uk/dgc/determ.html.

Clark, R. (1983). Reconsidering research on learning from media. *Review of Educational Research, 53*(4), 445–459.

Creswell, J. W. (1994). *Research design. Qualitative and quantitative approaches.* London: Sage.

Eisner, E. (1981). On the differences between scientific and artistic approaches to qualitative research. *Educational Researcher, 10*(4), 5–9.

Firestone, W. A. (1987). Meaning in method: The rhetoric of quantitative and qualitative research. *Educational Researcher, 16*(7), 16–21.

Fraenkel, J. R. & Wallen, N. E. (2000). *How to design and evaluate research in education* (4th ed.). New York: McGraw-Hill.

Glesne, C., & Peshkin, A. (1992). *Becoming qualitative researchers. An introduction.* New York: Longman.

Guba, E. G. (1981). Criteria for assessing the trustworthiness for naturalistic inquiries. *ERIC/ECTJ Annual Review Paper, 29*(2), 75–91.

Guba, E. G., & Lincoln, Y. S. (1988). Do inquiry paradigms imply inquiry methodologies? In D. M. Fetterman (Ed.), *Qualitative approaches to evaluation in education* (pp. 89–115). New York: Praeger.

Jonassen, D. H. (1996). *Computers in the classroom: Mindtools for critical thinking.* Englewood Cliffs, NJ: Prentice-Hall.

Kulik, J. A. (1984). Evaluating the effects of teaching with computers. In G. Campbell and G. Fein (Eds.), *Microcomputers in early education.* Reston, VA: Reston.

Kulik, J. A., Kulik, C., & Cohen, P. (1980). Effectiveness of computer-based college teaching: A meta-analysis. *Review of Educational Research, 2*(2), 525–544.

Kulik, J. A., Kulik, C., & Schwab, B. (1986). The effectiveness of computer-based adult education: A meta-analysis. *Journal of Educational Computing, 2*(2), 235–252.

Lincoln, Y. S., & Guba, E. G. (1985). *Naturalistic inquiry.* Beverly Hills, CA: Sage.

McCracken, G. (1988). *The long interview.* Newbury Park, CA: Sage.

McLuhan, M. (1964). *Understanding media: The extensions of man.* New York: McGraw-Hill.

McMillan, J., & Schumacher, S. (2001). *Research in education* (5th ed.). New York: Addison-Wesley.

Miles, M. B., & Huberman, A. M. (1984). *Qualitative data analysis: A sourcebook of new methods.* Beverly Hills, CA: Sage.

Patton, M. Q. (1988). Paradigms and pragmatism. In D. M. Fetterman (Ed.), *Qualitative approaches to evaluation in education* (pp. 89–115). New York: Praeger.

Patton, M. Q. (1990). *Qualitative evaluation and research methods* (2nd ed.). London: Sage.

Reeves, T. C. (2000, April). Enhancing the worth of instructional technology research through “design experiments” and other development research strategies. *Paper presented at the Annual Meeting of the American Educational Research Association,* New Orleans, LA.

Schwandt, T. (1989). Solutions to the paradigm conflict: Coping with uncertainty. *Journal of Contemporary Ethnography, 17*(4), 379–407.

Vierra, A., Pollock, J., & Golez, F. (1998). *Reaching educational research* (3rd ed.). Upper Saddle River, NJ: Prentice-Hall.

Werner, O., & Schoepfle, G. (1987). *Systematic fieldwork: Vol. 1, Foundations of ethnography and interviewing, 1.* Newbury Park, CA: Sage.

CHAPTER FOUR

THE LITERATURE REVIEW PROCESS IN e-RESEARCH

A few months spent in field research can frequently save a few hours in the library.
Anonymous

A quality research project benefits from and builds on the accumulated research knowledge of others and is further informed by the ongoing dialogue with those engaged in related research. E-research does not change this basic tenant of quality research, but it does provide new tools and techniques to increase both the efficiency and effectiveness of the researcher. In this chapter we discuss ways in which gathering and compiling an effective review of the existing literature works in a networked world and provide hints and techniques to assist the e-researcher in completing this task. We begin by reviewing the goals or objectives of the literature review process.

WHY DO A LITERATURE REVIEW?

The purpose of a literature review is to report published material on existing conceptual frameworks, theories, and previous research related to the topic under investigation. The most important contribution of a literature review is to identify why some of the literature is noteworthy and which literature has made important theoretical contributions to the field being studied. The literature review component of an effective e-research project is both a process and a product. As a process, the literature review serves to familiarize and educate the researcher—not only with the results but also with the theories, techniques, processes, styles, and instruments of other researchers. Because the e-researcher may be challenged by problems similar to those encountered in prior research, the results of a literature review can save time as well as effect a greater contribution to the knowledge base through building on existing information. Although an e-researcher may be either thrilled or deeply disappointed to uncover a completed study that answers many of his or her own research questions, a careful reading of the work almost always reveals hints and suggestions for ways in which further research is both necessary and important; thus, such studies can result in important and beneficial shifts and modifications to the research proposal.

In traditional research reports and thesis designs, the literature review is placed near the beginning of the document. This should not be taken as a sign that the literature review is completed before other parts of the study commence. In our experience, creating, fine-tuning, and editing the literature review is an iterative and ongoing process. As the research proceeds, new problems and questions arise that require investigation and input from others—documentation of these questions and their resolution in the literature review enhances the value of the e-research project.

A well-done literature review will not just document the results of earlier studies. Rather, it will reflect on all aspects of the research process. Further, an excellent literature review has specific characteristics that separate it from a good literature review. The defining characteristics that are present in an excellent literature review include the mention of

- the theory that guides the research and helps to frame the research question;
- the methodology used, including the development of techniques and tools used for analyzing and interpreting the results; and
- the means by which the results are disseminated.

As a product, the literature review will serve both you and subsequent researchers as a record of and a set of pointers to the research that you have extracted from the large base of possible knowledge. It represents your informed extraction and synthesis of the extant research and thus is itself a valuable contribution. The literature review will also guide future researchers in understanding why you made the research choices that you did, help others to uncover and recreate the research process, and disclose the literature that you found of greatest value in your research efforts.

ENSURING QUALITY OF THE LITERATURE REVIEWED

There are five basic elements that academic researchers require of information sources (Kibirige & Depalo, 2000). These are accessibility, timeliness, readability, relevance, and authority. The use of a network changes our approach to, and means of, assessing these quality indicators, but does not change their importance. Nor does the use of a network change the need to access the literature (e.g., books, microfiche archives, and paper-based academic journals) from established libraries at universities or other educational institutions.

Accessibility

The most dramatic impact of a network on the process of building a literature review is the increase in accessibility. For much research, the locale for creating a literature review has shifted from the stacks of the research library to the networked computer screen located in the home, office, or library. Until quite recently, a review of the formal published literature was a two-step process. The first step involved searching databases of published abstracts followed by the second step of retrieving the article from the paper or microfiche archives of academic journals, conference proceedings, and reference books. The Net has steadily eroded the time and effort required to undertake both of these steps by providing direct access to indexes, research databases, and to the full text of an increasingly large number of articles, reports, and scholarly books.

Accessibility is also increasing as a result of the surge of interest and product availability for wireless products. Although we are not swept up in the wave of hyperbole that paints a picture of e-researchers completing their literature review while relaxing on a beach, jogging on a sidewalk, or driving to work, we do acknowledge that the amount of valuable research information available "anywhere/anytime" continues to grow. Networked information also increases accessibility to resources that would require considerable travel time and effort. The use of Net-based video and audio telephones will allow researchers to meet with, share, and disseminate results with related researchers located anywhere that is "Net accessible." Accessibility for visually handicapped researchers also has increased with the dissemination of research results that conform to standards designed to improve Web page readability for handicapped users (Center for Applied Special Technology, 2001).

Timeliness

Increases in timeliness are both the bane and triumph of Internet-based search results. The ease of publishing preliminary findings, unreviewed drafts, and final documents on the Web, results in a proliferation of documentation, much of which is by its nature temporary and transitory. An older paradigm of research literature saw publication of only those materials that survived a rigorous peer-review process. This time-consuming and lengthy process has been blamed for the creation of bottlenecks that slow dissemination and replication of important research results. The most significant time losses occur in the exchange of articles between editors and reviewers. The use of email, coupled with the capacity for reviewers to comment on and edit electronically has already resulted in improvements to this problem. More radical concepts of review such as the provision for public participation in, and public review of, the peer review process are being developed by a variety of peer-reviewed educational publications (see the *Journal of Interactive Media in Education* at http://www-jime.open.ac.uk/). The use of the Net by authors to publish their own work (often referred to as the "vanity press") is a challenge to authenticity—but a boon to timeliness. Like many commentators (such as Harnad, 1996), we see the Net as not eliminating, but improving the speed and efficacy of the peer-review process.

Net resources are plagued with an expectation of currency that far surpasses that expected of paper publications. Since it is possible to update information on Web sites regularly, we have come to expect such continuous revision. However, many authors do not take the time and effort to maintain sites once created, and, thus, like a paper text the content soon ages—some less gracefully than others. It is becoming more common for Web designers to help readers by attaching a "last revised on date" indicator to their pages. In the absence of such an indicator or as an accuracy check, most popular browsers provide a way to display a limited set of information about the page (for example, right click and select "page properties" in Internet Explorer). This information includes the author's name and the date the page was last modified. Noting the latest date of any references quoted in the content can also check currency of academic publications. Obviously the more current the document the better, but old pages, like old wine, often have historical, if not legacy value!

Readability

Readability of Net-based literature can be improved in a number of ways from what is available in paper format. First, the text of much Net-based content can be modified by the reader's program to suit viewing preferences. The font can be enlarged for those with visual impairments, or compressed for those wishing to rapidly scan the content. The text can also be imported into word processors or text editors for further elaboration such as adding color or emphasis, changing fonts, and printing onto paper. Such manipulation would constitute copyright violation if the document was further distributed but is permitted for single, personal use by the e-researcher.

Net-based content also provides opportunity to raise the concept of readability to new levels, as the capacity for publication in multimedia formats becomes viable. Sound recordings, animations, video clips, and sophisticated computer models and simulations can be included in either peer-reviewed or popular research literature. As acceptance of e-research grows, the inclusion of such multimedia components of others' work in research reports will likely become commonplace. It should be noted, however, that care must be taken to insure the authors' own copyright for all media distributed in their presentations and/or publications (see http://fairuse.stanford.edu/ for guidelines on fair use in the United States and http://www.uottawa.ca/library/carl/projects/copyright/c-r-e.htm for a discussion of digital copyright issues from a Canadian perspective).

Relevance

The quest for relevance of literature review content seems little changed in an e-research context from earlier days. The increased capacity and efficiency of search engines (see Chapter 2) will help e-researchers reduce the time it takes to find and review potential content for inclusion in their literature review. However, the task of assessing relevance and veracity may actually increase in scope and difficulty for e-researchers as they are presented with a constantly increasing body of accessible information. Thus, increased skill and competency is required of the e-researcher. This higher standard for quality and relevance of the literature review is one of the many ways e-research promises to improve the efficiency and efficacy of the research process.

Authority

Finally, e-researchers must be able to authenticate the authority and thus attest to the reliability of the information that they review in their research reports. The capacity for easy publication of both valid and invalid information on the Net compels e-researchers to acquire a new set of critical evaluation skills. This topic is covered in-depth in the next section.

EVALUATING AND AUTHENTICATING NET-BASED INFORMATION

Either peer or editorial review authenticates much of the formal information that researchers use to build their literature review. The Net does not negate these valuable sources of authentication. Indeed, as noted earlier, the convenience and accessibility of the Net promises to improve both the speed and quality of the review process. However, the Net also provides opportunity for authors to directly publish their work and bypass any form of review. Of course, anyone can publish almost anything on the Net, resulting in what December (1994) refers to as an increasing amount of information that is a "thin soup of redundant, poor quality or incorrect information. . . . A flood of information unfiltered by the critical and noise-reducing influences of collaboration and peer review can overwhelm users and obscure the value of the Web itself." Sifting through the mass of advertising material, vanity publications, and gray writings to find credible and high-quality literature is an onerous task (Harris, 1997; Smith, 1997; Tillman, 2000)—albeit, it is becoming easier to find credible and peer-reviewed publications as articles from many scholarly journals are being published online. But even within the morass of non-peer-reviewed networked data are valuable nuggets of information. To guarantee the reliability and credibility of this information, specific criteria should be applied in evaluating the publications found. Hallmarks of what is consistently considered to be valuable, credible, and high-quality information that can be used when evaluating publications found on the Net are clustered into the categories of authority, accuracy, bias and objectivity, and coverage. Of course, determining what is valuable, credible, high-quality information is a slippery subject—what may be noteworthy in one field of study may be unworthy in another.

Authority

Although authority is not synonymous with truthfulness (if it were we would have had no reformations, revolutions, or paradigm shifts), a reference linked to an institution or writings of known authority serve as useful clues that the information is likely to be reliable and accurate. The authority can be deduced from indicators in the Web page. These include the host computer, which is the URL listed under the domain name of an established authority or institution such as a known university, government, or public agency. Other indicators include prominent links to the homepage of the corresponding organization, and whether you can follow these links. When you read further information about the organization, you feel confident that the Web site author is a credible source. For example, are the authors' names, email addresses, and telephone numbers provided in the page so that you can seek further information about the content? Are there links to the homepages of the authors so that you can check on their career path? Can you check for any peer-reviewed publications of the authors? Are there links within the document to other sites or information that you can check for sources of authority?

Accuracy

Accuracy is difficult to attest, especially if all relevant information is not provided. In our careers as academics, we regularly review materials submitted for publication. In the review process, we are allowed to request additional information (such as background or confirming evidence) before accepting an article for publication. If the Net-based information is a component of a peer-reviewed e-journal, then you have some guarantee that experts in the field have reviewed the data collection process, methodology, theoretical underpinnings, and analysis techniques, and thus, the probability of accuracy of results is enhanced. However, if the information has not been peer-reviewed, then e-researchers are forced to undertake this evaluation themselves. After reviewing the research processes described in this text, you should have some sense of the issues involved in claiming accuracy of your own work; these same criteria can be used to evaluate the presentations of the work of others. Although no guarantee, one way to assess accuracy is to look for the referencing of other known works in the text. Such referencing indicates that the author has read the works of other researchers in the field and thus has been exposed to the issues and the accepted methodologies in the field of inquiry.

The assessment of accuracy requires the skills of critical thinking coupled with a strong dose of common sense. If you find valuable information at a site, dig deeply within the site and associated links; often you may find further work that has been reviewed by the authors or other indicators of authority that will help you make a valuation of the information's accuracy.

Bias and Objectivity

Our postmodern colleagues convince us that no information is unbiased. However, quality Net information is clear about the source of any funding, organizational bias, or political or moral agenda. If such disclosure is not apparent, and especially if the topic has commercial, political, or religious implications, e-researchers must be vigilant to insure they are not being purposely misinformed or being provided with biased information. Clues to a biased perspective include overly strident language, links to sites with a known bias, absence of links or arguments from opposing viewpoints, and the absence of any linkage to unbiased authority references.

Coverage

As noted earlier, the rapidly expanding nature of networked resources makes it very difficult to determine when the e-researcher has exhaustively reviewed all relevant materials. The impossibility of covering everything produces a tendency for reference sites to tightly restrict the scope of knowledge that they attempt to explicate. Thus, the e-researcher is forced to review and examine resources on an ever-enlarging set of so-called boutique sites that are narrowly focused on a particular subset of information, or conversely to search through very broad (and often shallow) overview reference sites. Our only advice to ameliorate this problem is to use the search engines regularly and effectively, taking special care to review the most timely sites.

Additional Resources

There are many Net resources (mostly created by dedicated librarians) offering advice, checklists, and methods for asserting the authority, accuracy, and veracity of WWW-based resources. A list of a few of these resources is available at World Wide Web Virtual Library at http://www.vuw.ac.nz/~agsmith/evaln/evaln.htm.

FINDING SOURCES OF INFORMATION FOR THE LITERATURE REVIEW

The e-researcher uses the traditional sources of relevant literature including library-based books, journals, printed conference presentations, and the popular press. In addition, the e-researcher uses the growing body of literature that is available online. These sources can be divided into two groups, formal sources that are usually peer or professionally reviewed and informal resources that are gathered through discussion groups, conference presentations, and private correspondence.

Formal Online Resources

The skilled e-researcher uses a variety of search engines and searching techniques to scour the Internet for relevant materials. Often such searches begin with keyword searches in popular general-purpose search engines (such as Google.com) or scrolling down a hierarchical subject listing of sites (such as Yahoo!). The techniques for searching that are detailed in Chapter 2 will be useful in finding relevant information.

Online literature searches often progress to the searching of specific databases or Web indexes that focus on a particular field of study or topic. These so-called boutique search engines exclude references to unrelated topics. For example, an index that excludes all references to non-academic topics such as sports, gambling, television, and sex will eliminate large numbers of sites of little or no interest to an e-researcher. Examples of these specialized search engines include ProFusion (http://beta.profusion.com/), which provides vertical searches on ten different subject areas including arts and humanities; All Academic (http://www.allacademic.com/), which provides free searching and displays the full text of academic journal articles and book chapters; and an even more focused service, Education-line (http://www.leeds.ac.uk/educol/), which publishes only educationally related, full-text articles and conference proceedings from the United Kingdom.

Many of the textbook and journal publishers are also developing boutique search engines that provide selected readers (often those who purchase their textbook) access to electronic versions of articles and resources that are normally only available in paper format. For example, the parent company of the publisher of this book, Pearson Education, provides a service known as Content Select at http://ebsco.pearsoncmg.com/. Content Select provides access to approximately 25,000 articles in each of fifteen discipline areas. The articles can be searched using a natural language interface, and the full text of each article is available.

Finally, most of the popular education, social science, and humanities reference databases, including Educational Resources Information Center (ERIC) are now available for searching online (see http://www.accesseric.org/). ERIC indexes two types of documents, those published in peer-reviewed journals (the Current Index of Journals in Education [CIJE] with ERIC reference numbers beginning with EJ) and more informal research papers, conference presentations, and government documents (Resources In Education [RIE] with ERIC reference numbers beginning with ED). The full text of the CIJE journal articles must be obtained from the journal publisher. In an increasing number of cases these CIJE articles are online, but often paper copies must be obtained through campus libraries and interlibrary loan services or purchased through commercial library services that provide faxed copies of copyright materials, such as CARL at www.carl.org. The full texts of RIE documents are available in microfiche format at major university libraries, and the more current RIE documents are available through subscription or single-copy prices online at http://www.edrs.com/.

TIPS FOR FINDING FORMAL RESEARCH LITERATURE

- If you have trouble finding the full text of an article you have seen referenced by others, use Google (www.google.com) or one of the other search engines to find and link to the home page of the author. The sought-after article or an even more recent or relevant work may be available directly from the author's home page.
- If you have neglected to copy some important piece of information about a reference or wish to obtain a second quote, searching one of the full-text search engines such as Google, with a few words from the title (typed in quotations), often finds the text of the complete reference or perhaps even a copy of the full-text article.
- Be wary of the "~" sign in a URL as illustrated in the Web address www.ualberta.ca/~tanderso/. This often indicates that the site is a personal page of an employee that works for the organization, but such sites are usually unauthorized, private, and not official pages of the host site owner and thus may lack authenticity and be temporary.

Informal Online Sources

Our discussion on the creation of a literature review has focused, thus far, on reviewing and compiling information from the formal materials that are published on paper or online by researchers and academic or professional organizations. There is, however, a second source of valuable literature to review. This is the informal network of researchers who communicate, share, and build knowledge using both the older opportunities provided at face-to-face conferences and seminars and, increasingly, newer opportunities from a variety of Net-based tools (Hart, 1997). These informal communications constitute the "invisible college" of researchers who are supported on the Net via mailservers, personal emails, newsgroups, chats, and webcasts.

The informal discourse within the community of educational scholars was, before the development of the Internet, a private process that occurred through letters, telephone calls, and at professional conferences. This discussion has now evolved into public and text-based discourse. Messages can be supported on a variety of individual and group-based communications tools. The act of posting, using these text-based tools, forces researchers to articulate their arguments in discourse that is free of much of the trappings of status, gender, and distracting body language that can both illuminate and confuse face-to-face discussion. Finally, this mediated form of informal communication leaves a permanent, searchable record, thereby permitting motivated researchers to revisit and reanalyze discourse on their networked computers. We next briefly outline the most popular tools that support informal literature for review.

Email Lists

The most popular tool to support these informal networks is currently the ubiquitous email list. Lists are usually owned and managed by professional organizations, institutions, research teams, or dedicated individuals inspired by a variety of service motivations.

Most often, membership in academic lists is both free of charge and open to anyone with an interest in the topic. However, membership is always a privilege and never a right. The list owner has the power and is expected to expel anyone whose contributions to the Net are deemed to be offensive to or not supportive of the mailing list membership. Most lists are unmoderated in the sense that the list owner does not preview each posting before it is distributed to the group. This allows for faster exchange and less tasks for the list owner but leaves the list open to abuse through inappropriate posting by any member.

These lists can be used to ask and answer particular questions and relevant research issues and/or read to gain an understanding of the issues, major theories, activities, and personnel involved in a particular research field. Novice e-researchers often subscribe to a large number of email lists in an initial burst of enthusiasm. However, participation in a stimulating exchange of relevant information can all too easily disintegrate into a flood of unread emails and overflowing mailboxes. Thus, efficient e-researchers regularly measure the value of each list to which they subscribe to insure that they are getting information of current value.

Finding an appropriate and relevant mailing list can be a challenge to the e-researcher. There are a number of databases that attempt to gather data and provide subscription information on these lists. For example Dianne Kovac's *Directory of Scholarly and Professional Conferences* lists 375 discussion lists related to education (see http://www.kovacs.com).

The tips provided in the following section are a subset of list netiquette (etiquette rules and practices designed specifically for communicating via the Net) provided by such groups as the HTML Writers' Guild at http://www.hwg.org/lists/netiquette.html or detailed in the official *Internet Engineering Task Force Netiquette Guidelines* (RFC 1855) at http://www.ietf.org/rfc/rfc1855.txt.

Usenet Groups

A second source of informal discussion is the venerable Usenet group. Access to Usenet groups is usually provided by your Internet Service Provider (ISP) and is commonly accessed via the "news reader" functions built into popular Web browsers. Usenet groups provide much of the functionality of the email discussion group, with one major difference. Contributions to a Usenet group are not distributed via email, but in a separate stream of information that circulates throughout the Internet. One participates by reading any of the 50,000 or more groups one wishes to subscribe to. If a subscriber is short of time, the unread messages merely accumulate on the ISP server and are eventually deleted. The messages never overflow the subscriber's mailbox.

Most Usenet groups are unmoderated in the sense that anyone can post anything to the lists. This has resulted in very high levels of spam, or unsolicited messages of a commercial, political, or religious nature. Excessive spam in some newsgroups (many users argue that even one spam message is excessive) has effectively made many Usenet groups useless for their intended purpose with the result that many group members dropped their subscriptions. For this reason, much scholarly discussion has migrated from Usenet groups to public or private email lists.

Usenet groups are organized hierarchically (much like Internet domain names), however unlike domain names the major grouping is listed first, with each subsequent grouping listed after the major topic group. The major top-level groups describe the nature of underlying newsgroups in the hierarchy; they include categories such as "comp," "humanities," "misc," "news," "rec," "sci," "soc," "talk," and the designation "alt" for more informal groups. For example, most of the Usenet groups related to education are located under the alt.education hierarchy. A recent glance at the Usenet group alt.education.research revealed six postings during the past two days—two of them spam postings related to real estate purchases!

TIPS FOR EFFECTIVE USE OF EMAIL AND USENET RESEARCH GROUPS

- Search for a Frequently Asked Question (FAQ) list that may be stored at the list homepage or posted regularly to the discussion group. Many of the Usenet groups' FAQs are linked through the Internet FAQ consortium at http://www.faqs.org/. These lists are designed to inform new users about frequently asked questions and to help prevent regular readers from rereading responses to questions that have been dealt with on many previous occasions.

- Use quotes to reference only relevant material from a previous post to which you are responding. A brief quotation is useful to provide context; however, long inclusions of past comments only waste bandwidth and add to screen clutter.
- Follow the discourse for a few weeks before posting comments or questions yourself to insure that your particular question is relevant to the interests of the list members.
- If in doubt about the appropriateness of a potential posting, email it privately to the list owner for feedback before posting it publicly.
- The use of HTML coding and the addition of attachments to postings always add to the size of the message and may result in messages that cannot be read by all members of the list. A better solution is to post an announcement of the availability of the resource to the list, Usenet group, or virtual conference and to post longer or multimedia messages and files to a Web site where the interested reader can selectively retrieve them.
- Create a separate file folder in your mailbox for information you are sent when first subscribing to a new list. These first subscriber information postings will tell you how to resign or suspend your membership in the list—information that may be relevant but very difficult to find when you wish to resign from the group or change your email address.

Virtual Conferences

The first "virtual conference" on the Internet was organized in 1992 for the International Council for Distance Education (Anderson & Mason, 1993). Subsequently, virtual conferences have proliferated and continue to provide a forum for professional development that is much more cost-effective and accessible than their face-to-face equivalent (for example see http://www.rmrplc.com). Virtual conferences are time-delimited in that they use combinations of synchronous and asynchronous tools to support presentation and dialogue for a limited period of time and usually on a particular topic (Anderson, 1996). Like their face-to-face counterparts, virtual conferences usually include keynote presentations, promotional displays, and small group discussions. Such conferences provide ideal means for e-researchers to gain low-cost exposure to major spokespersons in their field. Announcements of upcoming virtual conferences can be found on appropriate mailing lists, Usenet groups, or the home pages of sponsoring organizations.

Direct Email

Writing directly to an expert in the field may be a useful way for the e-researcher to gain invaluable access to the "informal network." The use of powerful search engines usually allows one to enter the expert's name (in quotations and possibly with a key word appended, if the name is very common) and find a Web site with relevant information, including the expert's email address and phone number. However, the novice e-researcher should be careful not to abuse this availability and should utilize such contacts only when other, less demanding forms of communication have been exhausted. Most experts whom you would like to reference in your literature review are very busy people—if they were not, you probably wouldn't be interested in their work. In addition, most experts write books, publish articles, and create Web sites so that you can gain access to their ideas and comments. Attempts by the novice e-researcher to short circuit the process and go directly and personally to the expert, without checking their public work, will likely be interpreted as bothersome and not be answered.

As an example of an inappropriate request, we recently received an email from a graduate student studying in a foreign country. The email noted that the student had read one of our articles, liked it, and wondered if we could send more information. Since we had no idea which article was read (we have been publishing for many years), we were not inclined to even answer the letter. Alternatively, legitimate, well-informed, clearly written, and polite questions and concerns may not only be answered, but may be appreciated and lead to further contacts with experts in the field.

Filtering Messages for Others

It is impossible to follow all of the discussion groups and Web sites that may have information relevant to your field of study. Thus, many successful e-researchers develop informal networks of friends and colleagues who filter relevant information from their own explorations of the network and forward appropriate messages, links, or referrals to them. This filtering can become institutionalized as the researcher sets up a formal or informal mailing list for messages or references that contain information relevant to the members of the list. In the early days of networking, prior to the Internet, this transporting of information between networks was referred to as *porting* and porters were celebrated as "Unsung heroes of the Network Nation!" (Masthead, *Netweaver Magazine*).

Making Effective Use of the Informal Network Resources

To maximize the effectiveness of an inquiry, an e-researcher must be careful to ask a question or request assistance in an appropriate manner. As in any conversation, the researcher must be sure to use a manner and tone that is polite, respectful, and appreciative. In addition, e-researchers must insure that they have done their own literature review and research work before asking others to do it for them.

For example, a question such as "Does anyone know anything about school dropout for a research paper I'm doing?" will likely not result in any assistance and will certainly let the members of the group know you have a great deal to learn about both the subject and the etiquette of Net-based discussions. A refined request such as "Tinto's model of student dropout seems to be used often in postsecondary, but an ERIC search turns up only a single study in a secondary school context. Does anyone on this list (Usenet group, or virtual conference) know of any work, using Tinto's model in this area or have any ideas why it is not appropriate?" This latter phrasing illustrates that you have done some research and thinking and may well be a useful contact and serious e-researcher.

Citing Net-based Resources in the Literature Review

There are a number of formats for referencing documents and correspondence obtained from the Internet. In general the format for most styles follows that prescribed for the referencing of paper-based documents, with the addition of the Uniform Resource Locator (URL) and the date of access of the document appended to the end of the reference. For example, in American Psychology Association (APA) format the equivalent paper reference is followed by the words:

> Retrieved on *date* from the World Wide Web: *http://site address*.

Some citing guidelines (notably APA) do not encourage private emails, unarchived list postings, or postings to Usenet groups in the reference bibliography, because obtaining a copy of the correspondence may be difficult or impossible for the interested reader. Instead, these guidelines suggest referencing such private or difficult to retrieve material as "private email correspondence from *name* on *date*" or "posting to *list name* on *date*" within the text of the document. Other guides suggest that this information be kept and made available to the interested reader and that it be referenced in the bibliography in the format:

> Anderson, T. (16 September 2001). Subject: When will our book be published? [email to H. Kanuka], [Online]. Available email: heather.kanuka@ualberta.ca.

For more information related to the format for citing electronic references, the World-Wide Web Virtual Library maintains a listing of sites entitled *Electronic References & Scholarly Citations of Internet Sources* at http://www.spaceless.com/WWWVL/.

It is important to learn and consistently use the format in which your e-research results will eventually be published. Making use of consistent notation of all relevant fields from the very beginning of the research process will save you a great deal of time in the long run. To aid in this data organization process, a brief discussion of personal reference management software appears in the next section.

PLAGIARISM AND NETWORKED SOURCES

Most academic writing has liberal doses of direct quotations from the works of others. This practice lends authenticity to the literature review and, done properly, can even enhance the readability of the literature review. However, it is imperative that the work of others be properly acknowledged. Even if a quotation is not used directly, ideas that are paraphrased by the researcher need to be credited to the original source. Given the pervasiveness of ideas, papers, reference sources, and commentaries on the

Net, e-researchers may feel they are drowning in a bewildering and immense sea of information, sources, and references. They may even have trouble remembering where or even if the idea or quotation they have gathered came from another source or is original work. There is no easy solution to this problem, except to remember that quality research is systematic. An electronic or paper notebook (see personal reference management software in the next section for an example) to record quotes and ideas, as well as their source, is an essential tool for all researchers and can be especially important when beginning a literature review.

Plagiarism, or the act of presenting the work of others as if you created it, is not a new problem for e-research, but one that the availability of the Net makes both easier to commit and to detect. As a result, the ease of cutting and pasting from the Web has been blamed for an increase in plagiarism. Although we do not doubt that ease of transcription may lead unscrupulous or naïve students to plagiarize the work of others in essays and assignments, we doubt that it is a significant factor in inadvertent or blatant plagiarism by serious e-researchers. Plagiarizing of the ideas or works of others has been around since the days of quill pens and any careful examination of this behavior will likely lead one beyond facility of transcription. Indeed, this section on plagiarism is short, as we believe the issues and sanctions associated with plagiarism have not changed from traditional research to e-research.

It is often tempting to extract and use a direct quote that is cited in the work of an author that you are reviewing. This too is generally not a good practice. The main reason for this cautionary advice is that the author you are taking the quote from may have taken the quote out of context from the originating source. Specifically, the author may have used the original work in ways that buttress his or her own argument, but may not present the full argument from the original author. Further, it may not make use of the work of the original author most effectively for your purposes. The most effective approach is to obtain, read, and then either paraphrase or quote the work of the original author directly, thus allowing you to make your own, original decision as to the value of the quotation or reference and to select the correct amount of content to quote. The Net makes this search for original authors easier, as entering the quotation or at least the original author's name and the year of publication may return the full text of the original reference. If the original publication is not available online, you should look for a paper-based copy at a public library or a library at an academic institution. If the original text is not available or held at that particular library, almost all libraries offer interlibrary loans.

As noted earlier, this practice of searching the Net for the direct quotations of others can also serendipitously lead to additional papers that have quoted the same author. With luck, persistence, and good searching technique, one reference often leads to a trail of relevant links that very quickly appraises the e-researcher of relevant literature related to the question under investigation. However, one must always remember that, at least at the time of this writing, many of the major journals and seminal writings are not available on the public Net. Thus, any comprehensive research makes use of online- and CD-ROM-based indexes and direct searching of paper-based copies of relevant journals.

In an interesting legal description of plagiarism, Standler (2000) notes that plagiarism also includes taking credit for material that was written collaboratively or by others—in particular graduate students or others employed as assistants to original authors. Standler cites a 1993 case of a professor who was dismissed for publishing material that was originally developed by both a coauthor and graduate student (without attribution). This issue of fairly sharing recognition of collaborative work is complicated and covered in more depth in Chapter 6, Collaborative e-Research. We have found that the roles of participants in collaborative work, the order of authors on any published document, the right to present papers at conferences from collaborative work, and other issues of appropriate recognition should be discussed openly before the research project commences—and should always be open for further discussion as the research proceeds.

As noted earlier, detecting plagiarism is also made easier by using the Net. Typing a suspect phrase into a search engine like Google.com, can often uncover the original source, or perhaps another author who has directly quoted the phrase in question. In addition there are commercial sites that purposively index scholarly papers and thousands of student essays and allow academics or teachers to search (for a fee) their databases of articles, books, and essays for plagiarized phrases (see for example http://www.turnitin.com/). An excellent resource on plagiarism can be found at Indiana University's Writing Tutorial Services at http://www.indiana.edu/~wts/wts/plagiarism.html. This Web site is a useful overview that includes examples of quotations and paraphrases to both adopt and avoid.

Personal Reference Management Software

Most serious e-researchers soon conclude that there must be an easier way to manage the long lists of references that they accumulate and must format correctly at the end of each of their research reports. A first step is to judiciously cut and paste from earlier documents and, with the insert function of a word processor, manually alphabetize new references. However, as one continues to create documents, the need to consistently reference key resources and to change format style for different publications, along with the frustration and errors involved in rekeying references from existing electronic databases, often motivate the e-researcher to acquire and use tools specifically designed to aid in this process. These tools are referred to as *reference management software*.

Reference management software is designed to assist the researcher in managing, entering, retrieving, and printing a wide variety of reference citations in an equally large number of format styles. Unlike traditional database software, reference management software allows data to be entered in specific fields for different types of references. For example, the required fields to properly reference a chapter in an edited online book are different from those needed to reference an online conference proceeding or email posting. Finally, these software packages allow authors to sort references by any classification system desired. For example, you could categorize references by chapter title in your thesis or research report, thereby being able to export, select, or sort quotations easily and effectively.

Personal reference management software is useful for both e-researchers and traditional scholars. Like many software applications, new versions of reference management software are becoming Net-enabled. This means that they can connect to and search library catalogs and databases (including ERIC and other educational reference databases) and import selected references into the researcher's private reference collection without the time-consuming and error-prone task of rekeying the entry. Net-enabled packages also allow formatting of reference lists in HTML for publishing on the Net, and some allow multiple researchers at different locations to add to and extract references from a common database. There are many reference management packages available in the commercial and shareware market (see http://www.wisc.edu/wendt/help/win.html). Free trial versions of the two most popular commercial products are also available to researchers at these sites:

ProCite: http://www.isiresearchsoft.com/pc/pcdownload.html
EndNote: http://www.endnote.com/ENdownload.htm

SUMMARY

The quantity and quality of both formal and informal sources of information available and useful to the e-researcher increases daily. The development of searching skills, coupled with the increasing sophistication and artificial intelligence of search engines, creates a tremendous advantage for the e-researcher over those working without networked tools. This chapter provides useful tips, hints, and suggestions for maximizing the effectiveness of the literature review process.

The selective review and synthesis of the relevant literature almost always results in savings of time and effort for the researcher as well as improvements to the quality of the research study. Equally important, quality literature reviews help us "stand on each other's shoulders" and see further into the problems and opportunities challenging the researcher.

REFERENCES

Anderson, T. (1996). The virtual conference: Extending professional education in cyberspace. *International Journal of Educational Telecommunications*, *2*(2/3), 121–135.

Anderson, T., & Mason, R. (1993). The Bangkok Project: New tool for professional development. *American Journal of Distance Education*, 7(2), 5–18.

Center for Applied Special Technology (2001). [Online]. Available: http://www.cast.org/bobby/.

December, J. (1994). Challenges for a webbed society. *Computer-Mediated Communication Magazine*, *1*(8). [Online]. Available: http://www.december.com/cmc/mag/1994/nov/websoc.html.

Netweaver. Electronic Networking Association (1991). *NetWeaver* 7(3).

Harnad, S. (1996). Implementing peer review on the net: Scientific quality control in scholarly electronic journals. In R. Peek and G. Newby (Eds.), *Scholarly publication: The electronic Frontier* (pp. 103–108). Cambridge, MA: MIT Press.

Harris, R. (1997). Evaluating Internet research sources. [Online]. Available: http://www.sccu.edu/faculty/R_Harris/evalu8it.htm.

Hart, R. (1997). Information gathering among the faculty of a comprehensive college: Formality and globality. *Journal of Academic Librarianship*, *23*(1), 21–27.

Kibirige, H., & Depalo, L. (2000). The Internet as a source of academic research information: Findings of two pilot studies. *Information Technology and Libraries*, *19*(1). [Online]. Available: http://www.lita.org/ital/1901_kibirige.html.

Smith, A. (1997). Testing the surf: Criteria for evaluating Internet information resources. *Public-Access Computer Systems*, *8*(3). [Online]. Available: http://info.lib.uh.edu/pr/v8/smit8n3.html.

Standler, R. (2000). Plagiarism in colleges in the USA. [Online]. Available http://www.rbs2.com/plag.htm.

Tillman, H. N. (1998). Evaluating quality on the net. [Online]. Available: http://www.hopetillman.com/findqual.html.

CHAPTER FIVE

ETHICS AND THE e-RESEARCHER

Penetrating so many secrets, we cease to believe in the unknowable. But there it sits nevertheless, calmly licking its chops.

H. L. Mencken, American editor and critic

Researchers associated with academic institutions need to submit an ethics proposal prior to conducting their research. Researchers who are associated with private or commercial research functions will also need to think and plan very seriously about the ethical implications of their e-research. Hence, it is fitting to begin a discussion here of ethical procedures for e-research. As an e-researcher, you will encounter a number of dilemmas, issues, and problems with respect to ethics. These issues pertain to all types of research, but they have a tendency to acquire added and more complex twists when undertaken in an electronic format. Irrespective of the size, complexity, or methodology employed in your research, you must always adhere to ethical and moral principles. We believe that when all is said and done ethical research is really more about creating and maintaining respectful relationships with the participants of the study than about formalized codes of ethics and internal review board rules and guidelines. Unfortunately, many of the existing principles for face-to-face-based research do not adequately account for significant differences encountered when conducting research on the Net, nor do many of the ethics review committee members understand how e-research is actually conducted and, hence, may not recognize an ethically compromised Net-based study. As such it is up to us, as competent e-researchers and principled human beings, to define and practice ethical behavior. This requires personal integrity and self-regulation, which includes openness and honesty about all aspects of the study, as well as reflection on our actions before, during, and after conducting a research project.

This chapter is not about following codes of ethics or preparing for institutional ethics review boards. All academic institutions have prescriptive guidelines defining what constitutes ethical behavior to which all researchers associated with these institutions must adhere. Nor is this chapter an attempt to provide a definitive moral platform to guide research conducted on the Net. Rather, the chapter is designed to bring to your attention the ethical complexities of e-research that must be understood and integrated into the practice of an e-researcher.

Before we begin a discussion on how the Net complicates ethics, it is important to acknowledge that there are few hard-and-fast rules that categorically define ethical research, however there are a few agreed-upon principles. These principles include: (1) voluntary informed consent; (2) privacy, confidentiality, and anonymity; and (3) recognizing the elements of research risk (Bickman & Rog, 1998). In practice these principles can conflict with each other, and the researchers will then need to balance carefully the importance of advancement of understandings and knowledge and the need to guard against potential harm to the research participants (e.g., loss of dignity, self-esteem, privacy).

HOW THE NET COMPLICATES ETHICS

Ethical concerns are becoming increasingly multifarious in our postmodern society, which is defined by complexity, multiculturalism, and media saturation. Researchers are expected to understand the basic principles of good research and be cognizant with respect to any proscriptive codes of ethics. Ultimately, however, ethical conduct depends on the individual researcher. "The researcher has a moral and professional obligation to be ethical, even when research subjects are unaware of or unconcerned about ethics" (Neuman, 2000).

In any new field of study, time and experience are required before it is possible to infer the appropriate definition and extent of ethical behavior. Infamous studies of potentially harmful deception (Milgram, 1963) in social psychology illustrate the need for ethical behavior by researchers and the usefulness of institutionalized guidelines to both define and enforce ethical practice by researchers.

The study that perhaps best brings to our attention the immediate need to establish ethical protocols for Net-based research is the Rimm study reported by Thomas (1996). This long-term research study involved an analysis of data about users of text-based erotica files that was collected via analysis of particular Usenet posts from the alt.binaries hierarchy. The research study also included a summary of the statistics on Usenet readership. Readership data was obtained from the private files of users on a large university computer system. The study was described by the researcher (Marty Rimm, who was at that time an undergraduate student) to be scientific, comprehensive, and the first of its kind. The study involved three main data-gathering techniques. The initial pool of subjects was identified from approximately 1,000 Bulletin Board Systems (BBS). From this pool, ninety-one were chosen and thirty-five were used. Descriptions of pornographic files were then downloaded for analysis by a linguistic parsing software script. At least half of the BBSs were not accessible to the general public (e.g., proof of age was a requirement for access). At the researcher's request, the system operator collected other data including demographic details (age, sex, nationality, marital status, position, department, and other confidential information) of the users without asking the users' permission that allowed the researcher (Marty Rimm) to track approximately four thousand individuals who accessed erotic and/or nonerotic Usenet groups once a month or more.

Among the many ethical issues illustrated in this case (such as gathering data from privileged sources for which there was no evidence that permission was attained), is the continued debate over what is a public forum and what is a private forum. While there is general consensus that Usenet groups are public forums and anyone can read them, it is less clear if studying those who subscribe to the newsgroups can be done without informed consent or loss of personal integrity, dignity, and respect for privacy. Are online interactions on bulletin boards and Usenet groups public, or are they private conversations that occur in public spaces? And if the conversations are private, but occurring in a public space, are researchers intruding? And if we do agree that researchers are intruding, what is the nature of the intrusion as it relates to harm that may or may not result from the research and in light of the benefits that may be realized from the findings of the study?

As the Rimm study illustrates, the Net has become the focus of an extensive range of ethical concerns as it evolves into a modern agora in which contrasting ethical interpretations and actions are played out. This context is further complicated by characteristics of the Net that are unique and largely unknowable within physical environments. These include the capacity of individuals to retain various degrees of anonymity, the capacity to horde, steal, and retain objects with no physical embodiment, the blurring between public and private domains, the possibility of participating in sexual experiences with no physical contact, and other forms of interpersonal activity that have few parallels in the physical world. These evolving scenarios and the actors (both physical and virtual) create the fascinating context in which the e-researcher works. To date, there are no clearly defined criteria for appropriate ethical behavior for all e-researchers or all e-research activity. For many behaviors and challenges we experience on the Web, we search for successful and appropriate rules from the pre-Net context to use as analogies and models that we can apply to define appropriate ethics for the Net. Existing rules provide a good starting point, but they are not sufficient to capture all of the peculiar ethical nuances and concerns of Net-based research activities and subsequent research.

One way to overcome many of these issues is to develop a full set of ethical guidelines and practices specifically designed for the Net. However, because the field and methodology of study, as well as the actual context of activity are changing, there is need for caution before formalizing permanent ethical standards that may not meet the long-term needs of either researchers or participants. Currently, most efforts to prescribe ethical behavior in Net-based contexts attempt to apply existing ethical codes of practice. We explore both the value and limitations of this type of projective ethics throughout this chapter.

Different Applications Present Different Challenges

As described in Chapter 1 (Figure 1.1), there are two quite distinct ways to use the Net for research. Both ways present ethical challenges for the e-researcher. In the case in which e-research methods are used to study behavior that does not take place on the network, but the network is used as a means to contact, observe, survey, or interview participants, the ethical issues are more directly related, and analogous, to non-networked research. In this case, ethical guidelines can, generally, be ported from existing ethical guidelines. Some of the procedures involved in obtaining and verifying consent and providing for security and privacy are unique to the network, but, generally, updating existing guidelines to a networked context is relatively straightforward. However, when applying e-research to study behavior that takes place on the networks, ethical issues become more complex. In these virtual contexts, issues of identity, anonymity, privacy, and protection of virtual self are difficult to transfer to the online environment, and direct analogies from non-networked research ethics become stretched and in some cases nonfunctional. The following sections discuss these difficulties as they relate to existing ethical guidelines and principles.

Standing Ethical Guidelines and Principles

In addition to dignity, privacy, self-esteem, and our own values, ethics revolves around the behavior of the individual in regard to that demanded or accepted by a larger group (Thomas, 1996; Thomas, 1999). These dictates from the larger group are often proscribed as rules of conduct for members of particular professions or organizations. Traditionally, the principles for such "right" conduct in most societies are derived from sacred texts or oral teachings. However, Western societies are characterized by diversity of culture, where there is no one universal teaching to provide us with these guidelines. Societies and groups wishing to act with particular authority are forced to look to sets of commonly held and defined values to determine what is correct behavior in both the general and the individual case.

As mentioned, ethical behavior stems from commonly perceived and held values. With respect to research, the commonly perceived and held values generally relate to the following three areas: autonomy and respect for other persons, the reduction of potential to harm, and, conversely, the potential for beneficence and justice. Researchers and their professional bodies, such as the American Psychological Association, or funding bodies, such as the Canadian Government Granting Councils, have built on these values to create sets of ethical guidelines for activity in the physical realm. These are detailed by organizations such as the American Psychology Association (APA) at http://www.apa.org/ethics/code.html. While proscribed for practicing psychologists, many researchers from other disciplines (e.g., education and the social sciences) usually adhere to these general principles as well. We outline these principles here, adjusting them toward a generalized perspective for e-researchers.

Competence. E-researchers should strive to maintain high standards of competence in their work. They need to recognize the boundaries of their particular competencies and the limitations of their expertise and provide only those services and use only those techniques for which they are qualified by education, training, or experience. In areas in which recognized professional standards do not yet exist, researchers should exercise careful judgment and take appropriate precautions to protect the welfare of those with whom they work. Moreover, they should maintain knowledge of relevant scientific and professional information, and recognize the need for ongoing education.

Integrity. As e-researchers seek to promote integrity in their research, they are honest, fair, and respectful of others. In describing or reporting their qualifications, they do not make statements that are false, misleading, or deceptive. E-researchers should strive to be aware of their own belief systems, values, needs, and limitations and the effect of these on their work. To the extent feasible, they attempt to clarify for relevant parties the roles they are performing and to function appropriately in accordance with those roles and avoid improper and potentially harmful dual relationships.

Professional and Scientific Responsibility. E-researchers should uphold professional standards of conduct, clarify their professional roles and obligations, accept appropriate responsibility for their behavior, and adapt their methods to the needs of different populations. Further, they should consult with, refer to, and/or cooperate with other professionals and institutions to the extent needed to serve the best interests of their research participants. Just as they are for any other person, moral standards and conduct are personal matters for the e-researcher, except when their actions compromise their professional responsibilities or reduce the public's trust. When appropriate, they consult with colleagues to prevent or avoid unethical conduct.

Respect for People's Rights and Dignity. E-researchers hold appropriate respect to the fundamental rights, dignity, and worth of all people. They respect the rights of individuals to privacy, confidentiality, self-determination, and autonomy, mindful that legal and other obligations may lead to inconsistency and conflict with the exercise of these rights. Moreover, they are aware of cultural, individual, and role differences, including those due to age, gender, race, ethnicity, national origin, religion, sexual orientation, disability, language, and socioeconomic status. They try to eliminate the effect of biases based on those factors on their work, and they do not knowingly participate in or condone unfair discriminatory practices.

Concern for Others' Welfare. E-researchers seek to contribute to the welfare of those with whom they interact professionally. In their professional actions, they weigh the welfare and rights of their research participants, and other affected persons. When conflicts occur among colleagues' obligations or concerns, e-researchers attempt to resolve these conflicts and to perform their roles in a responsible fashion that avoids or minimizes harm, they are sensitive to real and ascribed differences in power between themselves and others, and they do not exploit or mislead other people during or after professional relationships.

Social Responsibility. E-researchers are aware of their professional and scientific responsibilities to the community and the society in which they work and live. They apply and make public their knowledge of their profession or field of study to contribute to human welfare. They are concerned about and work to mitigate the causes of human suffering. E-researchers comply with the law and encourage the development of law and social policy that serves the interests of their research participants and the public. They are encouraged to contribute a portion of their professional time for little or no personal advantage.

For most types of research in physical contexts, following these principles is relatively straightforward. However, Net research provides a different kind of research format—one that transforms our conceptions of time, space, and physical environment. In turn, our understanding of how to follow ethical principles changes with respect to maintaining privacy, confidentiality or anonymity, voluntary and informed consent, and recognizing elements of research risk.

PRIVACY, CONFIDENTIALITY, AUTONOMY, AND THE RESPECT FOR PERSONS

Privacy refers to the research participants' right to control access of others to themselves. Confidentiality refers to an agreement as to how the data collected in the study will be kept private (or confidential) through controlled access to the data collected. The terms of confidentiality are usually tailored to the needs of the participants. For example, for certain participants simply changing the name may be sufficient to provide confidentiality. Alternatively, it may also be necessary for the researcher to use pseudonyms for the geographical setting and type of employment to ensure confidentiality with other participants. Anonymity refers to processes or safeguards that are implemented to hide any unique characteristics (e.g., names, addresses, affiliated institution) that could be used to personally identify a subject. New researchers often, incorrectly, exchange the terms *anonymity* and *confidentiality*. It is important to understand the difference between these terms with respect to research and to use them correctly. The difference between anonymity and confidentiality is that with anonymity, steps are taken by the researcher to insure that the participants' identities are not revealed to the researchers (e.g., mailed surveys), whereas with confidentiality, the researcher does know the participants' identities (e.g., face-to-face focus group interviews), but takes steps to keep their identities confidential. Respecting a participant's need for privacy, confidentiality, or autonomy is a fundamental way in which a researcher can show respect for a person—indeed, it is a requirement of ethical practice among education researchers. This respect is shown most clearly by allowing the participants to share in the decision making that affects them. To make decisions accurately and knowledgeably the respondent must be informed of all the relevant details of the research and, in particular, be provided with an opportunity to refuse to participate.

These guidelines can and should be used for Net-based research as well. However, e-researchers also need to be cognizant that other people may have access to data that is kept on an Internet server and, hence, the same assurances for privacy, confidentiality, and anonymity cannot be provided by the e-researcher. For example, server maintenance personnel will have access to the data that resides on the server, and these individuals will need to guarantee that they will not share or distribute any data to which they may have access. The case study by Thomas (1996) cited previously illustrates the power that system administration staff have to gather and release private data. Hackers, or unauthorized persons, may also have access to stored data and thus are always a looming threat to safely securing data that resides on an Internet server. This threat is twofold: accessing and making public data that is collected or destroying data through distributed viruses. E-researchers will need to advise the participants that they cannot absolutely guarantee that data will not be accessed, used, changed, or destroyed by others. They will also need to provide details outlining the steps they are taking to attempt to provide privacy, confidentiality, or anonymity. Roberts (2000a) and Witmer (1998) have observed that there is sometimes a lack of understanding by both research participants and researchers with respect to the technical and storage capabilities of Internet technologies. Specifically, they note that there is an elevated "risk of exposure of the subject's identity and the potential accessibility of their personal information to others" (Roberts) and, as such, the participants should be made aware of this by the researcher. At this point, the participants can make a decision to participate, or not, based on this information. Further, if the security of the data does become compromised, the e-researcher will be somewhat better protected from humiliation, a possible ruined career, and legal action if he/she has informed the participants of this risk.

Finally, if e-researchers are dealing with sensitive data that, if made public, could bring harm to the participant, they will have to make the difficult decision of whether or not it is even ethical to use Net-based communication. The e-researcher has the option to use Net-based communication software that encrypts correspondence between researcher and subject (this software is discussed in the next chapter). E-researchers may also wish to routinely encrypt sensitive files (such as digitized audio interview transcripts) that are stored on personal or group servers. The stand-alone encryption program PGP (Pretty Good Privacy), available on the Web at no charge, encodes and decodes files, thereby protecting the privacy of files and electronic mail. A Frequently Asked Questions file explaining PGP use is available at http://cache.qualcomm.com/getpg.htm.

Another of the complexities and corresponding problems that e-researchers encounter with respect to privacy, confidentiality, or autonomy, is dealing with how to obtain informed consent from online participants. The following section provides a discussion of the issues, problems, and dilemmas facing e-researchers when obtaining consent from online participants.

OBTAINING CONSENT FROM ONLINE PARTICIPANTS

We begin the discussion of means to obtaining consent by reiterating the need for the e-researcher to gain the trust and support of all potential participants. This support can be effectively achieved in an introductory note that outlines the purpose of the research, the details of the research process, what is expected of participants, and the steps that will be taken to protect privacy and confidentiality. The box includes an example of an informed consent form at a western Canadian university.

EXAMPLE OF AN INFORMED CONSENT FORM FOR RESEARCH PARTICIPANTS

Dear Participant:

The computer conferencing software you will be using for your courses this term is an educational software system in the beta stage of development. In order to improve upon this new software, data will be collected from the courses. Research will focus on two main types of analysis: communication patterns and discourse analysis. User feedback through surveys and/or interview data may also be collected. This study is separate from your course work and the data collected will in no way be used for course grading purposes.

Please read the text below and, if you agree, indicate your consent by signing the form and submitting it to the instructor or by submitting it online. The online form requires you to fill in your name in place of your signature. If you have any concerns or questions that you would like addressed before completing the consent form, please send an e-mail to [*email address*].

The University and those conducting this project subscribe to the ethical conduct of research and to the protection at all times of the interests, comfort, and safety of subjects. This form and the information it contains are given to you for your own protection and full understanding of the procedures involved. Your signature on this form or online submission of this form will signify that you have had an adequate opportunity to consider the information, and that you voluntarily agree to participate in the project.

The objective of the research project is to develop tools to support advanced models of learning and to manage, structure, and evaluate courses that are being developed to run on the e-software platform. This involves the conceptualization, implementation, and evaluation of tools to support and enhance collaborative learning. For research purposes, the system will collect the following data: (1) computer-generated usage data, (2) conference transcripts, and (3) virtual "artifacts" (e.g., common file areas, Web pages). Research will focus on two main types of analysis: communication patterns and discourse analysis. User feedback through surveys and/or interview data may also be collected. The research team greatly appreciates your cooperation in our study.

Having been asked to participate as a subject in this research project, I understand and agree to the following:

> The computer conferencing software (e-software) is an experimental system being developed and will be used for some of the activities in my course
>
> Institution:
> Course:
> Course Title:
> Instructor(s):

- Computer-generated usage data of student use of the e-software will be collected.
- Transcripts of user contributions will be saved and stored.
- Virtual "artifacts" created by users in online courses will be saved and stored.
- This consent form is requesting permission of the faculty members, teaching assistants, students, and industry-based participants for the use of the data described for research purposes.

- All uses of this research data will remain anonymous and confidential. Confidentiality will be maintained by use of pseudonyms. No real names will be mentioned in reports or publications related to the data.
- Copies of the results of this research will not be immediately available to students. As the studies using this data are completed, the results will be published and may be obtained on request.

As an industry-based participant/student/teaching assistant/faculty member using e-software in a course, I give my permission for the computer generated usage data, conference transcript data, and virtual artifacts data collected by the conferencing software to be used for research.

I understand that I may withdraw my permission at any time. I also understand that I may register any concern or complaint I might have about the experiment with the dean of this university [*name, email, address, and phone number of dean*].

Name
Email:
Date:

If you would like to comment on your experience as a participant in this project, you can use the Subject Feedback Form.

Note on this consent form that the purpose of the study is identified, participant expectations are outlined, confidentiality and anonymity are explained, and a contact for further questions is identified. While this consent form was designed to be completed either as a paper-based form, or as an online form, email is also often used for obtaining consent. Generally, email is the most cost-effective and timely way to communicate with potential respondents and it is also more personal than a pointer to a Web site that explains details of the study. Moreover, requesting that the respondent's email program send a receipt when the recipient opens the email can enhance the urgency of the message. An automated request from the e-researcher's email program will trigger a request for permission to email this notification to the potential respondent and will likely result in increased response rates. Dillman (2000) recommends sending such a request for participation prior to transmission of the actual research instrument. This politely informs potential respondents of their opportunity to participate without overloading their mailbox through distribution of unsolicited mail.

We can also see from the above example that the *construction* of consent forms for Net-based research is, essentially, very similar to other traditional forms of research. However, the problem of *obtaining* consent for Net-based research is often much more complicated. Specifically, because the medium lends itself to supporting fluid communities that are often in flux and transient, obtaining consent, which typically includes dissemination of results and/or member checks and debriefings, can be a challenge for the e-researcher. King (1996) observes, "given that cyberspace communities are tenuous conglomerations of individuals where membership changes frequently, even asking for permission from the group is often no assurance that all members studied will feel they gave informed consent." Research in these communities requires the development of unique guidelines that are functional within this emerging context. Sharf

(1999) developed the following set of four ethical guidelines for researchers working with these types of informal mail lists or Usenet groups.

1. The researcher should be sure that the research has the potential to benefit both the researcher and the group that is the subject of the research.
2. The researcher should make clear his or her identity, role, purpose, and intention.
3. The researcher should obtain explicit permission before directly quoting words of anyone in a publication.
4. The researcher should seek ways to maintain an openness and communication with all participants. (pp. 253–254)

Since a list owner or moderator manages most Usenet groups and active mailing lists, the appropriate place to begin the type of communications outlined by Sharf is with the list owner. Collaborating with the list owner will often result in higher participation rates and the study may be able to be refined so as to better serve the needs of the list owner and participating members of the online community, as well as the e-researcher.

We often analyze the transcripts of educational classes delivered online (see, for example: Kanuka & Anderson, 1998; Rourke, Anderson, Garrison, & Archer, 2000). During one such research project we attempted to study the computer conference use by medical student interns. The conferencing was designed to provide both support and guidance from campus-based instructors. As is customary, we filed a request for ethical clearance of this research with our university's research ethics review committee. After approval, we emailed a form to all interns, which granted us permission to analyze the transcripts produced during the internship. In this case a single student refused to sign the form arguing that the researchers' review of their conversations constituted a breech of the privacy that they felt existed within this private conference group. There was little we could do but to abort the research project at that point, since arguably even excluding this student's comments required a review and analysis of the transcript. More typically we find that acquiring informed consent forms, returned either electronically or in paper format, is easily obtained from the majority of students. We are careful to follow normal protocol of explaining that allowing for transcript review is not compulsory, that participants may withdraw from the study, that individual privacy will be safeguarded, and that there are no apparent risks to the participants. However, we often have problems when individual students, although they do not refuse to participate, do not respond positively to our request for an email confirming their willingness to participate. Have these students refused to participate and thus analysis of any information from these individuals should be perceived as unethical? Or has the email been lost in transport? Or have the students dropped out of the course? This creates a problem with limited solutions for the e-researcher.

The above-noted problems aside, it is usual for a high proportion of participants to complete and return permission to participate via emails, and rare for respondents to explicitly refuse to participate. A solution may be found by contacting the nonrespondents through telephone or regular mail, but often such information is deemed to be private and not available to the researcher. A second alternative is to exclude from the study only those participants who explicitly refuse participation through notifications to the researcher. In this case, those who respond favorably or who do not respond at all are assumed to have given permission for participation. A third alternative is to selectively delete from the analysis the messages posted by those who have explicitly refused to participate as well as those who have not responded. This is a difficult task, however, as often components of previous messages are quoted in subsequent messages, making extraction of particular messages very challenging. The safe option to this dilemma is to follow the third course and eliminate (if possible) all the comments except those who have explicitly given their permission to participate. In practice, extra efforts using the first alternative and rigorously pursuing a nonresponse is probably the best use of e-research time. Some researchers avoid this dilemma altogether by publicly announcing their participation to the online group, but only requesting formal permission from those whose writings they are intending to directly quote from in published results. This issue of informed consent for analysis of online activity will likely remain contentious for some time.

OBTAINING CONSENT ELECTRONICALLY

Unique ethical issues related to Net-based research also revolve around identifying research subjects and authenticating their responses. These issues are not unique to Net-based research but tend to become more complex when using the Internet and, hence, more problematic. For example, the process of acquiring consent usually involves signing a consent form in which the researcher outlines the relevant components of the research. In some cases consent is implied by the completion of a survey or questionnaire. Normally, a signature authenticates consent; however, many potential respondents do not (at least at the time we write this book) use digital signature technologies that insure encryption and authentication. Thus, e-researchers may collect emails or Web forms that, in a technical sense, do not have the legal weight of a signed consent form. However unless the researcher has reason to believe that the participant has an incentive to misrepresent him/herself, these forms are generally deemed to be acceptable notice of consent. E-researchers are encouraged to use authentication software for both participants and themselves. Authentication software also effectively eliminates third-party interference. These services are provided at relatively low cost through Certificate Authorities and public key infrastructure firms such as www.verisign.com.

E-researchers who obtain consent over the Net also have to be aware of the risk of possibly attracting vulnerable populations to their study. As Roberts (2000a) points out, important demographic details, such as age, may be concealed by potential participants. This may lead to vulnerable populations (e.g., children or persons of diminished mental capacity) being recruited and included in a study without the researcher's knowledge. Schrum (1995) maintains that this alone presents serious problems in obtaining some degree of informed consent and considers this to be the most difficult ethical issue of online research. While the e-researcher will need to acknowledge this as a looming possibility (or a limitation) to conducting Net-based research, Roberts

(2000b) maintains there is a counter argument. While attracting vulnerable participants is an ever-present possibility, the Internet also has the ability to access participants who might otherwise be unable to participate or who traditionally may not have been able to have a voice in research projects. For a variety of reasons (e.g., geographic, disabilities, situational) researchers are sometimes not able to access specific people or populations. In certain circumstances, Net-based research can provide greater inclusivity by accessing these populations.

Some researchers who wish to obtain consent have creatively used the forms feature on Web pages to obtain information. Figure 5.1 is an example of an online consent form by Nora Boekhout (http://www.teacherwebshelf.com/) at Simon Fraser University (for consent form see http://modena.intergate.ca/personal/boekhout/technologyincurriculum/ethicsforms.html). While the information on the form is standard for Simon Fraser University, notice that this online consent form has a section for a witness whereby the e-researcher may follow-up and verify the participant through the witness information. While there are no guarantees that the witness is credible (or even exists for that matter) this does provide another way to authenticate the research participants. Also note the active nature of required participation as contrasted with the way most of us casually click past license information (without reading) when first using new software packages purchased or downloaded from the Net.

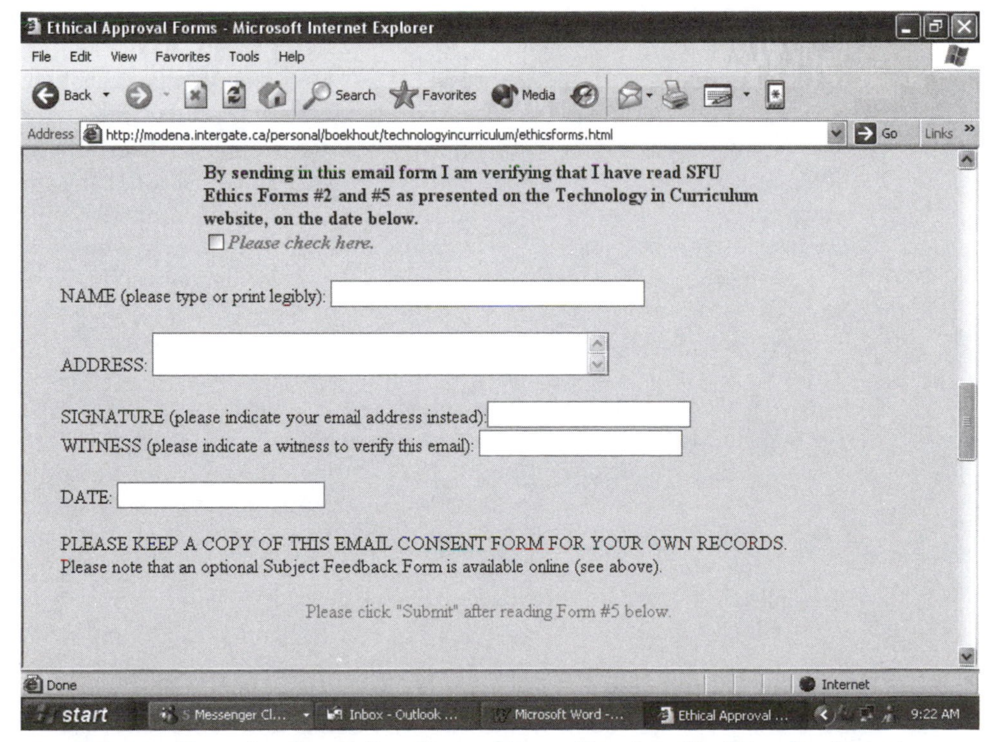

Ethical Approval Forms - Microsoft Internet Explorer

File Edit View Favorites Tools Help

Back Search Favorites Media

Address http://modena.intergate.ca/personal/boekhout/technologyincurriculum/ethicsforms.html Go Links

By sending in this email form I am verifying that I have read SFU Ethics Forms #2 and #5 as presented on the Technology in Curriculum website, on the date below.

☐ *Please check here.*

NAME (please type or print legibly):

ADDRESS:

SIGNATURE (please indicate your email address instead):

WITNESS (please indicate a witness to verify this email):

DATE:

PLEASE KEEP A COPY OF THIS EMAIL CONSENT FORM FOR YOUR OWN RECORDS.

Please note that an optional Subject Feedback Form is available online (see above).

Please click "Submit" after reading Form #5 below.

Done Internet

start Messenger Cl... Inbox - Outlook ... Microsoft Word -... Ethical Approval ... 9:22 AM

FIGURE 5.1 Example of an Online Consent Form (Developed by Nora Boekhout.)

Finally, it needs to be noted that there are certain circumstances when the Net should probably not be used to obtain consent. These circumstances include situations where the consent of guardians of minors or that of persons of diminished mental capacity is required. We advise against this for the protection of *both* the e-researcher and the participant.

WHEN IS CONSENT NEEDED? THE PUBLIC VERSUS PRIVATE DILEMMA

Informed consent is needed in almost all types of research with two notable exceptions. First, consent is generally not required to study an activity that is nonintrusive and takes place in a public space. For example, it is not necessary to obtain consent when undertaking naturalistic observations (for example, when studying linguistic patterns of fans' chanting at a football game). Neither is it usually necessary to obtain permission when studying a public record or archive. For example, it is not necessary to obtain permission to study the public speeches of politicians, perform content analysis of newspapers or other mass media, or to study the public record of proceedings from a legislature. It is possible to argue that this notion of public space is appropriately extended to the study of activity on public newsgroups, mail lists, chat rooms, or virtual reality environments (e.g., MOOs, MUDs). Specifically, as these kinds of online spaces are open for anyone to join and, hence, can be interpreted as a public spaces, informed consent from every participant is not required since the researcher is often not participating and, thus, not affecting the interaction that takes place.

Or is it a public space? This interpretation is not as straightforward as some e-researchers would like it to be, as the sense of what is public or private is defined not by the technology, but by the perception of privacy and inclusion that is maintained by the participants. Imagine, for a moment, that you are in a public park and you need to use the public washroom. As you are leaving this public facility you notice there is a video camera in each of the washroom cubicles. How do you think you might feel to learn that this is part of a research project? As King (1996) notes, with this kind of example "The sense of violation possible is proportional to the expectation of privacy that group members had prior to learning they were studied." For example, studies with virtual self-help groups have shown remarkable candor among participants and the publication of this content has been viewed by some participants as a violation of the privacy of the group (Sharf, 1999). An additional factor determining private space is the degree of intimacy that the researcher is studying. King notes that, generally, activity in a public place does not require informed consent. For example, noting how people are sitting on park benches. Nevertheless as Waskul and Douglass (1996) point out, if one installs a tape recorder and records conversations that take place on that park bench, a much different level of consent is required for ethical research.

Waskul and Douglass (1996) remind us further that "ethical considerations should entail an interplay between codes of conduct and an intimate understanding of the nature of the online environment." To behave ethically requires explicit and expert knowledge of the context within which the researcher functions. The Net is made up of a diverse set of technological and cultural contexts. For example, the ethics of analyzing the interaction in a large public discussion board sponsored by a media outlet such as the *New York Times*, call for far different means to protect privacy than research involving private emails. Further, codes of conduct may apply differentially to different types of research. For example, the study of anonymous language use in public online chat rooms and the publication of results requires different levels of individual disclosure than a study that is focused on identifying appropriate teacher/student interventions during an instructional class using the same Net-based chat technology. Thus, even though the technology is the same, different standards of ethical research behavior are required for these different research investigations.

To help the e-researcher determine when and what type of consent is required, many of the formal professional and research granting bodies provide guidelines that can help address some of the gray areas of ethical research. The 1994 Canadian Code of Ethical Conduct for Research Involving Humans (http://www.nserc.ca/programs/ethics/english/policy.htm) defines research participants as "living individuals or groups of living individuals about whom a scholar conducting research obtains (1) data through intervention or interaction with the individual or group, or (2) identifiable private information." Applying these guidelines can be helpful in determining when naturalistic observations (as, for example, noting the length of posting or language used in public Usenet groups) become personal interventions. If the researcher has no interaction or intervention with the participant and if there is no disclosure of private information, then it is generally not necessary to obtain informed consent from the participants. Unfortunately, ethical issues are sometimes very complicated in Net-based research, making it unclear how to apply existing consent guidelines. In these cases, judgment calls must be made to defend choices that require or dispense with requirements for consent. The American Psychology Association ethical code for researchers (Draft 6.1 at http://www.apa.org/ethics/) notes that "before determining that planned research (such as research involving only anonymous questionnaires, naturalistic observations, or certain kinds of archival research) does not require the informed consent of research participants, psychologists consider applicable regulations and institutional review board requirements, and they consult with colleagues as appropriate." In keeping with this guideline, it is advisable that the e-researcher consult with colleagues and institutional review boards prior to dispensing with consent.

REDUCING THE POTENTIAL TO HARM

The second core value that underlies e-research is to insure that the e-researcher avoids, through the research process, possible harm to research participants or non-participants who are affected by the researcher's activities. The most common form of harm comes from inadvertent or purposeful exposure of the participants in ways that are perceived by those involved as damaging or hurtful. Examples of harm may include not only physical injuries but also loss of privileges (an inability to participate in an activity), inconvenience (i.e., wasted time, frustration, boredom), psychological injuries (insults, loss of self-esteem, embarrassment), economic losses (job, entrance into programs), or legal risks (Bickman & Rog, 1998). Further, it should not be assumed that it is only individuals that can be harmed by such exposure.

The most common and usually the safest way to avoid harming individuals or groups is to ensure that the appropriate steps have been taken to attempt to protect the identity of participants in any publications or documentation of the research process. This can be effectively accomplished by ascribing direct quotations to pseudonym names, gender, and/or ages—for example, "a teenaged male." However, in some cases this may not sufficiently hide personal or group identity. For example, it may be possible to determine the school or classroom involved in an educational research project through knowledge of the researchers' employment or through details of the context provided by the researcher. A second alternative is to obtain permission from any participants to quote their words. However, this type of individual disclosure may reveal the identities of others from the same group who have not granted this right of publication. Furthermore, Herring (1996) notes that copyright laws generally ascribe ownership to the creator of all original works including emails, chat, and computer conferencing postings. Thus, copyright lawyers suggest that the direct quotation of these works requires the permission and the identification of the authors or at least the adherence to fair use conventions that allow for the quotation of limited amounts of such copyright content as long as the owner of the work is appropriately recognized. While this may be an alternative under certain circumstances, it should also be noted that the researcher cannot provide confidentiality or privacy and at the same time follow legal copyright laws—leaving this to be yet another ethical difficulty.

TIPS FOR ETHICAL e-RESEARCH

- In the first instance, understand and interpret ethics principles by analogy to those developed for the offline world.
- Develop and implement new guidelines only when a clear case can be made that offline proscriptions are either unworkable or inappropriate. Any new guidelines must support the underlying values of all research that include privacy and confidentiality, respect for persons, reduction of potential to harm, and potential for beneficence and justice.
- Be prepared to spend time and energy discussing evolving ethical issues with other researchers, research funding bodies, and professional organizations.
- If in doubt, discuss concerns or alternatives with members of both the research community and the community being investigated.
- Insure that you recognize any possible risks that may occur as a result of the research by reflecting before, during, and after the project has been completed.
- Use the request for notification of reception feature found in many email systems when sending first letters of invitation to potential participants, but do not use it for regular or ongoing communication, as it delays and may inconvenience participants, resulting in discontinuation of their participation.
- Use the filtering function of email to automatically store returned permission-to-participate forms in folders dedicated to the research process.

- Develop and maintain supportive contact with list owners, moderators, or major contributors to established virtual communities, before commencing any formal e-research study.

SUMMARY

The discussions in this chapter underscore the realization that there is no single procedure that allows for the protection and safeguard of confidentiality, privacy, or anonymity and at the same time supports the full copyright protection of e-research participants. As such, e-researchers are forced to use personal judgment and the counsel of other researchers and members of Net communities to analyze the particular circumstances of their own research and to determine appropriate levels of conduct to insure that no harm results from the research. Unfortunately, there are often large gaps between the experience and expectations of e-researchers and virtual community members. Gaining more experience in the use of Net-based research is helping to reduce these gaps, but even so, there continue to be instances in which the institutional perspective brought by many researchers is far different than that lived by the online research participants. This gap creates boundless opportunities for misunderstandings and suspicion. Allan (1996) notes the challenge of applying ethical guidelines based on the Golden Rule that underlies much ethical behavior in the offline world. In order to "do unto others as you would have them do unto you" there is an applied assumption that you share a common understanding of the ways in which others understand their behavior and activity in the online world. Allan notes that "this is why the 'golden rule' breaks down particularly in cyberspace—currently, there is little ground for presuming that one's own perceptions, values and wishes as a researcher correspond to those of the other participants involved."

The resolution of these fundamental ethical problems will only happen after extensive dialogue between members of both the Net communities and the research community. With time, experience evolves and so too will different degrees of acceptable practice—depending, partially, on the nature of the research (for example examination of posting lengths versus amount of personal revelation), the types of participants (students in compulsory courses versus those participating as hobby), and the degree of personally identifiable material being analyzed (video transcripts versus text chat). For now e-researchers are forced to begin the search for ethical guidelines in the more familiar offline context, apply those ethical constraints that make sense and are doable in the online world, and then proceed cautiously, openly, and honestly, in new research domains as they are presented.

REFERENCES

Allan, C. (1996). What's wrong with the "Golden Rule"? Conundrums of conducting ethical research in cyberspace. *Information Society, 12*(2), 175–187.

Bickman, L., & Rog, D. J. (Eds.) (1998). *Handbook of applied social research methods*. Thousand Oaks, CA: Sage.

Dillman, D. (2000). *Mail and Internet surveys: The tailored design method* (2nd ed.). New York: Wiley.

Herring, S. (1996). Critical analysis of language use in computer-mediated contexts. *Information Society, 12*(2), 153–168.

Kanuka, H., & Anderson, T. (1998). On-line social interchange, discord and knowledge construction. *Journal of Distance Education, 13*(1), 57–74.

King, S. (1996). Researching Internet communities: Proposed ethical guidelines for the reporting of results. *Information Society, 12*(2), 119–127.

Milgram, S. (1963). Behavioral study of obedience. *Journal of Abnormal and Social Psychology, 67*, 371–378.

Neuman, W. N. L. (2000). *Social research methods: Qualitative and quantitative Approaches* (4th ed.). Boston: Allyn & Bacon.

Roberts, P. (2000a). Ethical dilemmas in researching online communities: "Bottom-up" ethical wisdom for computer-mediated social research. [Online]. Available: http://www.com.unisa.edu.au/cccc/papers/refereed/paper40/Paper40-1.htm.

Roberts, P. (2000b). Protecting the participant in the contested private/public terrain of Internet research: Can computer ethics make a difference? [Online]. Available: http://www.aice.swin.edu.au/events/AICE2000/papers/rob.pdf.

Rourke, L., Anderson, T., Garrison, R., & Archer, W. (2000). Methodological issues in the content analysis of computer conference transcripts. *International Journal of Artificial Intelligence in Education, 11*(3). [Online]. Available: http://www.atl.ualberta.ca/CMC/publications.html.

Schrum, L. (1995). Framing the debate: Ethical research in the information age. *Qualitative Inquiry, 1*(3), 311–326.

Sharf, B. (1999). Beyond Netiquette: The ethics of doing naturalistic discourse research on the Internet. In S. Jones (Ed.), *Doing Internet research* (pp. 243–256). Thousand Oaks. CA: Sage.

Thomas, J. (1996). When cyberresearch goes awry: The ethics of the Rimm 'Cyberporn' study. *The Information Society, 12*(2). [Online]. Available: http://venus.soci.niu.edu/~jthomas/ethics/tis/go.jt.

Thomas, J. (1999). Balancing the ethical antinomies of Net research. *Iowa Journal of Communication, 31*(2), 8–20. [Online]. Available: http://venus.soci.niu.edu/~jthomas/ethics/iowa.html.

Waskul, D., & Douglass, M. (1996). Considering the electronic participant: Some polemical observations on the ethics of on-line research. *The Information Society, 12*(2), 129–139.

Witmer, D. F. (1998). Practicing safe computing: Why people engage in risky computer-mediated communication. In F. Sudweeks, S. Rafaeli, and M. McLaughlin (Eds.), *Network and Netplay: Virtual groups on the Internet* (pp. 127–146). Menlo Park, CA: AAAI/MIT Press. [Online]. Available: http://commfaculty.fullerton.edu/dwitmer/vita.html.

CHAPTER SIX

COLLABORATIVE e-RESEARCH

Perhaps more than anything else, a collaborative online project like Postmodern Spacings demands that you realize that at any moment the project could either explode in a hundred directions or collapse into silence and a blank screen. Personally, I have found that challenge quite rewarding.

Mark Nunes, 1997

Many important research projects are large enough to require the energy, commitment, skills, and expertise of more than one e-researcher. In addition, many research problems are based on regional or geographical contexts, in which collaboration across distance is critical. Interestingly, these disbursed projects are often those of most interest to provincial, state, and national funding bodies.

The Net's particular strengths lie in its support for communication and for sharing information across distance and time. It should therefore come as no surprise to learn that Net-based collaboration tools offer the e-researcher a great deal of opportunity to improve the effectiveness and efficiency of e-research teams. In addition, the Net serves as an accessible repository for data, personal and collaborative memos, and other documentation useful in creating, informing, and authenticating the research process.

In this chapter we discuss some of the tools currently available and the potential cost and time savings provided by their use. We also explore new technologies based on peer-to-peer networking that promise to further increase the advantages afforded by effective team-based research.

The collaboration tools and techniques most useful for e-research teams are the same tools used by work, social, or community groups as they resolve problems or undertake large-scale tasks. These tools generally fall into five categories:

1. *Communication tools*—real-time, chat, audio, and video conferencing; private and group-based asynchronous email; computer conferencing; and voice and video mail.

2. *Data and document sharing tools*—shared workspaces in which files can be stored, exchanged, updated, and managed to avoid the problem of multiple authors altering the same document simultaneously. In addition, the means to search for documents by a variety of indexes (including keyword, date, and author) or to select documents containing a single word or phrase in the full text of the object is required.
3. *Application sharing tools*—shared working environments in which applications such as word processing, sketching, or data analysis tools allow team members at different locations to manipulate the same documents. This sharing should be supported both in real time and asynchronously, based on the evolving needs of the members of the e-research team.
4. *Project management tools*—calendars and scheduling tools that allow users to coordinate activities, set deadlines, and report and monitor progress on project tasks and objectives.
5. *Community management tools*—the ability to track members of the e-research group, their current activities, the last time they logged on or contributed, when new documents were added or deleted, and a push facility that sends announcements or invitations to participants via email.

There are a number of Net-based commercial and open source products designed to meet these communication and knowledge management needs. The majority of this chapter consists of reviews of these early products, highlighting how they are designed to accomplish the tasks previously listed. First, however, we look at ways that collaborative tools can enhance the e-research process.

TYPES OF e-RESEARCH COLLABORATION

Collaboration in research operates at many levels and in many types of processes. Etienne Wenger's (2001) characterizations of a "community of practice" can be useful in describing a wide variety of networked and face-to-face communities, and in thinking about e-research collaborations. Wenger argues that communities of practice share three characteristics: a common domain of knowledge, a community, and a practice.

1. The *domain* of the e-researcher includes, of course, the overlapping abilities associated with general research design and implementation and with using network tools both in the research process and for communicating. This shared level of competence distinguishes members of this community from others and provides both with technical skills and attitudes conducive to applying networking to solve research-related problems.
2. The *community* of the e-researcher is established via ongoing communication with the group. Members use their domain knowledge and skill to help one another, seek advice, develop grant applications and proposals, and

filter information for each other. This mutually assistant interaction, over time, builds trust and communication competence, which furthers the development of the community of practice.

3. The *practice* of the community is instantiated in collaborative work. In many ways, the community stays at a superficial level until a task or challenge, such as a collaborative e-research project, unites it with common tasks, timelines, and potential for recognition and reward.

Although the community of practice described above is the most common form for e-researchers, there are other collaborative-research relationships. For example, those involved in ethnographic research have a unique responsibility—to establish often intense social relationships with individuals or communities, to understand the world-view of their subjects (Hine, 2000). Collaborative action researchers need tools to effectively work with participants in researching problems of personal or local concern and to insure that researchers become partners in the research process. Collaborative research can also link multidisciplinary teams (at a single location or multiple locations) that work on multifaceted problems. Interaction between members from these different academic groups (Becher, 1989) provides challenges to effective communication and collaboration. Universities and governments currently stress the need for collaborative research between university scholars and private business. Again, successfully overcoming cultural barriers between these groups requires a high degree of communication among participants. In all of these cases and in many other variations of collaborative e-research, quality communication, data sharing, and provision for discussion and project planning are critical.

Riger (1997) describes the critical factor to collaboration between researchers and community activists involved in "action research" and the elimination of social problems. She notes that issues of trust, time frame, and talent often arise between researchers from one culture and activists from a local culture. Riger outlines the tools needed to overcome these hurdles, as follows:

> [W]hen you start to work together, create a decision-making structure that makes explicit what people's responsibilities and areas of control are. To do this, we need to have on-going conversations and negotiations between researchers and advocates. We need a forum in which we can begin to talk about these issues and identify our common interests. We need to create relationships, and structures to contain those relationships, in which agreement can be sought, and disagreement can be worked out. Only by such sustained efforts will the potential of collaborative research be fully realized.

Certainly Riger was not referring to Net-based environments and technology-mediated communication when she described her communication needs in 1997. However, it is uncanny how closely the major design thrusts in collaborative e-research tools mirror the needs expressed above. Here, as in other discussions, we see that issues of e-research are not much different than those found in earlier, pre-Net, collaborative research.

CHALLENGES OF e-RESEARCH COLLABORATION

In addition to its potential benefits, the Net does create some new challenges for collaborative research. For example, one application of the Net is to create an environment in which the challenges of distributed research groups and the needs of the community can be met. However, such a substitution of Net-based for real-life contexts presupposes Internet efficacy and access (to hardware, bandwidth, a space, and a time) by all the participants. Such tools or skills are not always found among active researchers even in today's modern universities and are much rarer in higher education institutions and research units in developing countries.

Cyber scholar Mark Nunes (see Nunes, 1997) provides an account of his experiences with Internet-based scholarly activities. They include collaborating on writing projects, planning conferences, and participating in lists and MOOs. Nunes outlines a host of benefits and overviews problems that result from a lack of commitment in cyberspace. He writes:

> In addition, the lack of physical "space" has a serious impact on the commitment of your online collaborators. *We* all showed up this afternoon. If four of us agreed to meet at 1:15 for some sort of online panel, I could almost guarantee at least one of us would be missing. In the Postmodern Spacings project, at times real-time discussion consisted of only two people. In fact, we never had more than half of the participants present at any one meeting. In a similar vein, online collaborative projects like Postmodern Spacings make closure a difficult goal. While the medium is wonderful for new openings, the looseness makes completion quite a task.

One could argue that because Nunes's group used synchronous groups excessively, a lack of commitment stemmed from forcing synchronous activity on busy people, but that would not be the full story. Research collaboration depends on frequent formal and informal conversation to be most effective. Most of us can only commit a certain amount of time in our lives for such interaction—too often the face-to-face one takes priority. The pure technical determinist might argue that an effective project management tool could eliminate wasted time, logistical complexity, and errors due to misunderstanding. The predilection for face-to-face interaction amongst almost all researchers we know constrains effective collaboration—but it usually does not stop the collaborative process. As we gain more experience designing and completing collaborative e-research projects, and the tools continue to improve, this barrier will be reduced, though never eliminated. As in all life/space decisions, trade-offs between convenience, cost, effectiveness, and time commitment are a component of the collaborative research process.

COLLABORATION TOOLS IN ACTION: A FAILED EXAMPLE

Most of the examples in this book document successful applications of e-research tools and techniques. The following example illustrates that success is not an assured outcome. In this example we describe the context and the tools of a collaborative e-research project.

This research team was funded for a two-year project to investigate and develop educational applications for next-generation, high-speed Internet networks. The researchers were located at seven Canadian universities, and their work focused on developing Net-based video conference applications, creating repositories for educational objects, and repurposing of educational video content for distribution over the Net. The project administrative team was located in one of the universities, while a single researcher or small team was located at the other universities.

In early discussions, the researchers noted the need for asynchronous communication, file, and project management tools. They selected a free Net-based product (CommunityZero) that provided these and a variety of additional tools (such as news features, synchronous chats, calendars, etc.) that could be used by the group. One of the principle investigators in the project set up a demonstration in which the original project application, a few updated notices, and an asynchronous discussion were established as a prototype of the community collaboration tool's potential. This prototype was demonstrated at one of the few face-to-face meetings of the group, and all agreed to use the system. However, many of the collaborators did not sign on to the system, nor did they respond to the application manager inviting them to do so. Soon, those who had signed on noticed that the asynchronous discussion had little new material and that no one was adding new content to the collaborative workspace. The site failed to achieve critical mass and within six months was removed by the Web site owners.

Why did the system not prove beneficial? Despite the need for collaboration tools, these application tools were perceived as less valuable than more readily accessible and familiar tools. Most of the administrative staff, who were located at a single site, had access to a variety of LAN-based services. Most of the remote participants were less involved in the project and thus did not interact with the collaborative team software on a daily basis. This particular project was just one of many workplace obligations for the remote and distributed group. Although the software had the capacity for the owner to push e-mail announcements to participants, there was no way to automatically alert all members when new content was added. Thus, users logged on to a remote system only to find that there was nothing new in most instances. Such negative feedback quickly extinguishes the desire to log on to external sites. After a few months of nonuse, many participants forget passwords and login I.D.s, making further participation impossible without negotiating with systems operators.

Thus, a collaborative system like any new intervention must, first, add a relative advantage (Rogers, 1995), second, be compatible with the current workload of all participants, and, third, require minimal effort to participate. The availability of more compatible means of communication (email and FTP sites) plus the lack of incentives for participants to log in on a frequent basis meant that the software did not add significant value to the project and thus was abandoned.

APPLICATIONS OF COLLABORATIVE SOFTWARE BY e-RESEARCHERS

As the example above demonstrates, the need for communication and collaboration permeates many aspects of e-research. This is most obvious when there is a team of researchers, but collaboration is also useful for the solitary researcher during those components of the research process when results, discussions, or questions must be shared with others.

Net-based collaborative software is relatively new, and we are just discovering ways that e-research teams can use these powerful tools. As noted in earlier chapters, the e-research process commences with selection and refinement of a research problem. Often this process is iterative, as various drafts are shared with sponsors, supervisors, or members of the research team. Placing initial drafts in a Net-accessible file space allows for controlled access to important documents. During the literature review process, a collaborative workspace is also useful for documenting, summarizing, and sharing insights from research. Each of the three software packages reviewed later in this section provides space for listing and annotating Web sites, databases, and other references found on the Net. The polling feature of these collaborative packages is handy for conducting quick surveys of opinions and priorities of team members. The calendar feature is useful for setting deadlines and for reminding members of real-time meetings and consultations. During the data collection phase of the research, the calendar is also useful for scheduling interviews and for circulating and archiving drafts of survey instruments or coding protocols. An important feature of much qualitative research is the memoing feature (Nunes, 1997), by which researchers document ideas, insights, questions, and observations during the data collection and analysis phases of research. Bogdan and Biklen (1982) extend the role of these memos in research to "the mainstay of qualitative research . . . a written account of what the researcher hears, sees, experiences, and thinks in the course of collecting and reflecting on the data in a qualitative study" (p. 74).

Quantitative data sets can also be shared in common workspace so individual members can run tests on the data without bothering other team members for access. Finally, in the dissemination stage, opinions and suggestions can be polled and final drafts of results and "to do" lists can be shared amongst members. Although they are not necessarily Web-based, Microsoft Word's editing tools provided convenient ways to suggests edits and add comments as we composed this book. These tools are also very useful when marking student papers and exercises. Considerable time can be saved when using Microsoft's editing tools by displaying the "reviewing" toolbar from the "view" and "toolbars" options. The review toolbar allows one to quickly add comments and edits, accept or reject the edits of coauthors, and turn the edit feature on and off.

There are a number of software packages on the market that are designed to support these functions. The first generation of these products creates a shared workspace on a central, Net-connected server. Individual users log on to access and to add to these central services. More recently, software has been designed to use the computing power of remote users more extensively and to allow team members to share resources and communicate through "peer-to-peer" technologies. The most infamous of these peer-to-peer packages is Napster, which revolutionized how commercial music is distributed. We review three of these products, not to endorse them, but to illustrate how these tools can be used to enhance the e-research process.

MICROSOFT'S SHAREPOINT™ TEAM SERVICES

SharePoint Team Services were introduced as components of the Microsoft Office, version XP and were also included with later versions of Front Page. SharePoint resides on a Windows server and provides a list of services, as illustrated in Figure 6.1. One of the unique features of the SharePoint service is the capacity for members of the team to alter the Web site directly from their Web browser, without having to create or upload documents or HTML pages. The communication services include threaded discussion groups that are presented in a format similar to typical newsgroups or computer conferences. Besides sharing documents, SharePoint provides customizable notification services using email to push notification to subscribers when information changes in either discussion groups or document libraries. SharePoint also has a polling feature that allows members to query each other and instantly display the results. As seen in the screen capture in Figure 6.1, SharePoint is integrated with other Microsoft Office products, and thus will be most useful for teams that already use this suite of products. For example, SharePoint itself does not provide a calendar feature, but can export items directly to the services built into Microsoft Outlook's calendar applications. SharePoint services must be installed on an internal company or institutional Web server and can be purchased from external Web service providers. As the services are built into the cost of the full-featured versions of Office XP, the cost for installation and operation is quite nominal; however, installation on a central server normally requires the cooperation of the information technology services of a central organization.

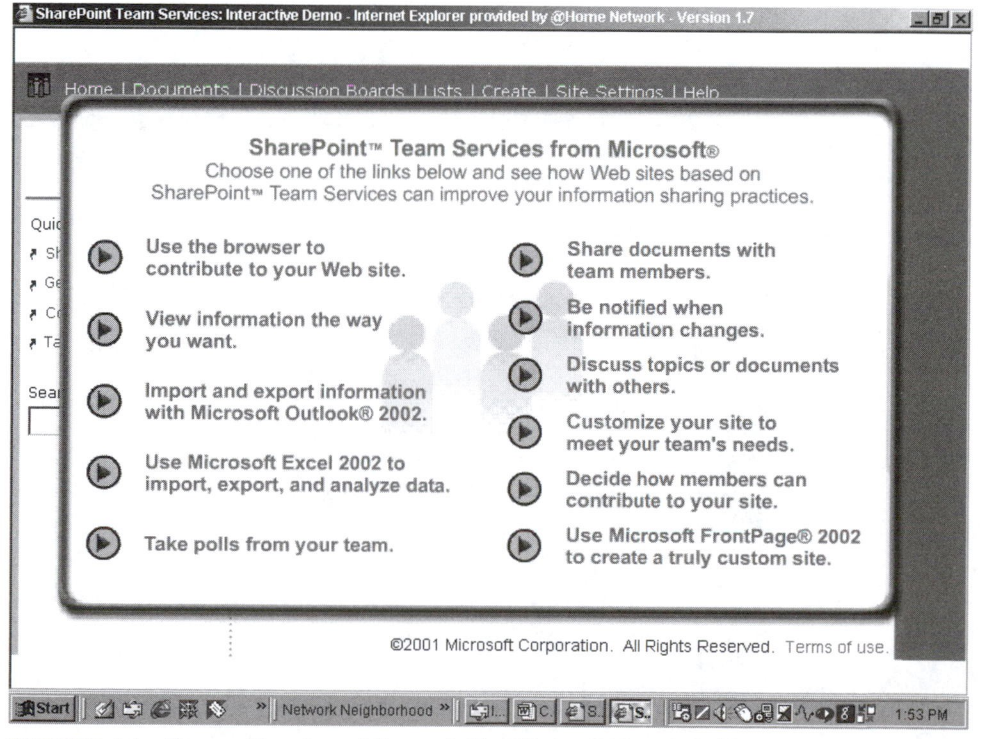

FIGURE 6.1 Screen Shot from Microsoft SharePoint.™ Reprinted by permission from Microsoft Corporation.

COMMUNITYZERO

CommunityZero supplies centralized collaborative services that give individual users access to any number of "communities"—some of which could be the focus of an e-research project. Unlike SharePoint, all CommunityZero communities are located on a single, central Web server. Individuals enroll for free and are allowed to participate in as many different communities as they wish to create or join. CommunityZero provides a larger suite of services to members than SharePoint and serves as a customizable portal for team members. Figure 6.2 provides a screen shot of a CommunityZero site that promotes the services provided.

CommunityZero provides asynchronous, threaded discussions; a "contributions" area where members can provide annotated links to sites or resources on the Web; a notice board feature for short announcements; and a list feature for creating itemized lists such as "checklists" and "to do" lists. CommunityZero provides real-time chat rooms and a series of "newsfeeds" from press agencies and other news organizations for team members. Like SharePoint, CommunityZero provides space for uploading and retrieving documents created by team members, but does not provide the notification services available in SharePoint that alert members when items change.

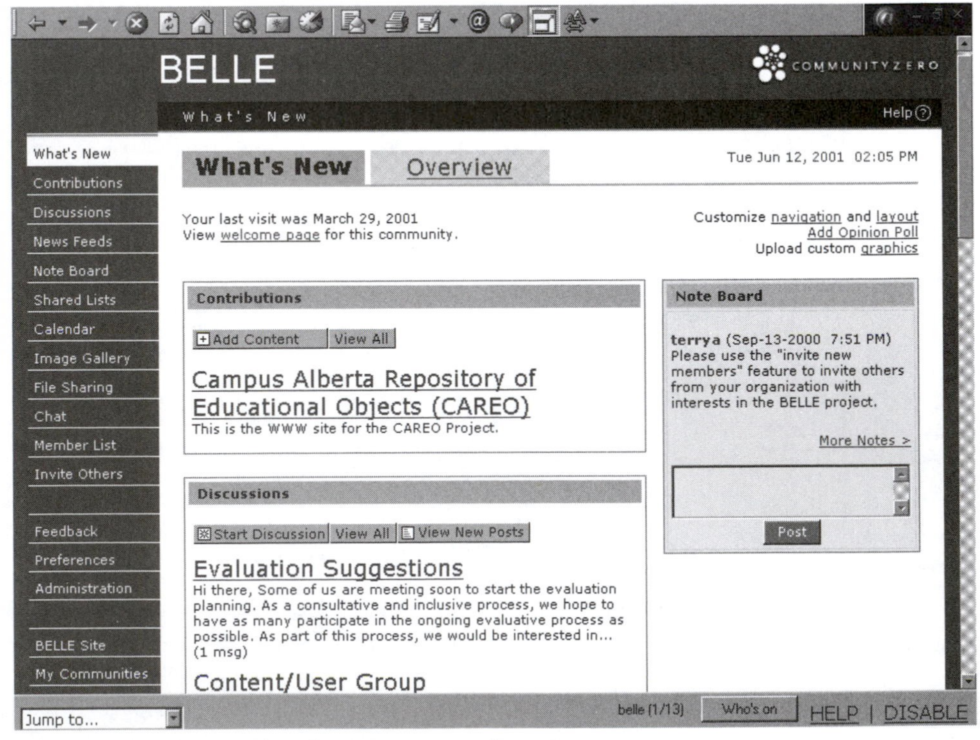

FIGURE 6.2 Screen Shot from CommunityZero.™

However, the creator of the community has the capacity to push a notice via email to new members, inviting them to join the community. CommunityZero provides a group calendar for each community, to which members can add or delete appointments. Like SharePoint, it provides a polling service to gather and summarize opinions from community members. Currently, basic CommunityZero core services are provided free of charge, but customized services with subscriber branding, enhanced security, and the capacity to host many communities are available on a fee-for-service basis.

GROOVE NETWORKS: PEER-TO-PEER COLLABORATION SOFTWARE

The final software suite we review offers a more radical means of providing collaborative services, one which Internet gurus have speculated will change the way we currently collaborate using the Net. The architecture of services originally provided on the Net and exemplified by both SharePoint and CommunityZero follow a model developed in telephone communication. In this model, all intelligence (e.g., billing information switching, directory services) is located at the center of the network, allowing for unintelligent devices (i.e., telephone hand sets) to connect to these services. Point-to-point technology takes an opposite approach and relies on the computing power of devices operating at the edge of the network to provide intelligent services, thus reducing reliance on central services. In the familiar Napster example, a central service merely tracks tunes from the disk drives of logged-on members—all transfer and sharing happens directly between these members. Other peer-to-peer services such as Aimster and Gnutella eliminate this central database service altogether, as members broadcast requests for specific files to their neighbors and transfer these files to member computers.

A company called Groove Network first applied this peer-to-peer concept to collaborative work. Their collaborative system, Groove software, works by downloading a suite of software to connect directly to other users, share files, and communicate without going through a central Web server. Shared files are stored on the local users' hard drive, and communication services, including multi-point text and audio chat, are supported by broadcasting communication directly to the other members of the research team from each machine. This approach will be attractive to those e-researchers who are not in a position to manage or to add programming to a Web server, and who are not comfortable with sharing or storing sensitive data on a commercial site. Groove also supports asynchronous threaded discussion lists and integrates with the users' default mailer for private email conversations. Video conferencing can be supported through integration with Microsoft's NetMeeting technology. Groove addresses the need for document control by insuring that two users do not edit the same document simultaneously. When documents are retrieved from the shared file space, any subsequent requests for editing of the document are not allowed. Instead, Groove creates a second copy with a slightly different name. This alerts the second user to its "in use" status, but still allows for editing, even though the two documents must be compared and merged before a single document is created. This comparison can be automated to some degree by using the "compare documents" feature

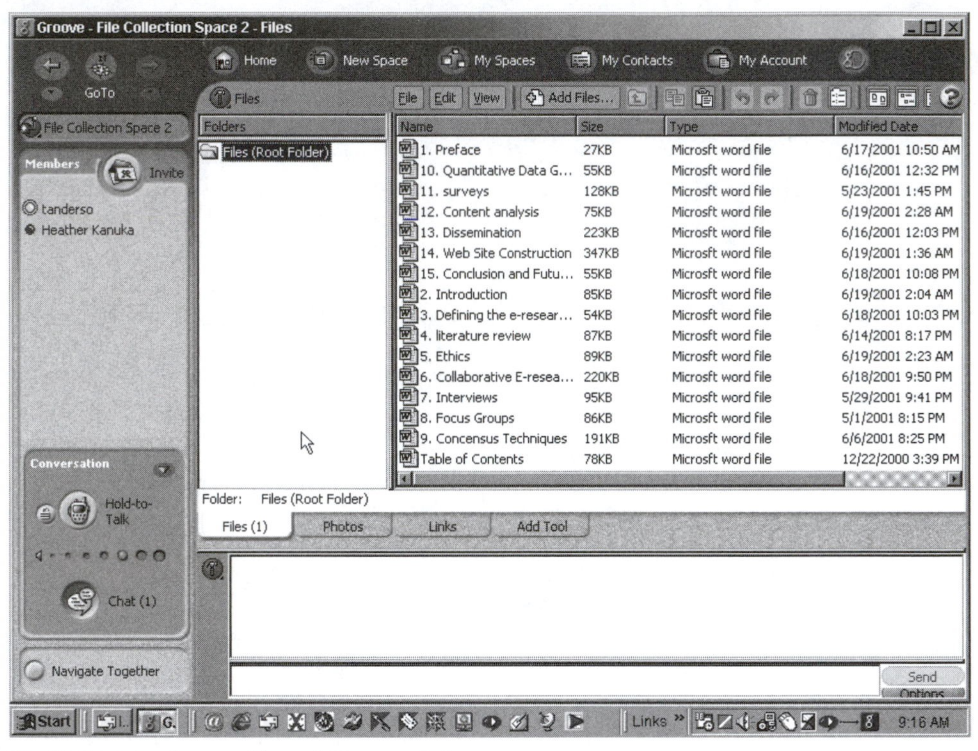

FIGURE 6.3 Screen Shot of Groove Software.

found in Microsoft Word and other full-featured word processing packages. Finally, Groove 1.0 supports a calendar and sketchpad and promises to support more extensive collaborative editing of word processing and spreadsheet packages in future releases. Groove is also marketed in a "light" version that can be downloaded for free. Larger, more functional enterprise solutions that support multiple users are available on a cost-per-user basis. A screen shot of Groove in use by the authors to collaboratively share work on this book is shown in Figure 6.3.

TIME TRACKING

Many projects require sophisticated tracking, scheduling, and cost and time allocation for administration and billing purposes. There are a variety of commercial and shareware software packages to aid teams in sophisticated levels of project management. However, small e-research teams are often able to coordinate their activities less formally through the collaborative projects cited previously or simply through regular email. One feature that is not provided in these collaborative projects is time tracking. Obviously, this information is critical if research is being done on fee-per-hour basis, but even if it is not, e-researchers should be able to measure, and thus more accurately control their time on various components of the research process.

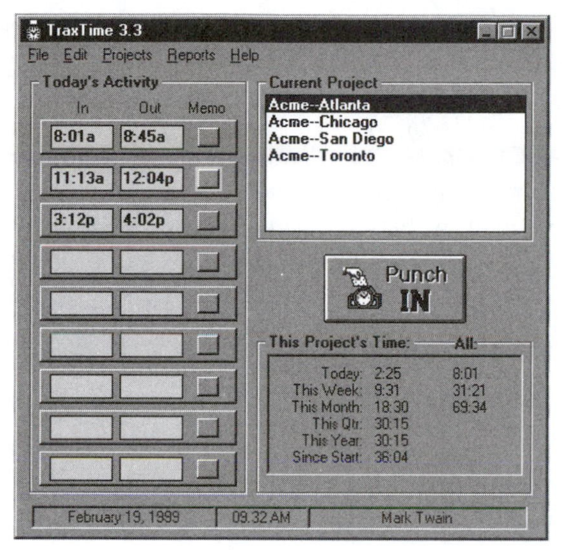

FIGURE 6.4 Screen Shot of Spud City's TraxTime Software.

Although there are many competitive products available, we concur with Riff Fullan's (1999) recommendation for shareware called TraxTime (http://www.spudcity.com/traxtime/traxtime.htm). TraxTime is available in either a single user or a networked manager's version, both of which allow for compilation of time spent by various team members. A memo can be added to each entry to provide supporting details. TraxTime produces a variety of customizable reports and has received excellent recommendations from a variety of software reviewers. A screen shot illustrating a typical time tracking task is shown in Figure 6.4.

APPLICATION OF COLLABORATIVE SOFTWARE BY e-RESEARCHERS

The need for collaboration permeates most aspects of the e-research project. This is most obvious when there is a team of researchers, but collaboration is also useful for the solitary researcher during those components of the research process when results, discussions, or questions must be shared with others.

Net-based collaborative software is relatively new, and we are just discovering ways that e-research teams can use these powerful tools. As noted in earlier chapters, the e-research process commences with selection and refinement of a research problem. Often this process is iterative, as various drafts are shared with sponsors, supervisors, or members of the research team. Placing initial drafts in a Net-accessible file space allows for controlled access to important documents. During the literature review process, a collaborative workspace is also useful for documenting, summarizing, and sharing insights from research. Each of the three packages reviewed in this chapter provides space for listing and annotating Web sites, databases, and other references found on the Net. The polling feature of these collaborative packages is handy for conducting quick surveys of opinions and priorities of team members. The calendar feature is useful for setting deadlines and for reminding members of real-time meetings and consultations.

In summary, there are a variety of Web-enabled collaborative applications that are capable of supporting an expanding list of group activities. It seems likely that these applications will become an increasingly important and valuable component of the e-research process. It is also likely that these applications will become more useful, as additional features are added and their functionality increased through user feedback. We also expect that increasing access to Net services provided by mobile devices will increase the ease and practicality of collaboration in research.

REFERENCES

Becher, T. (1989). *Academic tribes and territories—Intellectual enquiry and the cultures of discipline*. Milton Keynes, England: Open University Press.

Bogdan, R., & Biklen, S. (1982). *Qualitative research for education: An introduction to theory and methods.* Boston: Allyn & Bacon.

Fullan, R. (1999). Time tracking. [Online]. Available: http://www.bellanet.org/advisor/index.cfm?Fuseaction=view_article&TheArticle=30.

Hine, C. (2000). *Virtual ethnography*. London: Sage.

Nunes, M. (1997). Scholarly discourse and collaborative research online. [Online]. Available: http://www.dc.peachnet.edu/~mnunes/samla.htm.

Riger, S. (1997). Challenges in collaborative research: Trust, time, and talent. In University of Illinois at Chicago (Ed.).

Rogers, E. (1995). *Diffusion of innovations.* (4th ed.). New York: Free Press.

Wenger, E. (2001). Supporting communities of practice: A survey of community-orientated technologies. (1.3 ed.). Shareware. [Online]. Available: http://www.ewenger.com/tech/.

CHAPTER SEVEN

SEMI-STRUCTURED AND UNSTRUCTURED INTERVIEWS

Some things cannot be spoken or discovered until we have been stuck, incapacitated, or blown off course for a while. Plain sailing is pleasant, but you are not going to explore many unknown realms that way.

David Whyte

The research method e-researchers choose can often reveal their beliefs about what is valuable knowledge and, perhaps more importantly, their perspectives of the nature of reality. As discussed in Chapter 3, an objective of qualitative research methods is the discovery of patterns and the development of theories that expand understanding of complex social phenomena. When conducting qualitative research the researcher usually uses an in-depth inductive process. Semi-structured and unstructured interviews are the most common methods for achieving this deep understanding of complex social phenomena. The interview is a unique method for data collection in that the researcher gathers data through direct communication between individuals. This direct communication allows for customization of the questions, depending on the subjects' previous answers, their attitudes, and the trust that builds between the researcher and the participants. Such direct and focused interaction is necessary to pursue a deep understanding of the subjects' views and of the topic of investigation. In particular, interviews offer the researcher infinite flexibility in probing deeper by following leads and insights that may provide surprising new directions for both participants and researcher. This is the principle advantage of interviews over other kinds of research methods.

There are many different kinds of interviews used by e-researchers. In fact, there is considerable variation within the literature on types and definitions of interview genres. Fontana and Frey (1994), for example, describe nine types of interviews including structured, semi-structured, oral history, creative, group, postmodern, gendered, ethnographic, and in-depth interviews. Most of the literature, however, lists the most common kinds of interviews as structured, semi-structured, unstructured, and focus group (Borg & Gall, 1989; Cohen & Manion, 1994). In a structured interview the researcher asks the same sequenced and preestablished questions to a large number of respondents in a standardized manner, often with fixed response categories. Typically, there is no option for variations in response. While a structured interview, generally referred to as a survey, can be conducted one-on-one with the researcher, it is most commonly presented in a paper-based or online format to a large sample (see Chapter 11). The data from structured interviews are usually analyzed numerically using descriptive statistics such as means and standard deviations or multivariate statistics such as cluster and factor analysis, with the reliability of internal scales being calculated using sophisticated mathematical formulas such as Cronbach's alpha. Since these types of interviews are presented to large and carefully selected samples, the results are often evaluated in terms of their generalizability. Conversely, focus group interviews (see Chapter 8) are never conducted one-on-one or with a large sample; rather, they are conducted as a small group interview. The data are analyzed for themes and topics, and the researcher is usually not concerned with the generalizability of results. Rather, the data is evaluated for its ability to provide greater insights into the issue(s) being investigated. Alternatively, semi-structured and unstructured interviews are conducted one-on-one. While the most typical setting for semi-structured and unstructured interviews continues to be a face-to-face verbal interchange, there is an increasing opportunity for individual interviews to be conducted on the Net.

Whatever the format, interviews are a favorite methodological tool of educational and social science researchers. According to Fontana and Frey (1994), "interviewing is one of the most common and most powerful ways we use to try to understand our fellow human beings" (p. 361). Although, Patton (1990) suggests that the "quality of the information obtained during an interview is largely dependent on the interviewer" (p. 279). To obtain quality information, the e-researcher needs to not only be a skilled interviewer, but must also be able to transfer these skills to the Net environment. This chapter focuses on the interviewing skills and questioning techniques necessary to create engaging conversations for effective Net-based semi-structured and unstructured interviews.

UNSTRUCTURED VERSUS SEMI-STRUCTURED INTERVIEWS

Unstructured interviews are often referred to as in-depth interviews, open-ended interviews, or even ethnographic research. While we acknowledge that many qualitative researchers do not differentiate between ethnographic research and unstructured interviews (e.g., Fontana & Frey, 1994; Lofland, 1971), we do make this distinction. The frequently cited writing of Lofland maintains, for example, that in-depth interviews and ethnographic research go hand-in-hand. However, Net-based in-depth interviews typically do not use participant observation in natural settings, and in this context are considered to be fundamentally different from ethnographic research. As Internet technologies advance, in terms of cost and ease of use, we anticipate that in the not-too-distant future Net-based interviews will take place in virtual reality environments and make use of voice and video interaction. They will then allow e-researchers to conduct interviews and observe participants in their natural setting, thus making Net-based ethnographic research more commonplace. While this interview process is possible now, it is currently beyond the means of most researchers and their subjects in terms of the cost, required skills, and equipment.

An overview of the different kinds of Internet communication software is provided in Chapter 8 (Focus Groups). There are researchers who conduct ethnographic research in a Net-based context—where the objective of the study is to explore the social culture on the Net as well as the use of the Net for data collection. An interesting example of data collection can be found in an early, groundbreaking ethnographic research study about the psychology of online life, in Sherry Turkle's book, *Life on the Screen* (1995). For a variety of reasons (the primary one being financial), most researchers are exploring text-based asynchronous formats for interviewing. As such, this chapter focuses on text-based, asynchronous, and Net-based interviews.

Unstructured interviews provide the greatest potential for the researcher to achieve breadth and depth of data. This type of interview includes a small number of loosely defined questions (sometimes only one question) that provide openings for the participants to describe their views in their own language and style. There are no predetermined questions asked of each participant and no precise order of the questions; the interviewer converses with the respondent as questions arise. Usually questions are broad and open-ended, thus providing maximum opportunity for the participant to shape answers in a meaningful way. In turn, the interviewer clarifies the responses for deeper insights through paraphrasing, reflective comments, and follow-up questions (Snyder, 1992). Rapport between researcher and respondent and an understanding of respondents' experiences take precedence over data formatted into preestablished, coded categories.

Semi-structured interviews are usually conducted with specific topics in mind, from which questions are generated based on a theoretical framework. Typically, the interviewer works from an interview schedule that contains a series of preplanned and sequenced questions. These questions may be followed by less structured and open-ended probes (follow-up questions) to collect deeper understandings and insights. The main advantage of a semi-structured interview over an unstructured interview is that in the former there is both structure (ordered questions) and non-structure (open-ended probes). Thus the interviewer can both predetermine the data that will be gathered (in a structured interview) and follow the unexpected as it arises (in an unstructured interview).

INTERVIEWING SKILLS

Regardless of the type of interview format, forethought concerning the form, structure, and purpose of the interview is essential when using this method for data collection. An interview can take a variety of forms for a multiplicity of purposes. It can be a quick, one-time, five-minute exchange or multiple interactions extending over a number of days, weeks, months, or even years. Whatever the format, there are a number of steps the e-researcher should take prior to and during the interview. Some of these steps are challenging when using asynchronous text-based software to communicate, often making effective Net-based interviews more difficult to conduct than face-to-face interviews. However, this challenge is offset when travel expenses and the need to schedule with subjects are eliminated, resulting in significant savings of cost and time.

As in any form of interaction, familiarity with the participant's culture, values, and use of language greatly assists communication. Communicating in a text-based asynchronous environment is difficult enough in one's own language and culture. This difficulty is magnified when the e-researcher is not familiar with the participant's language (e.g., lexicon, syntax, phonemes) and culture. If a faux pas occurs as a result of inappropriate language use or lack of understanding of the culture, it may lead to misunderstanding between the participant and e-researcher and result in an inability to draw out relevant information. The e-researcher cannot use the body language, facial expressions, poignant pauses, or other paralinguistic clues provided during traditional interviews as cues to the subjects' deeper feelings. Subjects who are familiar with text-based communication may develop skills and techniques to overcome this limitation through the use of emoticons and other means of communicating affect in their messages, but many potential subjects may not have these skills.

Gaining trust is also essential to successful data collection in interviews. Even when trust is initially gained, it is often fragile, and efforts must be made to build on and preserve it. As the aim of the interview is to acquire an understanding of the participant's perspective through open and honest dialogue, it is important not only to establish but also to maintain trust throughout the interview experience. When conducting face-to-face interviews, establishing trust can take days, weeks, or even months of time in the environment, observing and often making only painstakingly small advancements in an attempt to integrate. How can the e-researcher achieve rapport and trust over the Internet?

The degree of trust necessary for successful Net-based interviews depends on the attitudes and skills of the participants and the sensitivity of the interview subject. The participant's attitude toward and knowledge of Internet technologies are critical to a successful Net-based interview. If participants have a bias against Net technologies, the medium will negatively influence their responses. According to Fontana and Frey (1994), the type of interview selected, the techniques used, and the way in which the data is collected will "all come to bear on the results of the study" (p. 370).

Ideally, participants selected for Net-based interviews should have considerable prior experience and a high degree of comfort in communicating using the Net. To reduce the challenges associated with learning new software, we suggest the use of personal email (as opposed to threaded discussion groups or other collaborative tools) to conduct the interview. This way, interview questions will appear as ordinary email from the researcher, and the techniques for responding, saving, or forwarding will already be familiar to most participants. If, however, the participant is new to asynchronous Internet communication technologies, or to a particular conferencing system, more time will be spent learning how to use the software than responding to the interview questions, which often lowers the insightfulness, quality, or usefulness of the communication.

The vulnerability that the participant may feel in sharing information also affects the ability of the interviewer to gain trust. For example, if the interview questions require the participant to share information that may be self-incriminating, the Net may not be an appropriate communication venue. Net-based communication is not as secure as the privacy of a personal face-to-face interview. Specifically, there are other people (e.g., server maintenance personnel and/or hackers) who may have access to the interview transcripts as they are stored on a system server or as they are intercepted in transmission. Although most research institutions require their staff to sign a confidentiality form with respect to any information they may have access to, data may, nevertheless, be less secure than with other forms of interview collection, such as researcher notes. Assuring confidentiality and explaining the techniques used to protect the privacy of participants are important components of obtaining informed consent and building trust. Ways to provide informed consent, to identify the risks of participating in research on the Net, and to reduce the risks through the use of encrypted software were explained in Chapter 6.

One step that you can take to determine if the Net is a suitable communication medium in which to conduct an interview is to spend time doing background work on the selected or potential participants. Much can be learned, for example, from reading personal Web pages or published works and/or asking people who know the participants. Of particular importance is to collect information that indicates whether the participants are comfortable communicating with asynchronous tools. If this information cannot be attained through these sources, you may want to consider conducting a brief, preliminary opinion survey about the Net. Creating and administering a survey can be done quickly using one of the commercial or free Web-based survey forms discussed in Chapter 11 or by including questions in a short email to potential respondents, and can be an effective way to determine if negative biases exist. Such a survey could ask for simple yes/no or agree/disagree opinions on such questions as:

- How long have you used the Internet for communication (e.g., email, mailing list servers, Usenet groups, etc.)?
- Do you think the Internet is a useful form of communication?
- Do you use the Internet for personal communication?
- Do you think the Internet is a reliable communication medium?
- Are you comfortable with expressing your personal opinions through Internet communication platforms, such as email?

Should any of these questions be answered with a negative response, you might want to re-consider selecting the participant(s) for Net-based interviews.

Additionally, it is important that the e-researcher consider whether or not nonverbal and contextual elements are essential to gathering and interpreting the data. There are four kinds of nonverbal elements considered by some qualitative researchers to be essential to the interviewing process. These include *proxemic*, *chronemic*, *kinesic*, and *paralinguistic* communication (Fontana & Frey, 1994). Proxemic communication refers to the interpersonal space used to communicate attitudes.

Chronemic communication refers to the use of speech patterns, such as pacing and the length of silence in conversation. Kinesic communication refers to body posture and movements. And paralinguistic communication refers to variations in pitch and quality of voice. Are these nonverbal elements essential to the interviewing process or can they be ignored or substituted in text-based interaction? When using text-based asynchronous communication software, these nonverbal elements are not present—so we must ask ourselves, how will this influence the data collected? Obviously, different types of data collection from interviews will be more or less suitable to different types of research questions. For example, questions related to highly sensitive and personal subjects will be more dependent on paralinguistic clues for interpretation than questions related to one's job or to experiences in public places (such as a classroom or a workplace setting).

Determining if the research question matches the data collection process requires the e-researcher to envision how these unique constraints of Net-based interviews will change the way the data is gathered and interpreted. Determining what types of interviews to conduct using asynchronous text and discovering the appropriate participants for text-based interviews are challenges for e-researchers. Due to these limitations, Net-based interviews are used by some researchers as a filtering technique for initial interviews that are then followed by more extensive interviews conducted by telephone or face-to-face.

Another limitation of text-based asynchronous interviews is asking the participants to take on the onerous task of writing the responses themselves. While we mentioned in an earlier chapter that a benefit of Net-based interviews is the elimination of the transcribing process, it must be acknowledged that this task is transferred to the participant. Most of us know from our experience communicating with email that when a complex concept requires explanation, it is often easier to simply pick up the phone and communicate the information verbally. As such, when considering using the Net for interviews, it is important to weigh the advantages and disadvantages of telephone and Net-based interviews—especially when the responses might include complex concepts. Alternatively, the advantages of conducting Net-based interviews include the ability to access geographically dispersed respondents more cost effectively than with telephone interviews, the ability to time shift to make the process more convenient for both participant and researcher, and (as already mentioned) the elimination of the transcribing process.

Once the e-researcher has made a decision to use the Net to collect interview data, trust should be built through establishing rapport with the participant. Establishing rapport requires the researcher to be able to "put him—or herself in the role of the respondents and attempt to see the situation from their perspective, rather than impose the world of academia and preconceptions upon them. Close rapport with respondents opens doors to more informed research" (Fontana & Frey, 1994, p. 367), and is discussed further in the next section.

Finally, in addition to the automatic transcripts that are created in text-based asynchronous interviews, e-researchers should keep a reflective journal consisting of their speculations, feelings, problems, and prejudices towards the interview process. Keeping a journal helps e-researchers become aware of their biases and assumptions.

Good qualitative research studies not only keep accurate records of the methods, procedures, and the evolving analysis, but are also self-reflective, resulting in a balance between reflective and descriptive material (Bogdan & Biklen, 1992). Fontana and Frey (1994) describe how reflective activity benefits the e-researcher: "As we treat the other as a human being, we can no longer remain objective, faceless interviewers, but become human beings and must disclose ourselves, learning about ourselves as we try to learn about the other" (p. 374). Becoming aware of and understanding our biases and assumptions through a reflective journal are essential activities that help us articulate not only what we do during interviews, but why. Knowing why is essential when analyzing the data, as our assumptions and biases influence what data we select and report as well as what insights we generate, and how.

INITIATING THE PROCESS

Inviting someone to participate in an interview is extending an invitation to participate in a conversation and build a relationship (Weber, 1986). The e-researcher normally begins the interview process with a letter of invitation. We suggest a paper-based, mailed letter on the e-researcher's affiliated institution letterhead. Because Net-based interviews are conducted in a virtual environment, the e-researcher should provide the participants with evidence that he or she is conducting valid research affiliated with a credible institution. Using institutional letterhead is one way to provide such evidence. The letter should reflect the nature of the research process, describe the purpose of the study, and include details with respect to what is being requested of the participant in terms of time and Internet resources. The language should be appropriate to the participants, not the researcher, and thus be simple, direct, and straightforward. The following is a sample letter of invitation.

Sample Letter of Invitation

[date]

Dear _______________:

I would like to invite you to participate in an **online** interview. The objective of this study is to explore the transformation that e-learning is having on higher education communities in North America. In order to fully understand the perspectives, needs, and concerns of educators like yourself, it is critical that your comments be heard and understood by researchers and decision makers.

I anticipate the interview will require approximately 10–15 minutes of your time for about 14 consecutive days (May 7–21), to respond to my questions. It is not necessary that you respond every consecutive day, but you should be prepared to respond at least every other day. You will need access to the Internet and an email address. If you are interested in participating in this study, please email me at [email address] or phone during the day at [phone number] prior to May 10th, 2003.

As an expert in the field, your participation in this study is greatly appreciated.

Respectfully,

[e-researcher]

Principle Researcher

If the e-researcher does not get a response to the letter of invitation from the participant within about a two-week period, the letter should be followed-up with an email message. This email should be brief (approximately one screen of text) and should make reference to the letter that was sent with another invitation to participate. If the e-researcher does not know the participant personally, the email should be formal, beginning with "*Dear* ________" and a closing with "*Regards,*" or "*Sincerely,*" as well as the e-researcher's designation in the signature line (i.e., Principle Researcher or Doctoral Candidate).

Once the prospective participant has agreed to participate, a friendly and somewhat informal message should be sent describing: the purpose of the study, the process used to maintain confidentiality, how the data will be secured, when and how the results of the study will be disseminated, and other administrative and ethical information related to the study.

Sample Letter of Confirmation and Consent

Dear [participant]:

Thank you for responding to my invitation to participate in this study. This email provides information about the nature of the research project and the procedures.

The study focuses on the transformation that open and flexible learning is having on higher education communities in Canada. The following three research questions are explored: (i) how does e-learning impact scholarship and research? (ii) how does e-learning impact teaching and learning? (iii) how does e-learning impact administration?

I have identified you for this study, because you are involved in implementing policies in relation to the integration of new learning technologies in higher education.

If you agree to participate, you will be requested to do the following:

• Respond to this email indicating that you have read and understood the purpose of the study and that you agree to participate.

• Participate in an online interview that will require approximately 10–15 minutes of your time for about 14 consecutive days (May 7–21).

All Internet communication has an element of risk—the possibility that others will intentionally or unintentionally access the data. However, I will take steps to provide confidentiality through placing the data on a secured server, and all names and identifying characteristics will be removed from corresponding reports and publications. No deception will be used, and you are free to withdraw from the interview at any point or refuse to answer any questions. The interview data will be destroyed after a period of five years unless permission has been granted for further use. A summary of the research will be posted on a Web site at the completion of the study, and I will email the URL to you. If you would like further information, you may contact me at [email and/or phone] or my supervisor [administrator, chair, or dean] at [email and/or phone].

If you agree to participate in this study, please reply to this email confirming that you have read and understood the purpose of this study, understand your rights as a participant, and agree to participate. Thank you.

Regards,

[e-researcher]

Principle Researcher

The email should be written in a conversational style in an effort to establish rapport and trust. As mentioned, it is important that the e-researcher take steps to put the respondent at ease and enable him or her to feel comfortable, setting the stage for a positive and responsive interview process.

The next correspondence should begin the interview process. The first way to gather meaningful data, prior to asking questions, is to establish an informal and friendly conversational tone (Kvale, 1996). Some people find that setting a friendly tone in Net-based interviews is not as easy (nor as familiar) as in face-to-face interviews. However, there are ways to facilitate this process, including the appropriate use of humor, self-disclosure, or narrative (Baym, 1995). We suggest that the first email posting should set the tone for the conversation between the e-researcher and the participant. We have also found that it can be useful to share our own uncertainty and nervousness in conducting Net-based interviews with participants.

The following is an example of a welcome message that sets a friendly tone. When the message is kept to one screen of text and is informal and friendly, the likelihood of facilitating a conversation, rather than only a sequential question-and-response interview, is increased. Depending on the characteristics of the participants, the e-researcher should use a writing style that is more conversational and friendly than academic.

Sample Welcome Message

Hello [first name of participant]:

Thank you for agreeing to participate in this interview. Further to my invitation letter, I would like to arrange a date to begin the interview. I was hoping we might begin Monday of next week (date), if this is convenient for you. I have about five questions that I would like to ask, and I anticipate that the responses to these questions should not take longer than about 10 minutes each. I also thought we could cover one question every second day, but I am flexible and could make an alternate arrangement if this is inconvenient.

If you need to contact me other than by email, you can call me at [area code and phone number] during the day or [area code and phone number] during the evening. I look forward hearing from you!

Regards,

[first name of e-researcher]

We suggest that the questions should not be presented to the participant at this point in the interview process. The rationale for this is that, typically, in unstructured and semi-structured interviews, the questions change based on earlier responses. As the interview progresses, for example, the e-researcher may wish to build on previous comments or rephrase questions so that they conform to the language of the participant. Moreover, during the interview, the e-researcher may discover an unexpected area that needs further exploration and is extremely relevant and enlightening to the topic.

ASKING THE QUESTIONS

Asking good interview questions is considered to be an art, because getting meaningful answers is often difficult and depends to a great extent on the wording and tone of the questions. Fontana and Frey (1994) maintain that no matter how carefully we word the question(s), there is always a residue of ambiguity. This problem is magnified in text-based asynchronous interviews. One of the most effective ways of reducing this ambiguity is to use good questioning techniques, which in turn will enable the e-researcher to obtain more accurate information from the participants and garner useful and meaningful data. No matter how much effort the researcher puts into the questions, there is always the possibility of misinterpretation or misunderstanding by the participant. Thus, it is essential that the e-researcher create an atmosphere in which participants are trusting and feel confident enough to seek clarification.

Once a friendly tone has been established through the welcome letter, it can be maintained by showing respect for the participant's opinions through supportive acknowledgments of his or her responses. For example, you could begin questioning with the following email:

> Hello [first name of participant]:
>
> Thank you again for agreeing to participate in this study. I'd like to begin with the following question:
>
> How does e-learning affect the way you design and teach courses?
>
> If you have any questions or need further clarification, please let me know through email or phone me collect at [area code and phone number].
>
> Regards,
>
> [first name of e-researcher]

Once the participant has responded to the question, feedback such as "Thank you for that last response" acknowledges the response and indicates that you are attentive, interested, understanding, and respectful of what is being communicated. You should also ensure that the participant has finished sharing prior to moving on to the next question. Knowing when the participant is finished is trickier in a Net-based interview than in a face-to-face interview, due to the absence of nonverbal cues. The e-researcher should not assume that just because a posting is sent that the participant has finished saying what needs to be said. For example, the time required to compose the message with the necessary explanation may be longer than the participant anticipated, and, as such, may be cut short. Because the e-researcher cannot "see" what is happening, a follow-up message should always be sent asking "Do you have anything else to add?" or "Do you think there is anything else I should know about this?" If the participant has anything further to say, this will provide an opportunity to expand.

Once rapport and trust have been established, the e-researcher will need to focus on the questions. Obtaining accurate and meaningful information over the Net requires carefully worded and articulate questions. One way to reduce the residue of ambiguity is to use words that make sense to the participants. Cicourel (1964), who first wrote about this, noted that many meanings that may be clear to the researcher, may not make sense to participants. The main cause of this foible is that the researcher has not been sensitive to the participants' context and worldview. According to Kvale (1996), to reduce the communicative ambiguity, the questions should be easy to understand, short, and without jargon. This advice is especially important in text-based asynchronous environments where the ability to clarify is reduced. For example, the e-researcher may ask a question to which the participant provides a lengthy reply that completely misses the point of the question. In a face-to-face interview, the researcher will know early on by the response that the question has been misunderstood, and can quickly clarify the misunderstanding. The e-researcher can reduce the odds of misunderstanding and gather useful data by adhering to the following guidelines:

- Familiarize yourself with the language and culture of the target participants.
- Using the communication software, pilot the interview question(s) to a few individuals (two or three) who have characteristics similar to (or the same as) the intended participants. Taking these actions prior to the interview will help identify problems with language usage and avoid a faux pas through insensitivity.
- Ask one question at a time.

This may seem like common sense. But Patton (1987), for example, points out a mistake that interviewers often make—putting several questions together into one question (sometimes referred to as a double-barreled question). Responding to double-barreled questions can be quite difficult, if not impossible. Consider the following question:

> Do you agree that the Internet is a useful tool for data collection, or do you think it is most useful as an information tool?

This sample question illustrates three types of problems. First, it asks two questions: (1) Do you agree that the Internet is a useful tool for data collection, and (2) do you think it is most useful as an information tool? Moreover, it might be difficult to answer if the participant does not feel that the Internet is useful as either a tool for data collection or as an information tool. Alternatively, the participant might feel that it is useful for both data collection and as an information tool. Hence, the participant might have difficulty answering this question given that there are two questions and an indication that an "either/or" response must be made between the two.

The second problem with this question is that it is not an open-ended question. Questions that begin with "*Do you*" or "*Would you*" allow the participant to respond with "yes/no" statements and, as such, do not provide the researcher with much insight about *why*. A better question format for the semi-structured interview is open-ended. Questions beginning with "*What do you think about*," "*Tell me your opinion about*," or "*How do you feel about*," allow the participants to respond in their own terms.

Finally, in the above sample, the questions are leading—particularly the first question. A question asking if someone "agrees" is value-laden. The e-researcher should be careful not to word questions as directive (with words such as *agree* or *disagree*) to guard against influencing the participant to respond in a certain way. A better way to word this question is:

> What is your opinion about the usefulness of the Internet?

If the researcher wants to know more about the participant's response to the use of the Internet as a tool, the initial question can be followed by an email with probing questions. Examples of effective probes include such questions as "*Can you build on that last idea?*" or "*Can you explain further?*" For example, an email might be worded in the following way:

> Hello [participant's name],
>
> Thank you for your response. You mentioned that the Internet is useful in facilitating critical thinking. Can you expand on this further?
>
> Thanks,
>
> [researcher's name]

Patton (1981) also suggests that the interviewer ask behavior questions prior to opinion/feeling questions. For example, questions such as "*How often do you use the Internet?*" or "*For what purposes do you use the Internet?*" should be asked prior to "*What is your opinion about the usefulness of the Internet?*" Asking behavior questions prior to opinion/feeling questions helps set the stage for expressing openness. Taking the time to follow this suggestion in a Net-based interview is especially important due to the lack of nonverbal cues to help guide the e-researcher in drawing out the participant's opinions and/or feelings.

Another suggestion offered by Cohen and Manion (1994) is to use a special technique called *funneling*. Funneling is a progressive questioning technique that acquires more in-depth information by building on the prior question. The following is an example of the funneling technique:

> Most of us know that the Internet provides access to information. However, some teachers believe that the Internet provides an invaluable information resource base for their students. Conversely, other teachers believe that because it is difficult to verify the reliability of this information, students should not use it as an information resource. What is your opinion?

The funneling technique is an excellent way to set a conversational tone for the interview and ease the participant into opinion and/or feeling kinds of question(s) and, thus, offset some of the formality that tends to occur in a text-based environment.

If, despite having used the funneling technique, you find that your participant's responses are not as in-depth as you would like, then you should follow with probes. Again, due to the characteristics of an asynchronous textual environment, you may find that responses from participants tend not to be as rich or as deep as in a face-to-face setting, for a variety of reasons (e.g., it is time-consuming to write a message that conveys an explicit opinion, there is a sense of uneasiness due to the permanency of the textual environment). However, probes can provide an opportunity for e-researchers to give cues to the participant about the level of response desired. This can be done in several ways. For example, we can follow up the prior example with:

> What Internet activities do you do with your students?

Alternatively, we can take words from the participant's response as a lead for further elaboration. For example, assume the participant answered the initial question with a response such as:

> Every so often I feel that the Internet might have information that my students might find useful.

We can see that this response does not provide much insight into the topic. In response to this, we can take a few key words and probe further. Using the above sentence, the following is an example of a linking probe:

> Thank you for your response Terry. Can you tell me more about those conditions under which your students might find the Internet useful?

As you can see from this example, the linking probe uses the respondent's own words ("*students might find useful*"). This kind of response provides a number of cues for the participant. First, it illustrates that you are attentive to what has been said and, second, it uses the participant's own words when asking for more in-depth information. This can often make the participant feel more comfortable and willing to elaborate further. Fontana and Frey (1994) note that the use of language and specific terms is important for creating a sharing of meaning "in which both interviewer and respondent understand the contextual nature of the interview" (p. 371).

If the e-researcher has sensitive questions, it is advisable to strategically place them around the middle of the interview. Asking sensitive questions might make the participant feel uneasy, intimidated, or irritated and may, in turn, result in avoidance by the participant. The problem of asking sensitive questions can be magnified in a text-based environment. For example, when asking sensitive questions in a face-to-face interview there are ways that the interviewer can soften the question through tone and body language. It is also easier for the interviewer to sense a good time to ask the question through observing the participant's reaction and immediately dropping or rephrasing the question as needed. Moreover, there are certain ethical responsibilities that the interviewer must consider when deciding whether or not to pursue a sensitive area. Unfortunately, the kinds of nonverbal cues that can alert the interviewer when to "back off" are absent in asynchronous text-based interviews. Once the question is asked, it is difficult to determine how the participant has reacted to it until a response is given (if a response is even offered). It is important then that the e-researcher takes steps to ensure that a sensitive question will not offend and that the participant feels comfortable enough to respond openly in a Net-based interview. While only the e-researcher will know whether it is the right time to ask sensitive questions, by carefully observing and being sensitive to the participant's prior responses, we suggest that sensitive questions be embedded in the middle of the interview in a way that naturally progresses from the probes. Of course this requires a careful line of questioning, including the use of a variety of probing techniques. A tremendous advantage of an asynchronous text-based interview over a face-to-face interview is that the e-researcher can take the time to carefully consider how to respond to, and build on, the participant's statements. A number of probing techniques that guide the interaction toward sensitive questioning can be achieved by linking probes and by funneling. Having an advance plan about how the interview will proceed will allow the interviewer to act on opportunities presented in the responses and to proceed confidently with sensitive questions.

ANALYZING THE DATA

The data analysis process begins with identifying the themes and topics and translating them into a narrative account. The approach to identifying themes and topics can be conducted in a number of different ways. Typically, the researcher will begin analyzing the data by reading it and getting a feel for the themes and topics. This process begins with the identification of recurring words and/or ideas, which are then flagged as possible themes or topics. If the data consists of only a few interviews (three to five) that are relatively short in duration, the researcher can read the data again (or a number of times) to verify themes and topics. Alternatively, if there are more than five interviews and the duration is extended, we recommend the use of qualitative software (e.g., NUD*ist, Atlas/TI) to help identify possible themes and topics. While extra time must be set aside to learn how to use qualitative software, if the data is extensive, you will save time in finding and organizing your topics and themes. Essentially, the way the data are analyzed will not differ from non-Net-based research. When the topics and themes have been identified, they are often verified by relating them to the literature. Often researchers further verify findings by providing draft copies of the original transcriptions and the analysis to interview participants. Participants are asked if the themes identified and the comments about them accurately reflect their ideas and comments. Whatever the approach, the results will help you interpret the topics and themes that emerged from the existing literature—this is considered interpretive research.

Distributed within the interpretation will be direct quotes from archived conference transcripts. Interpretive research clearly distinguishes between the participants' statements and the e-researcher's interpretation of them. The e-researcher has a great deal of influence over which data are analyzed and how they are interpreted. If the e-researcher has kept a reflective journal throughout the interview process, the interpretation is likely to become more insightful through grounding in the analysis of his or her worldview. Once themes and topics have been identified from the data, the e-researcher should analyze his or her reflective journal and draw out those personal elements that may have influenced the study. Questions that the e-researcher might consider include, for example, how his or her gender, age, background, interests, or race might influence the interpretation. Or how the Net as a communication medium might have influenced the interview results. When e-researchers keep notes on how asynchronous computer-mediated communication software might influence the interviewing process, they not only provide more responsible reporting of the data, but also help future e-researchers understand how the medium might influence the message. They can then make more informed decisions as to whether or not this medium is suitable for conducting semi-structured and unstructured interviews, as well as form a greater understanding of how to use it most effectively. Research is currently being conducted to determine the effects of online interviews.

Finally, note that creating research reports that use the hypermedia features of Net-enabled creation and distribution software offers new ways to interpret and disseminate the results from interview data and other sources of online data. For example, Mason and Dicks (2001) note how hypermedia presentation challenges the printed word as the best or at least the only media in which ethnographers report and disseminate their research results.

TIPS FOR CONDUCTING INTERVIEWS

- Prior to the interview process, consider how you will establish and maintain rapport and trust over the Net (e.g., a welcome letter, acknowledgement of responses).
- Keep a reflective journal on how the Net might be influencing the interview process.
- Word the interview questions so that they are short, easy to read and understand, and jargon-free.
- Post only one question at a time.
- Strategically place sensitive questions in the middle of the interview with the use of linking probes and funneling questions as leaders.

SUMMARY

Clearly, different kinds of interview topics are suited to different interview formats. The greatest advantages of a Net-based interview over a face-to-face interview include: the saving of time and expense for both researcher and participants, the ability to time shift to make participation more effective and less onerous, the simplification and greater accuracy of the data transcribing process, and the increased access to geographically dispersed participants. The disadvantages, however, are that it is more difficult to establish rapport, and the interviewer cannot observe as well as listen. Overall, our experience is that Net-based interviews are most effective when the number of questions do not exceed five (or do not exceed two weeks of online communication), the participants are comfortable using Internet communication technologies, and the topic being investigated does not deal with sensitive or emotional issues.

REFERENCES

Baym, N. (1995). The performance of humor in computer-mediated communication. *Journal of Computer Mediated Communications, 1*(2). [Online]. Available: http://www.ascusc.org/jcmc/vol1/issue2/baym.html.

Bogdan, R., & Biklen, S. K. (1992). *Qualitative research for education: An introduction to theory and methods*. Boston: Allyn & Bacon.

Borg, W. R., & Gall, M. D. (1989). *Educational research: An introduction* (5th ed.). New York: Longman.

Cicourel, A. V. (1964). *Method and measurement in sociology*. New York: Free Press.

Cohen, L., & Manion, L. (1994). Research methods in education (4th ed.). New York: Routhledge.

Fontana, A., & Frey, J. H. (1994). Interviewing: The art of science. In N. K. Denzin and Y. S. Lincoln (Eds.), *Handbook of qualitative research* (pp. 361–376). Thousand Oaks, CA: Sage.

Kvale, S. (1996). *InterViews: An introduction to qualitative research interviewing*. London: Sage.

Lofland, J. (1971). *Analyzing social settings: A guide to qualitative observation and analysis*. Belmont, CA: Wadsworth.

Mason, B., & Dicks, B. (2001). The digital ethnographer. *Cybersociology 6*. [Online]. Available: http://www.cybersociology.com/.

Patton, M. Q. (1990). *Qualitative evaluation and research methods* (2nd ed.). London: Sage.

Patton, M. Q. (1987). *How to use qualitative methods in evaluation*. London: Sage.

Patton, M. Q. (1981). *Practical evaluation*. Newbury Park, CA: Sage.

Snyder, S. U. (1992). Interviewing college students about their constructions of love. In J. F. Gilgun, K. Daly, and G. Handel (Eds.), *Qualitative methods in family research* (pp. 43–65). Newbury Park, CA: Sage.

Turkle, S. (1995). *Life on the screen. Identity in the age of the Internet*. New York: Touchstone.

Weber, S. J. (1986). The nature of interviewing. *Phenomenology and Pedagogy, 4*(2), 65–72.

CHAPTER EIGHT

FOCUS GROUPS

As the island of knowledge increases, so does the shoreline of ignorance.
George Silverman

An effective way of getting at the answers to questions that are not yet well defined and the topic is not yet well understood is through the use of focus groups. A focus group is a unique kind of interview, in that it draws data from a number of people in a manner that is nonquantitative (Neuman, 2000). Of course, before conducting a Net-based focus group, e-researchers will need to ask themselves two questions. First, why choose a focus group interview over other kinds of methods? Second, why choose a Net-based focus group over a face-to-face focus group?

With respect to the first question, the nature of the research question should dictate the type of research that is conducted (Mertens, 1998). Focus groups are commonly used to define the research topic and the research questions (Fowler, 1995). Focus groups can be used for both exploration and confirmation and are particularly effective for collecting data about attitudes, perceptions, and opinions. Focus groups can be especially useful for revealing the complexities of the problem, but can also be useful for evaluation purposes (most often program evaluations) to identify strengths, weaknesses, and needed improvements. They are not intended to reach a consensus among participants, to determine a plan of action, or to generate solutions and decisions. Rather, they stimulate in-depth exploration of a topic when little is known about the phenomenon of interest (Stewart & Shamdasani, 1998). As such, focus groups are particularly effective for gaining a more in-depth understanding of the topic, and, hence, a better definition of the research question(s). Thus, when beginning to explore a topic for investigation within the field of education, focus groups can effectively narrow the topic, define the research question, and identify the delimitations of the study.

The main assumption embedded in the focus group method is a belief that the decisions we make are socially constructed and grow out of discussions with other people (Patton, 1987). Hence, focus groups are effective at gathering data in a social context, in which individual members consider their opinions against the opinions of others. While the focus group interview was originally inspired in the 1950s as a way of obtaining consumer product preferences, this technique eventually found its way into educational and social science research methodology. It has been shown to have the capacity to garner rich and credible qualitative data. Further, according to Patton (1990), focus group interviews provide quality controls on data collection, as participants tend to question and eliminate false or extreme views. The result is a tendency to focus on the most important topics and issues and to assess the extent to which a relatively consistent, shared view exists among participants—as well as identifying inconsistent views.

This method is called a focus group interview because it is focused in two ways. First, the group participants are similar in some way (e.g., they have similar experiences of the topic being investigated). Second, the purpose is to gather data about a single topic (or a narrow range of topics). They are most often guided by open-ended discussion questions proposed by the researcher, with an emphasis on gaining insights through group opinions rather than on specific facts. This format is a convenient way to accumulate the individual knowledge of the members and to inspire insights and solutions that are difficult to achieve with other interview methods. A distinct advantage of focus groups is that they allow respondents to react to and build on responses. The result can be a synergistic and dynamic effect on group behavior, often resulting in data or ideas that might not have been collected in individual interviews (Stewart & Shamdasani, 1998). Moreover, because focus groups tend to provide checks and balances among group members to eliminate false or extreme views, it is fairly easy for the researcher to assess the extent of consistent and shared views (Patton, 1990). Given these advantages, according to Glesne and Peskin (1992), interviewing a group of people on a focused topic can be a powerful way to collect data. However, it should be stressed that focus groups do not represent feedback from a randomly selected population, but from purposely selected individuals. As such, the results from focus group interviews should not be generalized to other, larger populations.

Finally, Net-based focus groups are usually selected over face-to-face focus groups because of the need to involve individuals from several different geographic areas. The travel time and expense of bringing geographically dispersed individuals together is often prohibitive. The Net provides an environment whereby the researcher can conduct a focus group cost-effectively.

THE DIFFERENT KINDS OF NET-BASED FOCUS GROUPS

Net-based focus groups can be conducted on the Internet either synchronously or asynchronously and with text-based software and/or audio and video software. Table 8.1 provides examples of various kinds of Net-based focus groups classified by asynchronous, synchronous, text-based, and non-text-based distinctions. As this table illustrates, there are four kinds of Net-based focus groups: synchronous and text-based; synchronous and audio- and/or video-based; asynchronous and text-based; asynchronous and audio- and/or video-based.

TABLE 8.1 Samples of Net-Based Systems to Support Focus Groups

	SYNCHRONOUS	ASYNCHRONOUS
TEXT-BASED	NetMeeting ICQ FirstClass WebCT	Majordomo FirstClass WebCT Email groups
AUDIO- AND/OR VIDEO-BASED	Centra Latitude NetMeeting	Centra Latitude Wimba

The combination of media used in the focus group process makes it difficult to generalize about the characteristics of all focus groups. Nevertheless, what uniquely differentiates a focus group from an interview is the capacity of participants to share and build on the comments and concerns of other participants. Prior to the Internet, there was no such thing as an asynchronous focus group; although one could conceive of mail-based focus groups, researchers did not actively use the technique. The predominant forms of asynchronous communication on the Internet have been text-based email and computer conferencing. Currently we are seeing a rapidly evolving selection of more media-rich forms of asynchronous communication to conduct Net-based focus groups (e.g., www.wimba.com). On the synchronous side, text-based chats are the most common and accessible way to conduct real-time focus groups. This mode of interaction uses software such as ICQ, NetMeeting, or one of the numerous Java-based Web chat software programs to share the comments of participants as they type. Text can be enhanced by viewing objects, sharing applications, or sharing a common space through text-based virtual reality (VR) systems such as MOO or MUD (for frequently asked questions about MUDs and MOOs see: http://www.faqs.org/faqs/games/mud-faq/part1/) or through two- or three-dimensional VR environments such as Palace (e.g., www.thepalace.com) or virtual worlds (e.g., www.worlds.net). Finally, focus groups can be conducted using audio or video conferencing. Until recently, the required software, end-user hardware, and bandwidth have prevented use of these richer and more natural forms of communication on the Net. However, the development of multisite audio and video conferencing systems (see www.microsoft.com/windows/netmeeting/ and www.centra.com) and the availability of high-speed connections at home and in the workplace promise increased use of media-rich, synchronous forms of Net-based focus groups.

Currently, most Net-based focus groups are conducted using text-based asynchronous or synchronous software. Accordingly, this chapter focuses on Net-based textual focus groups. As broadband services proliferate and become more widely available and affordable, we will likely see an increase in synchronous and asynchronous Net-based video and/or audio focus groups. As these multimedia services are added to

Net-based focus groups, they will tend to be more like face-to-face focus groups. Consequently, conducting face-to-face focus groups will become increasingly relevant and useful to e-researchers who use video- and audio-conferencing focus groups.

ADVANTAGES AND DISADVANTAGES OF FACE-TO-FACE VERSUS NET-BASED FOCUS GROUPS

Only recently have researchers been able to use the Internet to conduct educationally related focus groups. Net-based focus groups offer both speed and reduced cost (Van Nuys, 1999). While Net-based focus groups are currently in the exploration and development stage, they appear to be especially effective at removing certain barriers that many researchers experience when conducting face-to-face focus groups. In particular, they can reduce or eliminate participation and cost barriers. For example, if the e-researcher and the participants are geographically dispersed, Net-based focus groups allow them to participate from their homes and/or offices, thus travel expenses are eliminated. Van Nuys's cost analysis indicates that, in addition to travel savings, there is also about a 20 percent cost savings in conducting the focus group, compared to face-to-face focus groups. For example, such costs as food, beverages, and room rental would not be incurred in a Net-based focus group. In addition to this benefit, online discussions can be automatically archived, eliminating the transcription process and transcriber interpretation error.

Finally, Net-based focus groups may also reduce power struggles that often occur in face-to-face focus groups as a result of conflicting opinions when there are perceived status differences among participants (Patton, 1990). However, it is not necessary for Net-based focus group participants to reveal their real identities to other members of the group. Given this ability to provide an alias for each participant (depending on the medium) and that Net-based focus groups have the ability to join geographically dispersed participants (thus reducing the likelihood of participants knowing each other), power struggles and confidentiality problems can be reduced if not eliminated.

Notwithstanding these advantages, early explorations with Net-based focus groups have met with mixed results with respect to the quality of the data collected. Van Nuys (1999) has observed, for example, that a drawback of text-based asynchronous focus groups is that quite often there is less depth in the participants' responses as well as a loss of paralinguistic cues (e.g., facial expression, body posture, gesture, physical distance from the interlocutor, intonation pattern, and volume). Paralinguistic cues, in particular, are considered to be a very valuable source of data in face-to-face focus groups—in addition to what is said. Furthermore, Van Nuys notes that Net-based focus groups tend not to be effective for exploring complex concepts. Alternatively, Van Nuys has also observed that in text-based asynchronous focus groups, participants tend to speak more freely, since they cannot see others. In particular, the responses may be more objective, as participants tend to get straight to the point and not to "beat around the bush" when they are not face-to-face, since responses are typed, rather than spoken.

In contrast, while "not seeing the participants" is seen as an advantage by Van Nuys, Jacobson (1997) contends that it is arguable that there is no such thing as an online focus group, only moderated online discussions "given the absence of that tell-tale body language." While not wishing to debate nomenclature, Jacobson maintains that Net-based focus groups are not a substitute for face-to-face focus groups. Rather, Net-based focus groups are "simply an additional tool in the box . . . and under the right circumstances, clients get a substantial bang for their buck (and they get to sleep in their own beds at night, too!)."

An example of a successful Net-based focus group is shared by Roger Rezabek (2000) (see http://qualitative-research.net/fqs/fqs-eng.htm). Rezabek conducted a focus group as part of a dissertation research project. He cited the following benefits of conducting a focus group over the Net:

> The individuals who participated in the electronic focus group lived in widely dispersed parts of the U.S. from Nebraska to Maine to Florida, and could not have been brought together physically unless a large sum of money had been available for the travel and time necessary. Although it might have been possible to conduct this exercise using video conferencing equipment, the cost of doing that would have also been substantial. The latter techniques would have allowed a focus group to work in a synchronous or live manner, and would have been possible within a limited amount of time—a half day perhaps over videoconferencing. Two work days, however, would have been necessary, including travel time, if everyone would have been brought together into one location. But expenses are a real part of research, and often, the most economical method becomes the best method to employ. The online focus group experience provided a very economical method to conduct this part of the research, and resulted in vital findings that helped focus and clarify the rest of the study. (Rezabek, 2000)

As expected, Rezabek also noted drawbacks, including "lack of timeliness from beginning to the end of the process, sporadic participation and loss of participation at times by certain members of the group, and variable interaction among the participants."

Another drawback to text-based focus groups is the inability to ask as many questions as in a face-to-face focus group. First, due to the amount of response time and additional time required to "get up and running," the number of questions that can be asked is often limited to a maximum of ten, with the optimum number being between three and five. When there are more than five questions, the time commitment increases—especially for asynchronous text-based focus groups—resulting in a greater attrition rate. More questions will also require better group processing skills to keep the discussion flowing and lively. In the Rezabek example, three questions were asked over the duration of two and a half months. Rezabek made the following observations:

> During that two and a half month period, three questions were addressed by the focus group, in addition to the housekeeping and getting acquainted aspects at the beginning. A lot can happen in more than two months, and one can forget what comments were made in April by the time your discussion gets to June. Although the timeframe could have been compressed, the discussion just didn't progress that rapidly in order to deal with each of the issues and questions in a shorter period of time.

> One of the reasons for the length of the discussions had to do with the sporadic participation that resulted when one member or another didn't participate for a week or two. Although that was allowed and understood, the loss of participants tended to slow the discussion down. Participants temporarily left the discussion because of such circumstances as attending conferences, final exam preparation and grading, semester break, etc. There is little time during the year when such activities will not affect individuals engaged in higher education. But the result was to prolong the online discussions somewhat. And, since the focus group was comprised of specific individuals, their input and reflection on the topic was important.

Finally, according to Fowler (1995), the data from focus groups are often diffuse and hard to work with. This problem becomes even greater with Net-based focus group data and in particular, text-based synchronous discussion data. Both text-based asynchronous and synchronous focus groups tend to suffer from fragmented discussions making data analysis difficult. This results in differences in typing speed among participants and confusion about taking turns. The key to avoiding, or at least reducing, fragmented threads is to have a clear set of objectives and a moderator who can keep the conversation focused, fluid, and on topic.

As with any new technique, experimentation to determine the effectiveness of Net-based focus groups involves an initial trial-and-error process. The following section is a discussion of what we currently know about the process and the resources necessary to carry out a successful Net-based focus group.

THE PROCESS

If e-researchers do not have prior experience in conducting focus groups, it will be very useful to introduce themselves to the process by observing both face-to-face and Net-based focus groups. Face-to-face focus groups can be difficult to facilitate in a way that results in useful data, but obtaining useful data in Net-based focus groups is even more difficult! If the e-researcher does not facilitate the discussion properly, the data will not be useful. When this happens, a number of problems can arise. First, most participants will be unwilling to volunteer a second time, resulting in an inability to collect data, which can delay—or even bring an end to—the research project. Second, when other e-researchers invite prospective focus group members, participants may refuse to participate based on their (or others') prior negative experiences. Finally, neither researchers nor participants have time to waste and doing so is inconsiderate—if not unethical. For these reasons, it is important that the e-researcher acquire the necessary knowledge and skills to facilitate a successful Net-based focus group.

GROUP SIZE

In a face-to-face focus group, the researcher will usually invite six to twelve participants. We have found that in an asynchronous text-based focus group the size should be reduced slightly (e.g., six to eight). The reason is that in a Net-based textual environment, reading the combined messages from twelve active participants can be onerous. The time commitment may become greater than expected, resulting in feelings of resentment or in withdrawal by some group members. Alternatively, the focus group should not be too small. Having less than four members makes it difficult to garner the critical mass of input and discussion necessary to build and hone collective ideas and reactions. We have also found that asynchronous Net-based focus groups tend to have a lower participation rate and a higher attrition rate than face-to-face focus groups. Given these factors, the e-researcher should consider inviting twelve to fifteen participants, anticipate that eight to twelve will agree to participate, and assume that three to five will drop out during the study. Of course, whether or not this occurs will depend on the characteristics of and commitment from the targeted group. The ideal focus group would be one in which the e-researcher has a good understanding of the characteristics (i.e., motivation, time, likelihood of commitment) of the targeted participants and is able to accurately predict participation. Unfortunately, this is not often the case, and the prudent e-researcher tends to over-sample the target population to insure adequate participation in focus groups.

ADVANTAGES AND DISADVANTAGES OF TEXT-BASED SYNCHRONOUS VERSUS TEXT-BASED ASYNCHRONOUS FOCUS GROUPS

As mentioned, online text-based focus group interviews can be conducted either asynchronously or synchronously. While there are advantages and disadvantages to both, asynchronous text-based focus group interviews tend to be more successful than synchronous text-based focus group interviews. Reasons for this include:

- Asynchronous group participants can take the time to reflect on postings, which can result in more thoughtful responses.
- Asynchronous focus group participants can respond to questions when it is most convenient, through a capacity to time shift.
- The ideal number of participants for asynchronous focus groups is larger, resulting in greater ability to determine shared views.
- There is a need for fast and accurate typing skills in synchronous communication (minimum of twenty words per minute is recommended), whereas this is not as necessary for asynchronous communication.
- Synchronous focus group interview topics need to be kept simple, because participants need to respond quickly. This ensures that the discussion thread is not lost.
- There is a need for more active and responsive moderating in a synchronous focus group, since the facilitator must think and act on the fly.

The main weakness of synchronous text-based focus group interviews, however, is that they can easily degenerate into noncontiguous discussions. Noncontiguous discussions occur when a posting that is built on one person's response appears at the same time as a posting based on a different response. This happens because of the time lag between postings and the fact that we all type and compose at different speeds. It is possible to follow noncontiguous postings when there are three to five participants, but this becomes increasingly difficult as the group size becomes larger. While using a round-robin process (allowing each person to comment in turn) can effectively reduce if not eliminate noncontiguous discussions, it will also eliminate free-flowing discussions that build on others' input. The primary reason e-researchers decide to use synchronous focus groups is the dynamic synergy that can be created during the rapid pooling of ideas. The result can be fresh and creative discussions not typically found in asynchronous focus group interviews. As such, combinations of round-robins and spontaneous postings with fewer numbers of participants are recommended as a technique to reduce noncontiguous discussions and fragmented conversations.

It should also be noted that synchronous focus groups tend not to suffer from an attrition problem the way asynchronous focus groups do. In synchronous focus groups, there is a commitment to participate with a set time and date, whereas asynchronous focus groups are not as time bound, making it possible for participants to procrastinate and rationalize that they will "get around to it later." It is ironic that "anytime/anyplace" seems to imply that participants have "anytime/anyplace."

Problems aside, both synchronous and asynchronous focus groups are becoming increasingly popular survey methods for e-researchers. Overall, Net-based focus groups can be an effective data-gathering technique that has most of the strengths of face-to-face interviews with fewer costs and greater accessibility.

PARTICIPANT CHARACTERISTICS

While it is often difficult for the e-researcher to have in-depth knowledge of the characteristics of the invited group members, it is essential to know whether or not the participants have access to the necessary software as well as being capable of and comfortable with using the Net. The group members must also be somewhat knowledgeable about how to interact in a Net-based textual environment.

An important goal when selecting the participants for a Net-based focus group is to get a sense of the diversity of experiences and perceptions related to the research problem, rather than to get a representative sample per se. Purposive sampling is generally used when the invited participants are based on predetermined criteria (e.g., past courses taken, geographic location, employment). As such, the data gathered from focus groups are not meant to be generalized to other populations. Rather, data are used to obtain greater insight into the research problem and to further define the research question(s). When selecting the group participants it is important to identify elements that might threaten group conformity. Hence, an important consideration in constructing focus groups is to invite participants who are reasonably homogeneous with respect to the topic to be discussed but who will also represent diverse experiences and perceptions relative to key issues being investigated. The group composition will influence the quality of data collected, and hence what is learned.

In addition to careful selection of focus group members, the concepts and questions presented should be as uncomplicated as possible. This is particularly critical for synchronous focus group interviews. Complex issues that require carefully articulated responses are often difficult to introduce and explain in a text-based discussion. The problem is compounded when we account for the difficulty that many people have with reading text online. Furthermore, a lengthy text-based prelude may result in some—or many—participants skimming through the information presented. Thus, we recommend that the e-researcher conduct Net-based focus groups on questions, issues, and concepts that can easily be described in a few sentences, or at most, one screen of text.

ORGANIZATION

Preparing for a focus group, in terms of question design and evaluation, is essentially the same as survey instrument design. Likewise, a Net-based focus group should follow the same general principles and procedures as a face-to-face group interview. The organization of focus group interviews can be divided into four specific activities in this order: (1) introduction, (2) presentation of the research procedure and timelines, (3) presentation of the interview questions and discussion, and (4) closure.

Prior to the interview process, the e-researcher will need to select a platform to facilitate online discussions. There are two types of platforms that can be used for asynchronous discussion—mailing lists and computer conferences. Computer conferencing systems have an advantage in that messages are retained in "threads" that can be searched, displayed, and in other ways organized by each participant. However the major disadvantage of computer conferences is that the focus group postings are not pushed to the participants' desktop. Rather each participant must remember to regularly go to the conferencing site, enter a password, and navigate through a new system to find, read, and post new messages. The maintenance of logon addresses, as well as the necessity of insuring participants can and do access the conference, often become major burdens for the e-researcher. For these reasons we recommend the use of simple mailing list programs for focus groups. Mailing lists

- are easily accessed;
- enable both the e-researcher and participants to post and receive messages easily;
- require relatively little administrative work;
- can eliminate the need for participants to spend time learning how to log on, as the e-researcher can easily add each group member to the listserv; and
- are cost effective (most are free, see http://groups.yahoo.com for an example).

The next step is to select participants. This is usually done by emailing invitations to participate in the study. How to best solicit maximum participation from participants will depend on a number of factors. Most people are bombarded with solicitation emails from a variety of commercial and noncommercial sources. As such, many people are deleting unread emails received from unknown senders. Hence, your invitation will have a greater chance of being read when sent as a paper-based, mailed invitation, rather than an email. Furthermore, the participant can better verify the authenticity of the e-researcher when an introductory letter is sent on letterhead from the researcher's affiliated institution. For these reasons, we recommend that the e-researcher begin the process with a paper-based letter on institutional letterhead. The following is a sample letter of invitation.

Sample Letter of Invitation

[date]

Dear _______________:

I would like to invite you to participate in an **online** focus group that will be of significance for educational researchers and practitioners who use the Web to facilitate learning. The study focuses on language practices and instructors' perceptions of those practices in online undergraduate courses in postsecondary institutions.

The online group interview will require approximately 10–15 minutes of your time for 14 consecutive days (May 7–21) to respond to my questions and read the responses of other focus groups members. You will need access to the Internet and an email address. If you would be interested in participating in this study, please email me at [email] or phone collect during the day at [area code and phone number] prior to May 10th, 2003.

As an expert in the field, your participation in this study is greatly appreciated.

Respectfully,

[e-researcher]

Principle Researcher

As with online surveys (see Chapter 7), once the letter has been sent the e-researcher should follow up with an email to the participants who did not respond to the invitation. This should be done within ten to fourteen days of the date of the letter. This email should be short (no more than one screen of text) with reference to the invitation letter and with another request to participate. If the e-researcher does not know the participants personally, the email should be formal, beginning with "*Dear* ________" and closing with "*Regards*" or "*Sincerely*" and the e-researcher's designation in the signature line (i.e., Principle Researcher or Doctoral Candidate). The follow-up email should be sent individually, rather than sent as a "CC" to all participants. The reason for this is twofold. First, the names of invitees should remain confidential, and second, the invitation to participate is much more effective when sent to each participant individually.

Finally, to increase the acceptance rate, Silverman (2000) suggests that creative energy be put into the wording of the topic to be studied. For example, Silverman asks us to imagine that we are being invited to a focus group. Which would you like to attend more: "Research Methods" or "New Advances in Research Methods," or "How to Conduct Research That is Cheaper, Better, and Faster," or "Ways People Have Found for Getting Beneath Surface Responses"? Further, Silverman found that when a topic is truthful and of great interest to the selected participants, participation rates routinely doubled and even tripled.

Once the e-researcher has obtained a sufficient number of participants and has selected the communication software, a friendly message to the participants should be sent outlining:

- the purpose of the study
- how confidentiality will be maintained
- how the data will be secured
- when and how the results of the study will be disseminated
- any other administrative and ethical information related to the study

This process should be followed by a request for the participants to indicate that they have received, read, and understood the purpose of the study and agree to participate. This process serves two functions. First, it will let the e-researcher know if all the participants are connected and can successfully post and receive messages, and second, it will provide the e-researcher with informed consent from each participant. When there is no response from a group participant the e-researcher should follow up immediately by an email or phone call to determine the problem. The following is a sample confirmation and consent message. Note that the sample group in this example is made up of university-based teachers, thus the complex language used in the sample is appropriate for this audience but would need to be made simpler for a more generalized audience.

Sample Letter of Confirmation and Consent

Dear focus group members:

Thank you for responding to my invitation to participate in this study. This email provides information about the nature of the research project and the procedures.

The study focuses on online language practices and instructors' perceptions of those practices in postsecondary institutions. The study will draw on data that I have accumulated in four years of my own online classroom studies. For this study, I am endeavoring to complement work in progress (which sets out to examine discourse in the online classroom), by situating online group talk and reading within cross-curricular experiences. The intent of this part of the research is threefold: (i) to develop schemes for the analysis of students' online writing in undergraduate postsecondary inquiry and in technological problem solving; (ii) to analyze the nature of students' online writing and technological problem solving in undergraduate classes; (iii) to characterize the online reading and writing practices in undergraduate online courses.

I have identified you for this study because you have taught an online undergraduate course. I am hoping to conduct an online focus group interview with you to elicit your beliefs about and plans for learning in the online classroom and possibly follow up with a case study of your students' online reading and writing during one term of study.

If you agree to participate, the following will be requested of you:

- Respond to this email indicating that you have read and understood the purpose of the study and agree to participate.

- Participate in an online focus group for approximately 10–15 minutes per day, for 10–14 consecutive days (beginning May 7th).

The focus group responses will be confidential and all names and identifying characteristics will be removed from corresponding reports and publications. No deception will be used. The online messages connected with the study will be kept on a secured server for the duration and will be destroyed after a period of five years, unless permission by all participants has been granted for their further use. A summary of the research will be posted on the researcher's Web site at the completion of the study. I will email the URL to each participant. It is important to note that while the data will reside on a secure server and the researcher will make every effort to ensure data are kept safe, there is always a possibility that unauthorized access to the data may occur (e.g., by hackers) and/or that the data may become damaged through viruses.

If you agree to participate in this study, please reply to this email confirming that you have read and understood the purpose of this study, you understand your rights as a participant, and you agree to participate. Thank you.

Sincerely,

[e-researcher]

Principle Researcher

Next, the e-researcher will take steps to make the group participants feel at ease and foster communication between the participants, e-researcher, and moderator (if this person is not the e-researcher). This can be achieved by beginning with a welcome message and then posing the first question with a request for a response from all group members.

The following is an example of a welcome message. Again, the message should be kept short (not exceeding one screen of text) and be informal and friendly. This will set the tone for discussion, rather than for simply a sequential interview.

Sample Welcome Message

Dear focus group members:

Welcome and thank you for agreeing to participate in this research project.

Today is the first day of the online focus group, and it begins with a question (see below). Every second day, for ten days, a new question will be posted (five questions in total). Following this will be two additional days for the "wrap-up." At some point each day you are asked to respond to the question and/or respond to someone else's response. As mentioned in the letter of invitation, confidentiality will be maintained and only summarized information will be communicated in any publication of this study.

If you need to contact me during this study, I can be reached by email [email] or by phone at [area code and phone number] during the day or at [area code and phone number] during the evening. If you have any technical problems, [name of technical support] will be available to help. His [her] email is [email] or he [she] can be reached at this toll free number: [area code and phone number].

The following is today's question:

> When teaching an undergraduate online course, how do you determine if a student's writing (e.g., online discussion posting) exhibits inquiry-based learning, decision building, and/or problem solving?

Definitions:

• **Inquiry-based learning** is an investigation or probe for knowledge, data, or truths.

• **Decision building** is arriving at a position or passing judgment on an issue that is reached after generating the alternatives, evaluating the choices, and assessing the consequences.

• **Problem solving** is an attempt to explain, decipher, or resolve something that is enigmatic, ambiguous, and/or cryptic.

I look forward to each of your candid and frank responses!

Regards,

[first name of e-researcher]

Principle Researcher

At this point, the e-researcher can be somewhat more informal with a writing style that is more conversational and friendly than academic. If there are any unusual terms, they too should be clarified in the welcome letter.

It is important that the questions are written clearly and completely, otherwise respondents will have to ask for clarification, which can divert the attention of the group, stall the discussion, and delay the entire process. The e-researcher should plan to ask about five questions, though the ideal number of questions is dependent on the complexity of the subject and the follow-up probes. Probes are follow-up questions designed to gather deeper and more insightful information based on the group's initial responses to a question. The more complex the subject, the more probing questions are required to reveal deeper insights. Thus, too many prepared questions can minimize the time available for probing, resulting in missed opportunities to enrich the data. Questions should also be open ended to avoid "yes/no" responses. "How" and "what" questions usually work best. Paramount to a successful Net-based focus group interview is a skillful moderator who can keep the discussion on topic and maintain a dynamic and synergistic flow. The next section provides further discussion on the role of a moderator in a Net-based focus group.

THE MODERATOR

Focus groups have been criticized because they are so dependent on both the personality and skills of the moderator facilitating the research. Arguably, this is both its strength and weakness. According to Silverman and Zukergood (2000), the difference between a skilled and unskilled moderator lies in the ability to interpret not only what happens in the group interview, but also what does not happen, what should have happened, and what might happen with careful and intentional planning.

Most often the e-researcher is also the moderator for online focus groups, due to both the cost of hiring a moderator and the lack of moderators who are knowledgeable and skilled in facilitating online discussions. In face-to-face settings, focus groups typically require two people: a moderator and a technical assistant—most often the researcher. The moderator will facilitate and guide the discussion while the researcher attends to other tasks (e.g., video or audio taping and note taking). Because such tasks are not necessary in Net-based focus groups, many e-researchers assume the role of moderator.

To begin the Net-based focus group, the moderator will state the purpose of the group and outline ground rules in a welcome letter. As the sample letter in the previous section illustrates, this process begins with an explanation of the purpose of the study, information on how to participate (i.e., instructions for responses and a timeline), and the establishment of an atmosphere of informality and openness. The introduction should also be worded in a way that encourages participants to be candid and honest and that implies that there does not need to be group consensus. In fact, the introduction might also include a statement about the need to get as many diverse opinions as possible to represent people who are not group participants. It is important for the moderator to set a tone that makes the group feel free to agree or disagree, ask frank questions, and make candid remarks. If none of the participants open the discussion, the moderator should then ask for a response by name. For example, the moderator might post a message such as:

> Dear All,
>
> As no one is jumping in to be the first to respond, why don't we begin alphabetically? So [name of one participant] why don't you take the lead in beginning this discussion?

Once the discussion begins, the moderator will usually avoid arguing with the participants and making them feel they are wrong. The moderator will also avoid praising specific comments. For example, comments such as "that's very interesting" or "excellent point" are evaluative; they indicate to participants who do not receive praise that their contributions are not as good. Other kinds of redirective feedback, such as "why?" can make a participant feel defensive. These kinds of comments can quickly and effectively shut down the discussion. It takes a great deal of skill to acknowledge the responses with enthusiasm while at the same time avoiding reinforcing any particular viewpoint or bias. In contrast, to get data that is not superficial or does not contain stock responses, the moderator must guard against making the participants feel that their contributions are uninformed or uneducated. Redirective comments (or nondirective probes) should act as a stimulus to elicit further information from the respondent. The following are examples of effective probes:

> Explain this further to me.
>
> Can someone say more about that last remark?
>
> Who can build on that last idea?
>
> How important is that concern?
>
> Does someone have a different perspective on this?
>
> What are your reactions to this last comment?

It is also the responsibility of the moderator to help make the participant comfortable in what may be a new and unfamiliar environment. Some participants new to Net-based communication software may feel self-conscious and uneasy writing in such a public manner. Whatever the reason, the moderator should directly encourage silent participants to contribute. After several unsuccessful attempts, a private email or follow-up phone call can be made to ensure that there are no technical problems and to provide verbal encouragement. One of the most effective ways to get everyone to participate is to make the group discussions fun by adding humor, noting personal characteristics of the participants, or in other ways personalizing the discussion. A fun Net environment will facilitate the interaction process and bring the discussion to life.

If the discussion is not moving in a timely and orderly manner, the moderator may wish to consider using a round-robin questioning process with each person's turn to speak identified. Once the Net discussions begin, it is important for the moderator to strive for a balance between letting the group members express themselves and keeping the discussion focused on the question. A skilled moderator can probe without breaking the flow or the pace of the group. If possible, focus group questions should begin with an easy and nonthreatening question. More difficult questions should be asked toward the middle and end or when the moderator senses that participants feel comfortable with the topic and online environment.

It cannot be stressed enough that a knowledgeable and skilled focus group moderator will lead active, dynamic, and productive Net-based discussions that are flexible, keep participants on topic, and ensure that no one person (or persons) dominate.

BRINGING CLOSURE

Once the questions have been asked and discussed, the moderator must bring proper closure to the group discussion. One way to do this is to not allow the discussion to extend beyond its scheduled end date. The second-to-last day should be set aside for the wrap-up activity, which typically involves a summary of the main points and the participants expressing final thoughts and/or positions. The wrap-up activity should be done by the moderator and e-researcher jointly (if the two are not the same) to determine the major themes and topics of group responses. These themes should then be presented to the group participants as a *member check*, which is a post-session debriefing. During the member check, the researcher will ask participants how they perceived selected issues. Corrections and revisions should be made accordingly and verified by the group, as an accurate representation, on the last scheduled day. Finally, the focus group should end with closing statements including a final opportunity to ask any outstanding questions and a "thank you" for participating.

ANALYZING THE DATA

Prior to data analysis, the e-researcher can do a few things that will make this process easier and more meaningful. First, as the discussion progresses, the e-researcher should take notes about the discussion based on his or her speculations, feelings, problems, ideas, agreement, and disagreement. In addition to this, the e-researcher should summarize the main ideas and make member checks during the interview as well as on completion. When the focus group has ended, the e-researcher and moderator should jointly interpret what was said, articulate hunches, identify patterns between the literature and the group discussion, and begin generating hypotheses. When writing the data analysis, each topic identified should be categorized under similar themes. When describing significant themes that emerged, samples from the online transcripts should be provided as supporting evidence. The article by Rezabek (2000) in *Forum for Qualitative Research* (at http://qualitative-research.net/fqs/fqs-eng.htm) provides an example of how to write the data analysis for a Net-based focus group.

A thorough review of the literature should also provide the e-researcher with a solid basis of information to compare with the themes and topics that have emerged as well as to clarify issues that are both congruent and incongruent with the literature. The literature can either be integrated with the themes and topics or written as a separate section, usually titled "discussion."

Finally, when reporting focus group results, in addition to an analysis of themes and topics, a description of the selection procedures should be provided. This should include the criteria for sampling; how the participants were identified; the percentage that agreed to participate, as well as the percentage that eventually did participate; and demographic data (i.e., age, gender, education, socioeconomic status, etc.).

Once the data have been analyzed, the e-researcher should have a greater understanding of the topic under investigation and be able to define the research question(s) for further study—the most common aim of focus groups in the field of education.

Online Resources

- Carter McNamera maintains an excellent list of readings, resources, and tips relating to focus group process at http://www.mapnp.org/library/grp_skll/focusgrp/focusgrp.htm.
- The commercial firm Net.surveys provides an online focus group hosting service that can recruit participants and provides virtual rooms where online participants can be exposed to a variety of multimedia Web-based resources for comment or discussion. See http://www.web-surveys.net/net.probe/.
- Bob Dick provides a nice summary and tips for conducting structured focus groups online at http://www.scu.edu.au/schools/gcm/ar/arp/focus.html.

TIPS FOR FACILITATING A SUCCESSFUL NET-BASED FOCUS GROUP

- Observe or particpate in a Net-based focus group.
- Invite participants who are comfortable with communicating on the Internet.
- Anticipate an attrition rate of about 50 percent.
- Choose and word your questions carefully.
- Plan your probing questions ahead of time, but be prepared to change them based on the group's discussion.
- Write a friendly welcome letter and set a climate where participants feel free to contribute frank and candid remarks.
- Use nonevaluative feedback through nondirective probes.
- Follow up with a phone call to silent participants.

- End the group discussion with a post-session debriefing.
- Thank all participants.

SUMMARY

Focus groups are generally used for in-depth and collaborative exploration of important issues and to redefine the research topic and the research questions. While Net-based focus groups have met with mixed results, their advantages over face-to-face focus groups are clear: they reduce or eliminate participation and cost barriers as well as overcome certain power issues between participants. However, effective Net-based focus groups will require a skilled moderator who can probe without breaking the flow or the pace of the group in an online environment.

REFERENCES

Fowler, F. J. (1995). *Improving survey questions. Design and evaluation*. London: Sage.

Glesne, C., & Peskin, A. (1992). *Becoming qualitative researchers: An introduction*. White Plains, NY: Longman.

Jacobson, P. (1997). On-line focus groups: Four approaches that work. *Quirk's Marketing Research Review, Article Number 0245*.

Mertens, D. M. (1998). *Research methods in education and psychology: Integrating diversity with quantitative and qualitative approaches*. Thousand Oaks, CA: Sage.

Neuman, W. L. (2000). *Social research methods. Qualitative and quantitative approaches* (4th ed.). Toronto, ON: Allyn & Bacon.

Patton, M. Q. (1987). *How to use qualitative methods in evaluation*. London: Sage.

Patton, M. Q. (1990). *Qualitative evaluation and research methods* (2nd ed.). London: Sage.

Rezabek, R. J. (2000). Online focus groups: Electronic discussions for research. *Forum for Qualitative Research. 1*(1). [Online]. Available: http://qualitative-research.net/fqs/fqs-eng.htm.

Silverman, G. (2000). How to get beneath the surface in focus groups. *Market Navigation, Inc.* [Online]. Available: http://www.mnav.com/bensurf.htm.

Silverman, G., & Zukergood, E. (2000). Everything in moderation. *Market Navigation, Inc.* [Online]. Available: http://www.mnav.com/evmod.htm.

Stewart, D. W., & Shamdasani, P. N. (1998). Focus group research: Exploration and discovery. In L. Bickman and D. J. Rog (Eds.), *Handbook of applied social research methods* (pp. 505–526). London: Sage.

Van Nuys, D. (1999). Online focus groups save time, money. *Silicon Valley / San Jose Business Journal, November*. [Online]. Available: http://sanjose.bcentral.com/sanjose/stories/1999/11/29/smallb4.html.

CHAPTER NINE

NET-BASED CONSENSUS TECHNIQUES

Bis repetita placent
The things that please are those that are asked for again and again.
Horace (65–8 BC)

Creating, sustaining, and improving social environments are challenging tasks that involve aesthetic, cultural, and affective considerations, as well as rational and scientific-based decision making. Much of the information needed to make informed policy decisions resides in the minds of professionals, administrators, researchers, taxpayers, and students. However, the views of these experts often are not readily available to the e-researcher and/or sometimes they provide conflicting advice. There are techniques to solicit and sample this individual knowledge (notably interviews and surveys), however, sometimes a consensus is needed to arrive at a single best solution. The use of the Delphi Method, Nominal Group Technique, and Consensus Development Conference, as well as other experimental techniques have proved to be effective means to achieve this kind of goal. The purpose of consensus techniques is to systematically solicit expert opinion to facilitate the clarification of issues—even in the absence of a group consensus (Linstone & Turoff, 1975). This method typically uses a carefully designed program of successive individual questioning generally conducted with written questionnaires.

The primary reason for using consensus techniques is to structure a group communication process that creates useful results based on a consensus by experts in the field. Specifically, it is not the *nature* of this method that determines its appropriateness in a research study; rather, it is the *circumstances* of the research that necessitates this kind of group communication process. Linstone and Turoff (1975) identified specific circumstances in which a researcher, wishing to obtain group consensus, may find other kinds of communication processes (such as a focus group or interviews) too restrictive. Some of these circumstances include:

- The research problem does not lend itself to well-defined systematic techniques; it can, however, acquire useful results from subjective judgments on a collective basis.
- The research participants will be representative of diverse backgrounds, with respect to experience and expertise, and are geographically dispersed, making frequent group meetings virtually impossible due to time and cost.
- Related to the prior point (that the participants will have diverse backgrounds), the experts may be uncompromising between opinions in a way that the communication process must be refereed and/or anonymity assured.
- The heterogeneity of the research participants must be preserved to avoid domination by some experts.

A number of related research techniques have been developed that gather and condense opinions from groups of experts, which we refer to as consensus-generating techniques. The most well known of these is the Delphi Method, which has been used for over fifty years to resolve a wide variety of policy, forecasting, and decision-making problems. Consensus techniques have mostly been used in face-to-face conference modes; however, we are seeing increased interest in their use at a distance using a variety of communications technologies. The Net, with its capacity to support a variety of synchronous and asynchronous, as well as group and individual communications modes, is an ideal environment to support existing and experiment with new varieties of consensus data collection. In this chapter we overview the ways in which these techniques have been used and discuss ways the techniques can be adapted for Net use.

Generally, consensus techniques work by soliciting the opinion(s) of experts (usually in some sort of individual format) on an important issue or question. The researcher sometimes provides background materials or suggested information references that participants can consult to better inform their position. The range of the group responses, along with their individual opinions, are then returned to the participant. The participant is asked to defend, explain, or change their opinions so as to move the group to a single-best answer or consensus. This process may be repeated two or more times and hopefully as individual differences are reduced, a consensus develops. An important feature of the process is the facilitation and encouragement of individuals to share the rationale for their opinions—especially if these differ from the group mean. This sharing is facilitated through distribution of the written rationale or comments to the survey questions (using postal services, fax, email, or Web) or through a structured discussion during a face-to-face meeting or real-time distributed meeting or conference.

The objective of the consensus process is to arrive at a single statement or answer that participants can agree on. Failing this unanimity, the process should clearly identify the nature and extent of opinion divergence. Generally consensus is sought; however, we are mindful of Mahatma Gandhi's observation that "honest disagreement is often a good sign of progress." A measurement of central tendency, the interquartile range (IQR), or the simple mean is usually used to determine the consensus of opinion for each of the questions posed to the group. Opposing opinions (those who fall outside the IQR and median or bimodal distributions) are also noted and shared with the group to ensure that critical opposing opinions are not ignored. The process thereby dictates a conceptual communication structure that relates the opposing opinions to the data and objective of the research project. Opposing opinions are not considered to be antithetical with objectivity; rather, opposing opinions actually serve objectivity. This technique, then, may not lead to a convergence of opinions; bimodal distributions will always remain a possible outcome. However, the resulting outcome, irrespective of whether or not an opinion synthesis occurs, may be more valid than other methodologies *because of* the acknowledgment and accommodation of opposing opinions. Through the progress of successive iterations, the consensus process works to evolve an informed and well-thought-out answer to a difficult question. The question is often of such complexity or deals with future forecasts for which there is no way to calculate a single correct answer. As such, consensus techniques can serve to gather and articulate communal wisdom, as well as serve a cohesive and community function, bringing diverse opinions together and allowing individuals to work as an effective group.

The consensus process benefits if participants are able to view their opinions in relationship to those of the rest of the group and are given an opportunity and motivation to argue and defend their opinions. The resulting dialogue allows individuals (and the group) to alter and refine their opinions, hopefully leading to an informed and wise consensus of all participants. On the other hand, there is a danger that the consensus process will capture only collective ignorance. However, the selection of informed and motivated participants coupled with clear goals, objectives, and processes, usually results in consensus agreements that gather and expand the wisdom of all members.

Consensus-building theory has evolved into a series of techniques known as consensus research with three methodological variations or processes—Delphi Method, Nominal Groups Technique, and Consensus Development Conference (Murphy et al., 1998). The Net provides ways to not only expand, but also improve, both the effectiveness and efficiency of these traditional forms of consensus research.

ADVANTAGES OF CONSENSUS TECHNIQUES

Consensus techniques for e-research are related to focus groups and offer many of the same benefits and challenges. However, they provide more formal structure than focus group discussions. They are more deliberately focused on achieving a single best answer or statistically revealing the extent of disagreement than the open-ended and qualitative nature of most focus group research. Moreover, consensus groups provide a number of useful advantages for e-researchers seeking a means to gather knowledge from a dispersed group of experts.

Advantages of Traditional Consensus Techniques

High-Quality and Informed Opinion. Consensus groups are usually purposively selected so that the participants are informed, interested, and capable of providing high-quality opinions. Participants in consensus groups draw first on their own experiences and opinions, and then build on that knowledge by considering the opinions and expertise of others. This creates an environment for social cognition that is likely to produce better decisions than those made by individuals and to arrive at negotiated consensus from expert opinions. As Langford (1972) notes, the consensus data gathering technique endeavors to make "effective use of informed intuitive judgment; it is designed to combine individual judgments systematically and thus obtain a reasoned consensus" (p. 21).

Safety in Numbers. Consensus groups are less likely to arrive at or support incorrect answers or ineffective solutions because they are working with the collective expertise of a number of experts with a variety of experiences.

Authority. Group decisions are more likely to be taken seriously than those of any individual. In addition, specific consensus techniques have been shown to be more reliable and valid than other forms of opinion gathering and synthesis.

Controlled Process. Consensus techniques provide a set of procedures that tend to mitigate the negative impacts of group behavior, such as coercion, domination by certain individuals, or premature consensus seeking. A structured process can eliminate these kinds of group behavior.

Supports Communication among Individuals with Polarized Views. Although consensus techniques may not always result in individuals coming to a unified position, they do create an environment in which polarized views can be democratically expressed and negotiated with equity. In some applications, anonymity is used to allow participants to freely state and argue their positions without threat of retaliation.

Credibility. Although these techniques are not without their technical critics, various mathematical techniques can be applied at each stage of the process to quantify individual and group opinions. The feedback of results to individuals allows participants to judge their opinions in relationship to the larger group. At the end of the process the extent of consensus can be accurately calculated and discussed.

Accessibility. Some types of consensus groups have evolved through the use of face-to-face meetings, and more recently these groups have been aided by the instant computation of the results of their decision using computers and software systems generally known as decision-making software. To overcome the time and space restrictions and costs related to face-to-face meetings, consensus techniques have also used postal mail or courier services to allow members to post and defend their reasons without meeting face-to-face. However, the inherent time delay, inconvenience, and cost of postal returns remain problematic.

Additional Advantages

To these advantages of traditional consensus techniques, a number of others can be added when the Net is used as the means of communication.

Time and Cost Savings. The interactive capacity of the Net can be adapted to provide instant feedback to participants as to the extent to which their answers are congruent with those of the other panel members. Even if such feedback is purposely delayed until a certain number of responses are obtained, the process of distribution of results and gathering of subsequent responses is made faster when done by electronic means than by the older postal-based techniques. Snyder-Halpern, Bagley Thompson, and Schaffer (2000) found both cost and time savings for email in a comparison Delphi study however, the postal system produced higher participation rates among invited panel members.

Equitable Time and Power Sharing. One of the advantages of consensus techniques mentioned earlier is their capacity to control domination by any individual in the group. This advantage extends to Net-based consensus techniques because the participants with power and status can be kept confidential through assigning aliases.

Broad and Diverse Opinions. Because participants in Net-based consensus building research can be located anywhere and generally can participate at any time, it is possible to call on participants from nearly any geographical location.

TYPES OF CONSENSUS TECHNIQUES

As often happens when communication practices and techniques are adapted between different media, there are considerable overlaps and some components of the process are not easily mapped to the new media. Thus, three of the types of consensus techniques described in the following sections are not "pure" types, but are general adaptations of methods developed earlier. The final technique described is unique to the Net.

The earliest consensus techniques probably evolved around the time of cave dwellers and their use of fire circles, where tribal members met to discuss and make group decisions. The technique was formalized in the 1950s and named the Delphi Method after the mythical Oracle of Delphi, who could be called on to forecast the future. The technique was designed to systematically solicit expert opinion to facilitate the clarification of issues—even in the absence of group consensus. In particular, it endeavors to make "effective use of informed intuitive judgment; it is designed to combine individual judgments systemically and thus obtain a reasoned consensus" (Langford, 1972, p. 21). Moreover, consensus data-gathering techniques and the Delphi in particular were designed to reduce the problems of domination and unequal participation experienced in many unstructured face-to-face encounters and to reduce the costs associated with place-bound interaction. Delphi was first used with multiple rounds of mailed surveys with the return of individual and group results amongst an expert group. In the 1960s the technique was adapted to face-to-face meetings and named Nominal Group Technique (Delbecq, Van de Ven, and Gustafson, 1975), and in 1977 a further refinement known as the Consensus Development Conference was developed by the United States Institute of Health (Murphy et al., 1998).

DELPHI METHOD

The Delphi Method shares a common heritage with the Internet. Both the early Internet (know as the ARPANET) and early work with Delphi at the Rand Corporation were funded by the United States military. Both projects were funded to help predict and survive nuclear attacks by hostile forces. Besides a common funding source, the Net in its earliest incarnations was used to refine and develop Delphi techniques.

The Delphi Method is the most popular of the consensus-building techniques. Because it was designed to facilitate consensus among experts, who remain anonymous to each other and deliberate without meeting face-to-face, it is most easily adapted to the asynchronous, anonymous, and ubiquitous nature of the Net. The Delphi Method can be used in a variety of ways; however, most commonly it works by sending email letters of invitation to selected participants. Within the email, the participants are often directed to a Web survey or are emailed a survey in which questions are presented and space provided for participants to type the reasons for their choices. After all participants have filled out the survey, the results of the group are analyzed then returned or presented to the respondents as feedback, together with reasons participants have provided to defend their choices.

The participants are then invited to reconsider their answers after consideration of group means and the arguments of others. The process is repeated two to five times until either the group reaches a consensus or the answers stabilize between rounds. Turoff and Hiltz (1995) describe other variations of classical Delphi techniques that allow for the continuous interaction common in forms of computer conferencing. However, they argue that there is not yet a true merger of the Delphi Technique with Computer Mediated Communications. In particular, only recently has the technology become available to support the interaction necessary to structure the communication within a single conferencing system. It is likely that customizable conferencing systems with support for voting, computational analysis, visualization of consensus states, and other advanced features will result in new forms of Delphi Methods in the coming years (Turoff, Hiltz, Bieber, Fjermestad, & Rana, 1999).

NOMINAL GROUP TECHNIQUE

Nominal Group techniques have, to date, rarely been used on the Net, though they have been used for face-to-face consensus building and research for over forty years (Delbecq, Van de Ven, and Gustafson, 1975). The Nominal Group Technique is similar to the Delphi Method except that interaction occurs in real time—traditionally, in face-to-face encounters. Classical Nominal Group Technique begins with a facilitator introducing the issue (usually ending in a question) and then allowing time (usually around five minutes) for participants to formulate and write down individual opinions on the issue. The facilitator then asks each participant in turn (round-robin style) to provide his or her answer or opinion. Usually no discussion is allowed until all ideas are captured and displayed (often on a flip chart). After all members have had an opportunity to participate, they are invited to discuss, clarify or provide rationale for their position. Members next vote on or prioritize the answers provided. This process may be followed by a second (and perhaps subsequent) round of individual estimates and voting. The process ends with consensus or a sense that the groups have stabilized and "agreed to disagree." The quality of the Nominal group is usually determined by the number of ideas or opinions generated and the degree of consensus on the best or highest priority item(s). Randall Dunham (1998) provides a useful user guide to Nominal Group Technique at http://instruction.bus.wisc.edu/obdemo/readings/ngt.html.

In a Net-based context, Nominal Group process can be facilitated using text chat, audio or video conferencing. Real-time computing resources can also be used both face-to-face or on the Net to calculate and display the degree of consensus within the group. Commercial companies such as Centra (www.centra.com) sell and lease audio, video, and text chat software that could be used for this type of real-time group process. Generally, smaller size groups are involved in Nominal Groups than in other consensus techniques. Each participant should be given time to speak. Delays while waiting for a turn may cause more dropouts in distributed, Net-based groups than in those in facilitated face-to-face groups. Net-based Nominal Groups could also be accomplished with anonymous participants interacting via text chat or audio conferencing—a celebrated feature of the Delphi Method that is, of course, not possible in a face-to-face Nominal Group.

To date, there have only been a few exploratory studies testing the efficacy of Net-based Nominal Group Technique. In a small study conducted by Pazos, Perazzoli, Jiang, Canto, and Beruvides (2001), researchers found no significant difference between the amount of ideas generated nor the satisfaction with the process between Nominal Groups conducted face-to-face and those that used a text chat environment on the Net. A finding of no significant difference is interpreted positively, as the Net-based approach offers convenience, accessibility, and cost savings compared to face-to-face groups. We anticipate in the near future that the availability of voice input and discussion will result in increased use of this form of structured, real-time consensus making for both research and less formal decision making.

CONSENSUS CONFERENCES

Consensus Conferences have been most fully developed in Denmark (see http://www.tekno.dk/subpage.php3?survey=16&language=uk), where they have been used to produce reports on controversial technology related issues. The process used in Denmark is to select randomly a sample of citizens who, over a three-day period, listen to expert opinion and then discuss and finally draft a consensus document designed to guide public decision making. To our knowledge this technique has been undertaken exclusively on the Internet, though certain portions of face-to-face consensus conferences have been webcast (see http://www.nih.gov/news/pr/oct2000/omar-25.htm), and there are certain similarities between consensus conferences and virtual conferences.

WIKI SYSTEM

A final emerging form of consensus-building technique that is native to the Net is the WIKI Web system designed by Ward Cunningham (http://www.c2.com/cgi/wiki?WelcomeVisitors). A WIKI site allows selected, or all, users to jointly (and anonymously if they choose) edit hypertext markup language (HTML) documents. This means that any user can edit, delete, add, or otherwise alter the page on which the group is working. This may seem like a formula for anarchy (like the Web?), but it captures some of the original freewheeling spirit of the Net and can support a unique form of reflective, anonymous, and open-ended discourse. Peter Mercel, an early WIKI developer and contributor, described the ambiance of a WIKI group as "insecure, indiscriminate, user-hostile, slow, and full of difficult, nit-picking people. Any other online community would count each of these strengths as a terrible flaw. Perhaps WIKI works because the other online communities don't" (undated WIKI page at http://www.c2.com/cgi/wiki?WhyWikiWorks).

The major difference between a Net-based discussion group and a WIKI is the communal creation of HTML documents. Thus, the output of the group discourse is a series of continuously changing documents, rather than a long discussion or a quantified set of consensual agreements. Consensus has been reached when all participants are satisfied with the text and the format of the group document.

The original WIKI software maintains some of the critical components of earlier consensus data-gathering techniques, but it is much more informal and spontaneous and lacks means for quantitatively calculating differences amongst panel members. WIKIs have been adopted by a variety of organizations and the process has evolved with the development of various sets of rules (such as restricted membership) for different purposes. For example, an interesting site related to architecture can be found at the Three Dots site at http://www.threedots.org/. Three Dots allows for voting and in other ways attempts to maintain a heritage that evolved from Delphi Methods. To our knowledge WIKIs have not been used as a tool in a formal e-research project—but they could be!

DEVELOPING A NET-BASED CONSENSUS-BUILDING RESEARCH PROJECT

The first step in any research design is to plan the operational steps. For a consensus study, this plan revolves around setting the research question(s), selecting a participant sample, deciding on the method(s) of participant interaction, deciding on the analysis techniques, and deciding how to disseminate results. We discuss each of these components in turn.

Setting the Research Question(s)

Many important education questions lend themselves to consensus-building research techniques because the questions have no single, self-evident, or universal answer. A good question for the consensus technique draws out the participant's experiences and opinion. In particular, the question should be designed to draw out the participants' opinions on an important, but controversial, idea or their suggested solutions to a complex problem. Hopefully during the rounds of discussion, background detail or personal examples will be brought out and these will be used as incentives for the participants to converge on a consensus of opinion.

Like a survey, there is no single correct number of questions that makes a good consensus study; however, if there are too many questions, participants may become fatigued and abandon the process. This is especially important when participants are not engaged in real-time activities and they can leave the task without fear of hurting the researcher's feelings by an obvious virtual "walk out of the door." Remember also that the participants will see these same questions at least two times, and perhaps as many as five times, so we suggest not making the survey or the individual questions so long that participants will be reluctant to participate in subsequent rounds. Careful timing with pilot subjects is useful to be able to accurately inform participants of the estimated time required to complete the assigned tasks.

Selecting a Participant Sample

Usually participants are purposively chosen because they have knowledge that is valuable in answering the research questions. The target audience for the research should be considered when selecting the participants and a sample selected that will be perceived as credible by these final arbitrators of the value of the research. Most of the techniques for focus groups (see Chapter 8) or survey samples (see Chapter 11) can be used to gather a sample for consensus-building study. Ethical issues related to privacy and confidentiality must also be addressed when soliciting participation (see Chapter 5). Invitations to participate can be sent by email (to save cost and time), but we suggest, in agreement with other researchers (e.g., Dillman, 2000), that an initial letter on the letterhead of the sponsoring or affiliated organization is more likely to garner high rates of participation.

Participant heterogeneity is also an issue in participant selection. Obviously, the participants should have enough in common to be able to knowledgeably discuss the research problem. If, however, the question is marked by deep polarization, it may be very difficult for the group to move to consensus. Alternatively, choosing only well-known proponents of a particular cause or issue involves bias and will likely not result in sufficient differentiation to stimulate discussion or defense of different positions. Finally, if the technique chosen allows participants to know and interact directly with other members (as often occurs in online Nominal Group processes), large differences in status may impair honest and open discussion. The number of participants in most Delphi studies ranges from ten to thirty—fewer than ten participants may result in lack of ideas and problems with reliability, and more than thirty well-chosen participants from relatively homogeneous groups rarely results in new information (Collins, Osborne, Ratcliffe, Millar, & Duschl, 2001). Generally, the panel of experts should be representative of diverse backgrounds with respect to experience and expertise. The heterogeneity of the participants must be preserved to assure validity of the results. That is, the possibility of domination by one or several experts, causing a bandwagon effect, must be removed. This can be achieved through ensuring that the end-of-round summaries include all voices. In addition, the researcher's views and partialities to certain problems should never be imposed on the group respondents—especially at the expense of other perspectives in relation to the problem.

The number who agree to participate may be considerably lower than the number who are approached—Delphi studies are notorious for requiring considerable time commitments. To keep those that agree to participate from dropping out, the researcher must attempt to walk a fine line between allowing a wide latitude in the contribution of information and summarizing each round. Specifically, the researcher should conduct the research in a way that will not result in an overwhelming amount of information that will require an excessive amount of time on the part of the participants when reviewing the summaries. How to limit the summaries for an efficient communication process without sacrificing the participant's contribution is an issue that brings ethics, validity, and trustworthiness into play. The researcher must use his or her personal discretion to decide what will be included in the summaries. Personal discretion can be translated to personal preference or personal bias. To be ethical and maintain validity, the researcher must state whose and what parts of the contributions were limited as well as why. To promote trustworthiness, Glesne and Peshkin (1992) suggest that the researcher enlist an outsider to audit the summaries.

Finally, the reliability is also related to the size of the group. That is, the reliability of the group responses increases with the size of the group (Dalkey, 1972). Yet, one should not be too concerned, in a statistical sense, about the group size because inferential statistics are not used (Dalkey in Shearin, 1995). That is, the objective in selecting persons to serve on a panel is to choose or find people having special knowledge or expertise in the research area. Allen (in Shearin, 1995) claims, for the reasons cited by Dalkey, a definitive sample size is not required for an effective study, but also states in another publication (Allen, 1978) that an ideal size is a panel of thirty people. This is also in contrast with Martino (1972) who writes that a panel of fifteen, consisting of a cross section of experts from a particular field, is sufficient for reliable results. According to Martino, if the researcher has fifteen or more responses to the questionnaire, the study can be considered to adequately meet the question of reliability. Similarly, according to Tersine and Riggs (1990), a panel of ten to fifteen members has been judged sufficient for producing effective results.

Formatting the Questions

Issues relating to formatting a Web or mail survey are covered in Chapter 11 and apply equally to the surveys used in an online Delphi. Figure 9.1 is an example of a Delphi question that was developed and used by Kathryn A. Kennedy from the University of British Columbia for a Ph.D. (2002) study related to rate of adoption of online courses.

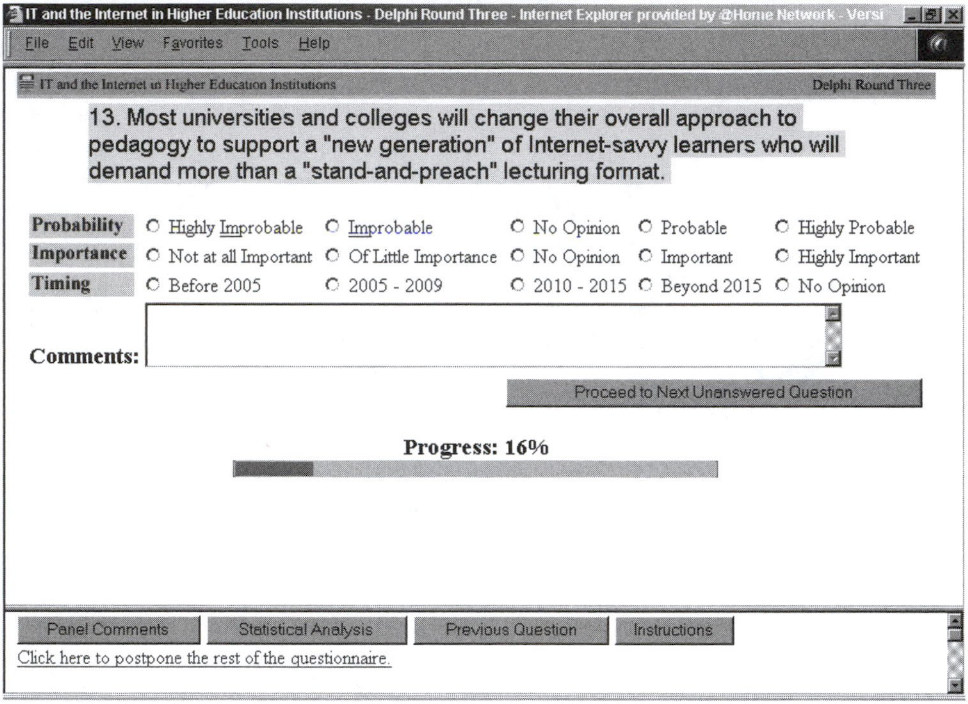

IT and the Internet in Higher Education Institutions - Delphi Round Three - Internet Explorer provided by @Home Network - Versi

File Edit View Favorites Tools Help

IT and the Internet in Higher Education Institutions — Delphi Round Three

13. Most universities and colleges will change their overall approach to pedagogy to support a "new generation" of Internet-savvy learners who will demand more than a "stand-and-preach" lecturing format.

Probability	Highly Improbable	Improbable	No Opinion	Probable	Highly Probable
Importance	Not at all Important	Of Little Importance	No Opinion	Important	Highly Important
Timing	Before 2005	2005 - 2009	2010 - 2015	Beyond 2015	No Opinion

Comments:

Proceed to Next Unanswered Question

Progress: 16%

Panel Comments | Statistical Analysis | Previous Question | Instructions

Click here to postpone the rest of the questionnaire.

FIGURE 9.1 Delphi Entry Form (With permission from Kennedy, 2002.)

There are a number of features of a well-designed Delphi that are illustrated in this example.

- The three 5-point Likert-type scales are distributed across the page and the formatting works well at a variety of text sizes chosen in the respondent's browser.
- There is a consistent format for all questions used in the study, thus reducing the cognitive load and allowing participants to move accurately and quickly through the survey.
- Three separate pieces of information are extracted from each question, thus probing more deeply about the issue, without forcing a larger number of questions or screen displays.
- Each question is downloaded separately from the Web server and the answers can be checked individually for incompleteness (if desired).
- There are a number of navigational aids allowing participants to control the order of the questions (if they so desire) and allowing them to complete the survey at a later date, if they are forced to leave the survey before completion.
- Headings that require ratings are highlighted until they are answered, then the highlighting disappears.
- A progress meter provides feedback to the respondent on his or her progress through the survey.

- There is a comments box under each question for elaborations or concerns.
- There is a help button (labeled instructions) on each page of the survey.

Distributing Questions

As mentioned previously, the e-researcher may distribute background materials to participants, but this is generally not necessary. Usually the participants have been chosen because of their expertise and thus are likely not in need of background briefing. Further, the selection of background information may result in undue influence by the researcher in the assessment of the participants' views and opinions. In addition, reading such material will add to the amount of time required to participate in the study and often results in only some of the members actually reading the material. The advantages and disadvantages of including the questions in an email survey as opposed to inviting participants to complete the questions online are the same as those discussed in the survey chapter (see Chapter 11). Either method can work effectively, and the decision may rest on the skills and access of the researcher to a sophisticated Web development and delivery environment.

Aggregating and Returning Results

Since the goal of consensus research is either to reveal the degree of consensus or to move the group toward consensus, feedback is provided between each round of questions, documenting and sometimes quantifying group progress towards consensus. There are a number of techniques for illustrating the central value and the amount of spread around the degree of consensus. These include the mean and standard deviation, as well as the median and interquartile range. The median and IQR statistics are less affected by extreme answers or outliers and less sensitive to skew, and thus are most often used with Delphi Methods. Even more sophisticated statistical techniques can be used including multivariate techniques, such as Multi-Dimensional Scaling that illustrate relationship and similarity of opinion in multidimensional spaces (Turoff et al., 1995).

Figure 9.2 provides an example of a portion of the information returned to participants after the second round of questioning. This information appeared on the screen directly below Figure 1 and can be scrolled to or linked directly from the buttons at the bottom of Figure 9.1. Note that a separate graph is provided for each of the three Likert-type scales associated with each question.

Features of an effective Delphi feedback form include:

- The question is repeated to refresh participants' memory of the exact wording of the question to which group answers are illustrated.
- A histogram is provided showing the results of the three different expert subpanels who are used as participant groups in this study (academics, administrators, and information technology professionals).
- The mean for each group is calculated and graphically displayed.
- There is a legend (top right) to explain headings.

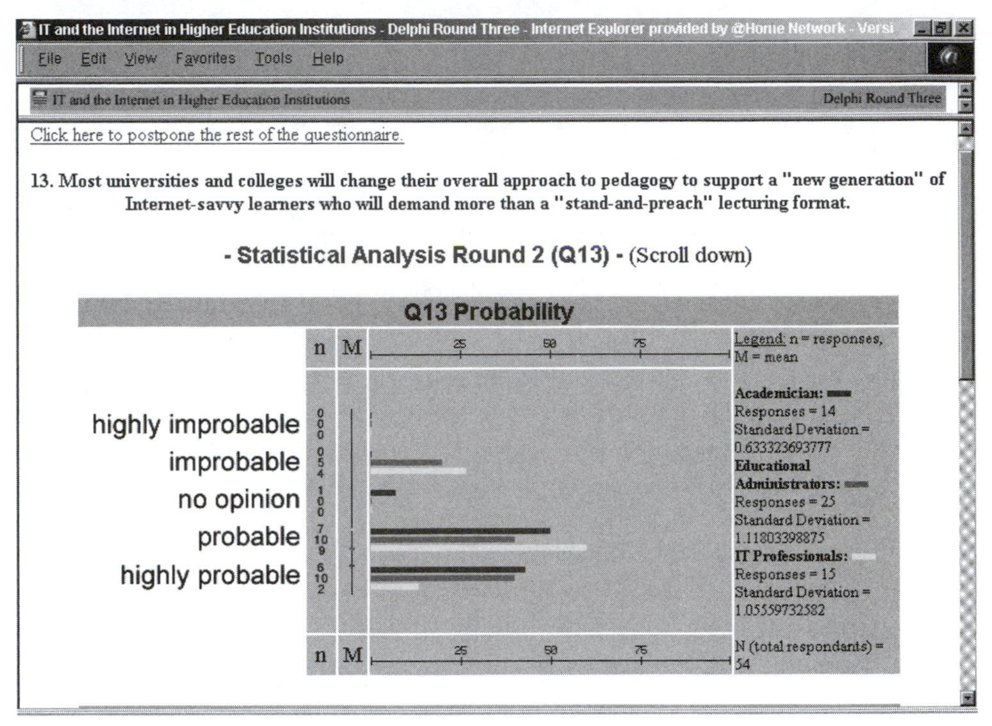

FIGURE 9.2 Statistical Analysis Response

- The total number of responses is provided along with their scores. Note the listing of standard deviation (SD) in the left column.
- In this example, Kennedy (2002) has not chosen to provide feedback to the participants that identifies their answers from the previous round, but rather provides the distribution of all responses by the participant's group and the other two subpanel groups. A copy of the participant's previous responses is provided by email, if requested.

Besides providing descriptive information to the participants indicating their own and the group's responses, these additional rounds can be used to modify or clarify the original questions, using feedback from the earlier round participants.

Finally, we note that words (as well as numeric displays of divergence) are also critically important in reaching consensus. In this example, Kennedy chose to extract and list these comments and arguments that are accessible in subsequent rounds by activating the comments button in Figure 9.1. She removed all personal information that could identify the respondents except the subpanel group to which they belong. Outliers are also identified with an asterisk.

Final Report

In all research, the researcher has a responsibility to provide at least a synopsis of the results to participants. Given the extended nature of the commitment of consensus-building techniques, it is even more important that the researcher take care to create and disseminate to participants a full and accurate summary of the results of the research. Delphi surveys in particular have been criticized for the time and commitment required of usually busy participants. A detailed final report seems a minimal incentive and more tangible rewards may be appropriate for participants.

CONCERNS WITH CONSENSUS RESEARCH

Throughout the history of the use of consensus research, there have been concerns noted with the technique, from both methodological and epistemological perspectives. We discuss these concerns here, while maintaining that there is a legitimate role for consensus research and noting areas in which the use of the Net ameliorates some of the concerns.

Some critics see the use of consensus techniques as nothing more than a pooling of ignorance or at least a dereliction of responsibility for finding empirical answers to questions or acting with conviction. Margaret Thatcher, the former prime minister of Great Britain, remarked that consensus is "the process of abandoning all beliefs, principles, values and policies in search of something in which no one believes, but to which no one objects." Of course, we disagree with this caricature of consensus and argue that the exploration of consensus clarifies and refines beliefs, principles, and values rather than abandoning them and is particularly useful when it draws together the opinions of experts. Consensus research methods often do reach consensus, but the method is also able to reflect and quantify disagreement where it exists among panels of experts.

There is also potential for experts to become fatigued with the consensus process—especially if the research design calls for many iterations. This fatigue can result in a "regression to the mean" if participants would rather agree than continue to publicly argue their beliefs or opinion. This problem can be alleviated to some degree by the researcher ensuring that as much information, argument, and exploration of differences is provided to the expert participants between each round. A clear sense of the number of rounds and the estimated length of time commitment should also be provided to participants.

Some have argued that the online anonymity that is usually associated with the Delphi Method is a license for irresponsible behavior (Kiesler & Siegel, 1984). While there is little evidence that such behavior occurs with any regularity, the use of Net-based systems may resolve this alleged problem. Turoff and Hiltz (1995) suggest the use of aliases in online Delphi research, where an alias can provide anonymity for the participants in relation to each other, but the researcher retains knowledge of the identities of the participants.

The powerful role of researchers in forming the questions, devising the means for analyzing, and presenting interim and final results, and their treatment of outliers and dissonants has been criticized (Stuter, 1996). But in Kennedy's 2002 research, the questions were developed and modified in cooperation with the participants. These criticisms are not unique to the Delphi Method; the e-researcher is always bound by ethical constraints to use the tools available in ways that reduce researcher bias and accurately reflect the participants' opinions.

Mathematically, the Delphi has been criticized for the process by which consensus is calculated. The use of means, standard deviations, and other mathematical entities with Likert-style agreement scales is in violation of the need for such numbers to be based on interval scales with a true zero. This criticism is not unique to Delphi and arises whenever Likert scales are used with opinion questionnaires. It is generally agreed that such mathematical calculation of central tendency is valuable in displaying and understanding group rater results, even if the justification is weak from a mathematical perspective. Providing anchor points and regularly spaced marks for each choice tends to build a rater's sense that there is a regular interval between the highest and lowest rating (Uebersax, 2001), and seems to be a best response to this general problem. John Uebersax maintains a site that describes a variety of traditional and new mathematical ways to calculate and display the degree of rater agreement at http://ourworld.compuserve.com/homepages/jsuebersax/agree.htm#basics.

Finally, some have criticized the use of Delphi to forecast into the future arguing that such "fortune telling" has little place in the empirical world of science. Sackman argued in 1974 that "the future is far too important for the human species to be left to fortune tellers using new versions of old crystal balls. It is time for the oracle to move out and science to move in" (quoted in Linstone & Turoff, 1975, p. 573). Unfortunately, neither Sackman nor any related critics have provided better tools for informing our actions today, based on a future that is un-seeable by traditional "scientific methods." It is only with hindsight that predictions and "best guesses" can be proved of value and we argue that the Delphi and other consensus techniques offer much better ways of decision making and thinking about the future than any other alternatives.

TIPS FOR NET-BASED CONSENSUS RESEARCH

- Much of the traditional methodology of the Delphi Method, developed since the 1960s, can be directly adapted to email or Web-based survey application. Chapter 11, on survey design, will be helpful in designing and implementing this type of electronic Delphi.
- Avoid sending out pre-survey reading materials or URLs to Web sites that may bias the opinion of your participants.
- Offer an incentive (such as a book or gift certificate) to participants who complete the full consensus process.
- Pilot test all surveys to eliminate errors and confusing language and to calculate the time to complete the tasks, so that you will be able to accurately inform participants of time requirements for participation.

- Use of Net-based multiuser audio and video conferencing allows for very cost effective means of reproducing classical Nominal Group Technique, however this type of process has rarely been tried, and its efficacy remains untested.

SUMMARY

The Net's attributes of speed, anonymity, and opportunity for discourse among distributed participants provide reason for optimism for the future of consensus research in a Net environment. The established techniques for conducting consensus research, including Delphi and Nominal Group techniques, can easily and cost-effectively be adapted to network environments. In addition, the continued development and use of customized computer conferencing systems, such as those described by Turoff and colleagues (1999), promise better tools for this type of e-research in the future.

REFERENCES

Allen, T. (1978). *New methods in social science*. New York: Praeger.

Collins, S., Osborne, J., Ratcliffe, M., Millar, R., & Duschl, R. (2001). What 'ideas about science' should be taught in school science: A Delphi study of the expert community. [Online]. Available: http://education.leeds.ac.uk/research/groups/cssme/AERA_delphi.pdf.

Dalkey, N. C. (1972). *Studies in the quality of life*. Lexington, MA: Lexington.

Delbecq, A. L., Van de Ven, A. H., & Gustafson, D. H. (1975). *Group techniques for program planning: A guide to nominal group and Delphi processes*. Glenview, IL: Scott Foresman.

Dillman, D. A. (2000). Procedures for conducting government-sponsored establishment surveys: Comparisons of the total design method (TDM), A traditional cost-compensation model, and tailored design. [Online]. Available: http://survey.sesrc.wsu.edu/dillman/papers.htm.

Dunham, R. (1998). Nominal group technique: A users guide. [Online]. Available: http://instruction.bus.wisc.edu/rdunham/MHR420/readings/ngt.html.

Glesne, C., & Peshkin, A. (1992). *Becoming qualitative researchers: An introduction*. White Plains, NY: Longman.

Kennedy, K. A. (2002). *IT and the Internet on higher education institutions. 2005–2015 A Delphi Forecast*. Unpublished doctoral dissertation. Vancouver, British Columbia: University of British Columbia.

Kiesler, S., & Siegel, J. (1984). Social psychological aspects of computer-mediated communications. *American Psychologist, 39*(10), 1123–1134.

Linstone, H. A., & Turoff, M. (1975*). The Delphi Method: Techniques and applications*. Reading, MA: Addison-Wesley.

Martino, J. P. (1972). *Technological forecasting for decision making*. New York: American Elsevier.

Murphy, M., Black, N., Lamping, D., McKee, C., Sanderson, C., Askham, J., & Marteau, T. (1998). Consensus development methods and their use in clinical guideline development. *Health Technology Assessment, 2*(3). [Online]. Available: http://www.hta.nhsweb.nhs.uk/fullmono/mon203.pdf.

Pazos, M., Perazzoli, V., Jiang, J., Canto, A., & Beruvides, M. (2001). Application of the Nominal Group Technique in an Internet versus a traditional environment. In Proceedings of the IIE Annual Conference, Pittsburgh: University of Pittsburgh. [Online]. Available: http://fie.engrng.pitt.edu/iie2001/rsrch/papers/2223.pdf.

Shearin, Jr. E. (1995). *Development of a definition and competencies for network literacy: A Delphi study*. Unpublished doctoral dissertation, Raleigh, NC: North Carolina State University.

Snyder-Halpern, R., Bagley Thompson, C., & Schaffer, J. 2000 Comparison of mailed vs. Internet applications of the Delphi Technique in clinical informatics research. In American Medical Informatics Association 2000 Symposium, Los Angeles, CA. [Online]. Available: http://www.amia .org/pubs/symposia/D200120.PDF.

Stuter, L. (1996). The Delphi technique: What is it? [Online]. Available: http://www.icehouse.net/lmstuter/page0019.htm.

Tersine, R. J., & Riggs , W. E. (1990). The Delphi technique. A long-range planning tool. In S. Deveraux Ferguson and S. Ferguson (Eds.), *INTERCOM: Readings in organizational communication* (pp. 366–373). Rochelle Park, NJ: Hayden.

Turoff, M. (1975). The policy Delphi. In H. A. Linstone and M. Turoff (Eds.). *The Delphi method: Techniques and applications*. Reading, MA: Addison-Wesley.

Turoff, M., & Hiltz, S. R. (1996). Computer based Delphi processes. In M. Adler and E. Ziglio (Eds.), *Gazing into the oracle: The Delphi Method and its application to social policy and public health* (pp. 56–85). London: Kingsley Publishers.

Turoff, M., Hiltz, S. R., Bieber, M., Fjermestad, J., & Rana, A. (1999). Collaborative discourse structures in computer mediated group communications. *Journal of Computer Mediated Communications, 4*(4). [Online]. Available: www.ascusc.org/jcmc/vol4/issue4/turoff.html.

Uebersax, J. (2001). Statistical methods for rater agreement. [Online]. Available: http://ourworld .compuserve.com/homepages/jsuebersax/agree.htm#basics.

CHAPTER TEN

QUANTITATIVE DATA GATHERING AND ANALYSIS ON THE NET

Discovery consists of seeing what everybody has seen
and thinking what nobody has thought.
Albert Szent-Gyorgyi

Large economic investments, press reports, and personal experiences each give evidence to an explosion of interest in the use of the Net for a wide variety of commercial and social activities. In educational applications, for example, these range from increased use of the Net in lecture halls to collaborative work by campus-based students distributed across the globe. Net application, however, becomes more critical when formal educational courses are delivered to students more or less exclusively on the Net, in a format often referred to as *distance education*, or more recently, *e-learning*. In this chapter we overview a sample of Net-based data-gathering applications and discuss ways in which e-research can play an important role by using techniques associated with quantitative research.

Quantitative research emphasizes the accurate measurement of phenomena and the testing of deductive inferences or hypotheses derived from established theory. Many quantitative researchers begin with an assumption that there is a measurable reality that can be reliably reproduced and measured across different instances of that reality. Even in the absence of these basic tenets of quantitative epistemology, researchers using mixed modes (qualitative and quantitative methods) often seek to find and measure phenomena that they can use to compare, contrast, or explain by references to the more subjective understanding of participants that they wish to understand and describe.

Quantitative data is used in many types of research designs. It is first gathered using either observations, measurements, or surveys. The data is then analyzed using a variety of mathematical techniques focusing on relationships between the data as expressed in descriptions, correlations, significant differences, or multivariate relationships between classes of data. In descriptive designs, observations are made and systematically gathered, but the researcher makes no direct intervention. There may be a single instrument of observation or data collection, such as a perception survey, a count of the number of times a participant uses a particular resource, or the scores on a test. Or multiple data sources may be gathered and analyzed for relationships among the data. The second type of design is one that involves more active intervention by the researcher and is generally known as experimental research. In these designs an active treatment is performed with the subjects and various before and after or control group comparisons are made—again based on measurement of quantitative data. Finally, quantitative data is usually a critical component of evaluation designs in which the measured attitude or performance of subjects is used to triangulate qualitative data gathered through interviews, observations, or interactions between the subjects and the evaluator.

There are many types of quantitative data that can be gathered from people using the Net and ways in which quantitative data can be gathered using Net-based tools from participant activity that does not take place on the Net. In this chapter we provide descriptions of two techniques for Net-based quantitative research. These are provided because they may be the most useful means of gathering quantitative data, but they are only examples of these two classes of quantitative data gathering. First we introduce the measurement of activity that takes place as participants interact with content stored on Web servers. Second, we focus on analysis of observations and measurements of activities that are captured by Web connected cameras (WebCams), audio recorders, and other remote sensing devices.

QUANTITATIVE STATISTICS ON INTERNET SIZE, USAGE, AND DEMOGRAPHICS

Often e-researchers will want to describe the context of their research or their methodology by describing the Net in quantifiable form. This is a challenging task, as the Net and its diverse applications are growing and evolving very quickly. Yahoo! maintains a listing of sites hosting Internet statistics and demographics at http://dir.yahoo.com/Computers_and_Internet/Internet/Statistics_and_Demographics/. A more select set of links is provided by the Library of Congress at http://www.loc.gov/global/internet/inet-stats.html.

From these we can see that the type of data most readily available include:

- Listing of the number and types of domain name registrations that provide an overview of the distribution and typology of hosts on the Net. These data are presented in tabular form (http://www.domainstats.com/) or in map form (http://www.zooknic.com/Domains/World_Domains.pdf)
- Percentage of people worldwide that are online (http://www.zooknic.com/Users/index.html)

- Total number of people online by continent (http://www.nua.ie/surveys/how_many_online/index.html)
- A weather-type map showing the latency or time delays experienced on the Internet from an historic or real-time view at (http://www.mids.org/weather/)
- Statistics on the so-called digital divide, or the current state of differentiated use of the Net by groups from different socioeconomic backgrounds, gender, and race at (http://www.internetpublicpolicy.com/digdiv.cfm)
- An updated list of recent surveys completed on Net behavior and activity by the IDC Corporation. This list links to worldwide information sources covering a wide range of issues, although there seems to be an emphasis on e-commerce applications. (http://www.nua.ie/surveys/index.cgi)

From these statistics we can gather an overview of Net usage, but usually the e-researcher is more interested in activity on particular sites. For this type of data collection, we move to a discussion of Web site analytics.

WEB SITE ANALYTICS OR e-METRICS

The explosion of programming and interest in the provision of online services and access to online resources creates a new arena for e-research. Many questions have emerged as a result. Who is using the site? What resources are they utilizing? How long are they spending on each component of a site? What are participants' perceptions of the value of the site? What suggestions for site improvement do users have? Are usage patterns different between new and experienced site users?

There is obviously no single research tool or methodology that provides answers to these and many other important research questions. The traditional means of assessing participants' perceptions, suggestions, and concerns through survey or interview research, coupled with evaluations of outcomes has provided answers to some of these questions. However, for other questions, the online environment itself provides a wealth of relevant data. The analysis of this data is a subset of the emerging (and somewhat over-hyped) field of study known as *data mining*. Two Crows Consulting describes data mining as "a combination of machine learning, statistical analysis, modeling techniques and database technology. Data mining finds patterns and subtle relationships in data and infers rules that allow the prediction of future results" (Two Crows Corporation, 1999). Clearly, the research possibilities for such analysis is great. A few of these benefits include the capacity to identify which activities and resources were used most (and least) frequently, the ability to record the length of time participants spend individually and on average using a particular resource, the ability to adapt the activities in response to data gathered on user behaviors, and the capacity to identify individual and group problems when accessing particular pages. The data from Net-based environments are, in one important sense, more accessible to the e-researcher than data from equivalent non-networked environments in that all interactivity, postings, and navigation are automatically recorded by the programs that create the Net-based environments. This section discusses means and ways to mine data from Net-based environments.

All activity that takes place on a Web site or in a virtual environment is normally logged or stored by the program owner. However, the difference between the promise of accurate and meaningful information and the reality of what one finds in the thousands of lines of raw data produced by a Web server log has inspired a host of Web analysis applications and even more customized solutions. These applications produce a wide variety of individual and summary data, some of which may be useful to the e-researcher. If, for example, one is studying the use of a dedicated educational suite of Web-enabled software, such as First Class, WebCT, or BlackBoard, the program may itself be gathering and presenting data on user activity. This is almost always the easiest data to access. However, most of the data collected by these programs is designed for educational purposes, rather than research purposes and, hence, may not be optimized for e-research. As such, the e-researcher may need to turn to one of the more sophisticated commercial or freeware tools designed to assist researchers in identifying and measuring the activities that users engage in while visiting a site. Unfortunately, most of these tools are focused clearly on the e-commerce market. The tools available, while interesting and of potential value for some types of e-research, may be too focused on analysis of behavior that is directly related to current or future sales prospects. Concurrently the prices of some of these products reflect their commercial orientation.

Aberdeen Consulting coined the term *insight-to-effort* ratio in regard to Web analyzer software to highlight the amount of effort required of the e-researcher to extract meaningful insights from the behavior of users of the site. Complex analysis information may be very time consuming and require special programming and data extraction skills. At the lowest level, a researcher can use simple text analysis tools to examine and extract data from the Web logs themselves. However these logs are usually overly detailed and not formatted for ease of understanding or analysis. In all likelihood, work spent analyzing raw server logs produces a very low insight-to-effort ratio. Alternatively, an e-researcher may choose to lease or buy a high-end Web analyzer package and achieve insights at low effort, though probably at a high price. The e-researcher's task, then, is to select a set of tools that provides a high insight-to-effort ratio without exceeding our often limited research budgets.

Beginning e-researchers might wonder just what type of information a Web server routinely captures. The Australian Web service, VSBWEB, provides a real-time analysis of a variety of Web sites that it supports. Reviewing the reports at http://vcsweb.com/logs/ provides a glimpse of the types of information available from the logs of a standard UNIX-based Web server and the output formatted using the open-source analysis program Analog (http://www.analog.cx/).

The basic features of Web analysis programs relevant to researchers include:

- Number of hits at specific pages.
- Amount of time between hits, thus indicating the time visitors spend at each page.
- Reviews of the path followed by subjects through particular educational sites.

- Demographics provided by a Web log such as type of browser used, domain name location.

The maintenance issues include:

- Number of errors of any kind encountered by users
- Link verification (should support a wide variety of links—http, ftp, mailto, image, applet, etc.)
- Site maps generated in Rich Description Format (RDF)
- Orphaned pages—those that are no longer connected to other pages on the Web site
- A graphical view of individual and summary statistics of navigation through your site
- Pages with slow download times
- Site reliability—when and for how long the site was not responding to requests for information
- A log of search items found in help or directory searches

These machine-gathered data are frequently combined with information provided by the user—typically when they first register at the site or through a standard educational registration process. In educational applications the researcher may have access to other demographic information including grades, prerequisite accomplishments, and scores on pre- and post-tests. Access to this personal information is of course controlled through ethical constraints and the e-researcher must obtain informed consent from participants (see Chapter 5). If e-research is being conducted on sites where personal information is not being gathered, it is still important to inform users of what information is being gathered and for what purposes. This information should be posted prominently in a privacy policy accessible from the first page a participant is likely to encounter. For help in creating such a policy, or to have your site assessed and credentialed as one that maintains privacy controls, you may wish to contact a non-profit privacy organization, such as www.truste.org.

The process of analyzing Web logs can be tedious as the volume and amount of irrelevant data translates into a great deal of preprocessing before analysis can commence. Zaiane (2001) lists the major steps in the analysis of educational Web logs:

- Remove irrelevant entries.
- Identify access sessions (to determine individual users).
- Map access log entries to learning activities.
- Complete traversal paths (what pages did the user request and in what order).
- Group access sessions by learner to identify learning sessions.
- Integrate data with other data about learners and groups of learners. (p. 61)

Fortunately, many applications require participants to log in, so that the activities of different users can be uniquely identified. This login identification is kept on the user's machine and information is passed to the Web server through the appendage of a *cookie* containing information about the user (see David Whalen's informative Frequently Asked Questions about cookies for a more detailed discussion of the technical, privacy, and security issues related to cookies at http://www.cookiecentral.com/faq/). Unfortunately, it can be very challenging to trace all the activities of different users. For example, users may leave the Web environment to search external sites, take breaks of indeterminate lengths during the session, or abruptly terminate the session for a reason that is not apparent to the researcher but is easily explained by the user. In addition, many users set their browsers to extract contents of repeated pages from the browser's internal cache, rather than repeating calls to the server, thus introducing discontinuities in the log. As we can see from these examples, analyzing Web logs presents a number of challenges to the e-researcher. Abrams and Williams (1996) describe four different means of accessing Web logs, including a client-side monitor that users install on their own machines to gather data on network usage. They also note how surveys and interviews can be used in conjunction with Web log analysis to further inform and explain some of the anomalies that arise when deducing user behavior solely from the Web logs. Forest Stroud also maintains a review of the commercial Web analysis software at http://cws.internet.com/reviews/analysis-reviews.html, and Web analysis software packages are regularly reviewed by ZDNet at www.zdnet.com.

Most of the sites studied by educationally orientated e-researchers are relatively small and frequented by a limited number of users. However, site mining information can also be gathered on large sites producing very interesting results. For example, Spink and Xu (2000) analyzed the results of user search behavior using the large, global Excite search engine that responds to over 30 million requests per day! They report summary data on the 30 billion requests to the Excite search engine between 1996 and 1999 and determined that only one in eighteen search requests used Boolean operators to refine the search. Of these searches, fully 50 percent made mistakes in the use of the terms according to Excite operation rules.

WHO IS REALLY VISITING MY SITE? PROBLEMS OF PROXIES AND ANONYMOUS USERS

Problems are emerging with respect to the increasing number of users who enter sites from behind a type of personal or corporate firewall known as a *proxy server*. A proxy server works by intercepting requests from an individual's machine, perhaps filtering, allowing, or disallowing certain sites, and then sending the request to the targeted Web site. The Web site returns the requested information to the proxy server, rather than directly to the end user. Thus, the Web server cannot determine who the real user was—an issue that is complicated if many users are accessing the same proxy server, such as on a large University campus. In addition, some users are willing to pay (currently about $5.00 per month) for privacy services, such as Anonymizer (http://www.anonymizer.com), that use a proprietary proxy server to filter information about individual use while accessing resources on the Net. These servers also sell anonymous and encrypted email and Web publishing services. It is unlikely that users willing to pay for such premium security will be frequent participants in e-research projects, but you may have occasion to run into such a disguised user. Our advice, if this happens, is to delete the subject and any data gathered from your study, unless you are after a very broad analysis of user behavior with no regard to individual or unique identities.

Like almost all e-research, usage analysis is most effective and useful when it is tied theoretically to previous studies and explanations of user behavior. Choo, Detlor, and Turnbull (1998), for example, describe how theoretical models of user search behavior are verified and elaborated on based on analysis of client-side user logs.

USE OF THE WEB FOR OBSERVATION OF NET-BASED ACTIVITIES

A common activity integrated into the preservice training of student teachers and other preprofessionals is to observe and document the activities of expert professionals as they interact with real clients, in real contexts. This practice has considerable value in that it lets the student (or researcher) observe real professional activity and provides a wide field of vision allowing students to focus and attend to particular details. In this section, we discuss ways in which the Web can be used as the eyes and ears of the e-researcher, providing observation and recording capacity anytime/anywhere.

The Net provides a much less expensive way to augment or replace direct human observation through the use of remote sensing devices including Web cameras (WebCams) and other forms of remote sensing devices. For example, a recent search of the AllCam (http://www.allcam.com) Web mega site provides links to 197 live Web cameras classified under the subject of education. Of these sites, fifteen were broadcasting live feeds from classrooms or lecture halls. These numbers show the popularity and increasing ubiquity of WebCams, but we are not suggesting that watching these public access cameras for twenty-four hours a day will do much for the e-researcher or for educational research other than give the researcher a mega-dose of eye strain! Rather, we are suggesting that WebCam techniques can be applied to create new forms of educational research.

Web-based observation builds on the data-gathering techniques developed for direct observation during professional practice. Direct observation offers the researcher a real-time look at behaviors that are only inferred from paper-and-pen-based surveys, personal recollections of events, and other indirect or time-shifted data-gathering techniques. It also allows the e-researcher to focus in detail on some particular aspect of the scene, which may not even be noticed by participants.

Steps in planning and executing a WebCam-based observation are similar to those involved in any study that uses direct observation of behavior.

- Determine a hypothesis, problem area, or behavior of interest, usually beginning with a theoretical basis for this interest.
- Locate a site for the observation.

- Develop a coding scheme and train additional observers to reliably identify instances of the behavior under study.
- Choose a scheme to systematically define or count the extent of the behavior. This is sometimes difficult as observers can become confused when trying to differentiate between the frequency and the duration of any behavior. Typical schemes include time sampling, running record, and event sampling.
- Quantify and tabulate results.
- Investigate and calculate relationships between observed behavior and other theoretically important variables.
- Report and disseminate results.

There are a number of technical and procedural differences that add complexity to the research when remote observations via the Net are involved in the data collection. These considerations relate to the type and detail of photographs needed, the acquisitions of appropriate hardware, software, and Internet connection, and the complexity of gaining approval and informed consent from participants.

The first decision facing e-researchers who are contemplating Web camera observations is to decide if still frame or video is needed. WebCams can be automated to take still frame pictures on a scheduled basis—say every ten seconds—and transfer these images to a storage device or a Web server. Alternatively, it is possible to gather full- or half-screen video images directly; however, this process requires much higher speed connections to the Net to both transmit and receive the signals. Television cameras capture video at thirty frames per second. Capturing, digitizing, and transmitting a typical 100-KB image thirty times a second creates a load of 3,000 KB a second. This is nearly 150 times the bandwidth supplied from a typical 56 KB modem, however, with higher speed Local Area Network connections, reduction of the size of the image and the number of images captured per second, and continuing improvements in compression techniques, it is possible to capture and stream live video. Deciding if the video is satisfactory for the objectives of the e-researcher is a challenge that is perhaps only resolved by trial and error.

Next, e-researchers must deal with the complexities related to the necessary hardware. The first task is acquisition and installation of the necessary hardware—usually a camera, mounted in the correct location and connected to a computer. There are a variety of very useful and detailed guides on the Net to aid in the selection of appropriate hardware. The AllCam Web site mentioned earlier provides tutorials of its own and links to additional tutorials. We were especially impressed with the informal but informative WebCam Cookbook site maintained by Sam Churchill at http://www.teleport.com/%7Esamc/bike/#Make. The WebCam can be connected by cable to a desktop or a portable computer. There are also a number of commercial firms who manufacturer custom WebCams with a dedicated computer built into the camera. Some systems also allow the viewer to remotely control the viewing angle and focus of the WebCam allowing for zooming in and closer view of behaviors of particular interest.

The e-researcher must then acquire and install the appropriate software on the WebCam system. Naturally there is different software for different operating systems, but in addition some WebCam software is designed for special purposes, such as security or animal watching, and only transmits when motion is detected. Software comes in a variety of commercial, shareware, and freeware distribution mechanisms. Again, a list at the AllCam site provides links to the major products available.

The next step is to obtain an appropriately sized Internet connection. Modem dialup connection provides only minimal service and most e-research applications will require higher speed connectivity on a continuing basis.

A final challenge is to arrange for informed consent by participants. It would be unethical to surreptitiously monitor almost any formal professional activity. Thus informed consent that details the nature and extent of the observation would have to be obtained from teachers and students, as well as parents of any minor students. The ethics chapter in this text (Chapter 5) provides some guidance in obtaining this consent.

SUMMARY

Since its inception, the Net has been plagued with exuberant and hyperbolic claims. Such sensationalism sells newspapers and has resulted in continuing public interest in the Net and its applications. However, this type of promotional and often self-serving propaganda has little place in serious e-research, thus, the need exists to gather and interpret information based on empirical data. This chapter has introduced three tools for gathering quantitative data via the Net or Net-based activity. This is a small start in a field that requires considerable and extensive e-research today and into the future.

REFERENCES

Abrams, M., & Williams, S. (1996). Complementing surveying and demographics with automated network monitoring. *Web Journal, 1*(3). [Online]. Available: http://www.w3j.com/3/s3.abrams.html.

Choo C., Detlor, B., & Turnbull, D. (1998). A behavioral model of information seeking on the Web—Preliminary results of a study of how managers and IT specialists use the Web. [Online]. Available: http://choo.fis.utoronto.ca/FIS/ResPub/asis98/default.html.

Spink, A., & Xu, J. (2000). Selected results from a large study of Web searching: The Excite study. *Information Research, 6*(1). [Online]. Available: http://informationr.net/ir/6-1/paper90.html.

Two Crows Corporation (1999). Data mining glossary. [Online]. Available: http://www.twocrows.com/glossary.htm.

Zaiane, O. (2001). Web site mining for better web-based learning environments. In T. Calvert and T. Keenan (Eds.), *Computers and advanced technology in education.* Calgary, AB: ACTA Press.

CHAPTER ELEVEN

SURVEYS

In God we trust. All others must bring data.
Anonymous

Creating and administering an effective e-survey involves a series of activities that work together as an e-research system. Each step is important to insure that the survey results are not only meaningful, but also accurately reflect the views of the target population. This book has been structured to guide you through the goal setting and information gathering, design, instrumentation, data collection, data processing, and report generation steps that create an effective e-research project. This chapter focuses on the instrumentation, data collection, and data processing components when the researcher's design incorporates survey techniques.

E-research offers a host of advantages, and a few challenges, for the researcher seeking to gain knowledge through survey research. Surveys are a unique form of investigation because, unlike experimental research, content analysis, or observation, they allow the researcher to make an accurate prediction of the characteristics of a large population by investigating the behavior of a smaller subset of that population. The advantages of e-surveys over paper or telephone surveys are the ease and economy by which Net-based surveys can be created, administered, and analyzed. Most of the challenges relate to creating the survey, as well as finding, identifying and providing sufficient incentive to potential respondents. In this section, we discuss solutions to these challenges and suggestions for maximizing this effective and efficient means of acquiring and analyzing information.

As a research technique, the participant-completed survey requires minimal direct participation by the researcher. As such, this "self-administered" form of data collection has inherent cost advantages over more labor intensive and intrusive data-gathering techniques. Telephone and face-to-face interviewing have, for the past thirty years, been the most widely used forms of survey data collection; however, they are both time and labor intensive. Dillman (2000) describes the impact of two important technologies on participants' behavior and their willingness to participate in survey research. First, there is a marked societal trend towards more automated forms of human interaction. People have become accustomed to dealing with machines at the bank, gas pump, transit station, and other mundane aspects of daily living. Thus, the public's capacity and willingness to interact with computer-based systems grows on a daily basis. Conversely, telephone answering machines coupled with enhanced security and privacy tools provided through the telephone have allowed the public to better screen incoming calls, making it more difficult to engage subjects for data collection using the telephone. Thus, there is considerable interest among researchers in benefiting from the economy, convenience, and utility of e-surveys.

WHY USE SURVEYS?

Before looking at the advantages of e-surveys, it is useful to review why surveys are the most popular means of acquiring a wide variety of perception, attitude, and behavioral data in education research. Surveys are used for three primary purposes:

1. *To provide descriptions of the target population.* For example, a survey can be particularly effective at gathering data that can be used to determine what percentage of school staff use the Internet for acquiring teaching resources.
2. *To determine the associations between data items.* Univariate or multivariate correlation analysis can be used to provide explanations or links between behavior and attitudes. For example, survey data can determine if students' use of networks is correlated with higher achievement.
3. *To explore questions or issues.* In an exploratory survey, open-ended questions and space for comments are often used to allow respondents the maximum freedom to reflect their thoughts and feelings. For example, a survey may be used to explore the perceived costs and benefits of a subject-based repository of educational resources.

WHY USE e-SURVEYS?

E-surveys offer a host of advantages over paper or telephone survey techniques. Such advantages include cost, time, and accuracy savings, enhanced presentation, immediate respondent feedback, increased survey opportunities, convenience, flexibility, higher return rates, and faster creation and delivery. Following is a short discussion of these advantages.

Cost Savings

The Net-based survey's most obvious advantage is its cost-effectiveness compared to surveys administered through the postal or telephone systems. Most paper-based surveys are created first electronically on word processors or with dedicated survey creation packages and later printed to paper before distribution through mail, newspapers or magazines. Delivery via the Net shortcuts this expensive process and allows surveys of almost any size to be both delivered to and returned by participants at negligible costs. In addition to delivery cost savings, e-surveys can be designed so that participant input is imported directly into analysis packages, saving the cost and potential error generation associated with data entry of mail or telephone surveys. Sheehan and Hoy (1999) report on a large-scale email survey involving 3,700 responses. It resulted in a 24 percent return rate at a cost of $470 compared to an estimated cost of $6,500 to administer the survey by paper and post. Perseus Development Corporation (2000), a creator of Web-based survey tools, provides comparative data on three types of data collection. They estimate that the cost to deliver a simple five-minute survey to 100 people at various remote locations is

> Telephone: $50 for telephone costs + $250 for interviewers + $250 to enter data = $550
>
> Mail: $100 for printing/postage + $400 to open envelopes/enter data = $500
>
> Internet: $50 to create/deliver form + $5 to convert data = $55

These examples suggest that the cost of e-surveys is approximately one-tenth the cost of equivalent mail surveys. However, experienced researchers caution that it is easy to underestimate the cost of time spent on programming when developing sophisticated, interactive e-surveys.

Time Savings

E-survey results typically are received by the researcher in much quicker time frames than those that rely on post delivery. GuideStar Communications (1999b), an e-survey company, claims that "on average 50% of e-Survey responses come in within 24–48 hours, and two-thirds within 72 hours." Faster return rates will be even more dramatic when international clientele are included in the e-survey. The rapid feedback, tabulation, and analysis are also very useful for researchers who are provided feedback immediately on any problem encountered by participants or the analysis software.

Increased Accuracy

E-surveys can be programmed to perform error-checking routines while the survey is being completed. For example, numbers can be checked to insure that responses fall within appropriate ranges, and if they don't the user can be prompted (politely of course) to reenter them. The survey can also be programmed to be adaptive, so that the type and number of subsequent questions depends on answers to previous questions.

Direct Participant Entry of Data

Since the participant enters the data directly, the researcher saves the effort and eliminates the potential for error involved in keying in data from completed surveys.

Enhanced Presentation

Web-based surveys and HTML formatted email can use color, graphics, animation, and sound at very low costs compared to creation and delivery of paper-based media. Surveys can even link to external Net resources, thus providing stimulation, explanation, or examples for participants.

Immediate Respondent Feedback

E-surveys can be analyzed automatically and the results displayed immediately for the respondents. These results can include normative data, comparing the respondent with others or simply presenting the participant with summary data of their contributions. Such information, provided very quickly, can be an important motivation to Net-based participants.

Increased Survey Opportunities

E-surveys can be presented to users using a wide variety of placement techniques. No longer are invitations to participate in surveys encountered only on trips to the mailbox, or as often as not during suppertime on the telephone! Pop-up surveys can be programmed to appear at certain times—for example, the e-survey can be programmed to appear immediately after a person utilizes a particular Web-based resource.

Increased Convenience

E-surveys allow increased time-shifted flexibility to respondents and researchers. Problems of schedule coordination and time zones, as well as prior and spontaneous commitments fall away when surveys can be completed "anytime/anywhere." Both theorists (Feenberg, 1989) and researchers (Anderson & Kanuka, 1997) have argued that forms of communication that occur asynchronously allow respondents to reflect on and time shift their responses, thereby increasing the quality of those responses. The time shifting provided to respondents may be the biggest reason for respondent appreciation of e-surveys. A 1999 survey of respondents to email surveys determined that 92 percent of the respondents preferred completing email surveys compared to paper and pencil surveys or telephone interviews (GuideStar Communications, 1999a).

Design Flexibility

Net-based surveys can be customized "on the fly," thus allowing the survey designer to reduce item response bias. For example it is possible to program the computer to word half of the surveys with a negative stem and half with a positive, or to change the order of progressive (Likert-type) scales from highest to lowest.

Higher Rates of Return

Although there is great variation in response rates to both paper and Net-based surveys, it is becoming evident that e-surveys can produce return rates as high as, or higher than, paper-based survey formats (Sheehan & Hoy, 1999; Yun & Trumbo, 2000). Kerns (2000) reports return rates of 40–60 percent on e-surveys that he has administered. Although we cannot say for certain why the return rates are higher, we can speculate, first, that it is likely attributed to the ease with which surveys and related introductory and reminder notices can be delivered into the private and convenient environment of the recipients' email boxes. Second, respondents know that survey completion involves relatively little effort (such as remembering to drop the survey at the post box). Third, the interested respondent can be motivated by instant or more accessible results of the survey—or other incentives, such as e-gift certificates and e-books. This potential for higher return rates is somewhat mitigated by the increasing quantity of email arriving daily in our inboxes. E-researchers are already finding that they need to insure their message stands out through effective labeling, use of an attention-grabbing subject line, and perhaps even using the paper mail to provide an initial invitation to potential participants.

Faster Creation and Delivery

E-surveys are bred in the "instant" world of network connectivity. Forms can be created instantly, linked to distribution systems automatically, and delivered at instantaneous speed. This results in Kerns (2000) claiming that "setup, data collection and reporting can be more than 60% faster than with a paper-based survey."

DISADVANTAGES OF e-SURVEYS

As with any technological innovation, there are disadvantages associated with the use of e-surveys. The challenge for the successful e-researcher is to design a research study that allows the research to benefit from the advantages of e-survey techniques, while minimizing the disadvantages. The disadvantages include response bias, lack of incentive, authenticity, security and confidentiality, respondent anger, and procrastination. The following sections outline these disadvantages.

Response Bias

Despite worldwide growth in access and use of the Net, there are still large populations who do not have access to this medium. In addition, the Net-accessible population is highly skewed towards English-speaking, well-educated, and affluent populations. This bias may not be problematic if the target population is known to be network users or their use of the network is a definition of membership in the target audience. However, when a full population is the target of research, a sample of those accessible on the Net will likely bias results.

Lack of Incentives

Researchers must develop compelling reasons for subjects to complete Net-based surveys. We are all familiar with the complaint of "information overload." Subjects who receive as many as a hundred email messages a day are as likely to delete as respond to a survey participant request unless the subject line, the content of the message, and any incentives both "hooks" and induces subjects to participate. Moreover, a recent survey by Gilbert (2001) shows that as many as 85 percent of users, at least occasionally, delete messages without reading them. A small number of users are also setting email filters to eliminate postings from all but well-known senders. These options are making it more difficult for the e-researcher to communicate with the targeted population.

Authenticity

Issues of authenticity plague all survey designs and may be exacerbated online. Unsophisticated designs make it difficult, or impossible, to determine if the participant replying to the survey is the one who was sent the survey. Further, it may be difficult to determine if subjects have replied multiple times to the e-survey.

Security and Confidentiality

Issues of anonymity are also exacerbated online (at least in the minds of some potential respondents). The e-researcher is forced to create a trusting environment by addressing directly issues of confidentiality, secure storage of results, and ethical research behavior. These issues are discussed further in the ethics chapter (Chapter 5).

Respondent Anger

Even the most well-crafted and inviting e-survey may be perceived by some respondents as aggravating *spam* (unsolicited and unwanted email). The response of a recipient of a mail delivered paper survey is usually to throw it away or return it unanswered. There is a small possibility that a disgruntled recipient of an e-survey may reply with a virus or Trojan horse email bomb, or inappropriately forward, alter, or in other ways misuse your e-survey. Until authentication and digital signatures become more widespread, there is probably little that e-researchers can do to eliminate this problem, other than to take standard procedures for protecting and checking their email and Web sites for viruses or other malicious attacks.

Procrastination

The advantage of time shifting can also encourage procrastination. Some users have noted the ease with which email can be glanced at and left unattended to at the bottom of a growing list of emails. Provision of an attention-grabbing subject line is critical to reduce this disadvantage.

CRITICAL ISSUES IN e-SURVEY DESIGN AND ADMINISTRATION

In this section we look at several key design issues that every researcher must address when using e-surveys. The task of the e-researcher is to minimize each of these errors to the greatest degree possible within the constraints of the available time and budget.

Reducing e-Survey Error

Every survey is subject to error. Even if one were able to survey each member of the target population, there may still be some error due to respondent misinterpretation of the questions or misrepresentation of themselves. However, since surveying all members is rarely possible, additional errors due to sample selection may also occur. Despite great care in selecting a sample, there will always be random variations in any population that may, quite by chance, bias even the most meticulously designed and administered survey. However, it is the responsibility of researchers to eliminate as much of the systemic error in their design and administration of the e-survey as possible. Next we describe the major sources of error, common to all forms of survey, with brief notations on the particular manifestation of the error in Net-based forms of survey research. Major sources of error reduce the value, veracity, and impact of any survey—including those conducted online.

Frame or Coverage Error

Coverage error occurs when only a particular subset of the target population is included in the survey. The sampling frame is the list or source of names from which the sample is drawn. If this list does not contain all of the members of the population, and especially if some groups or individuals are systematically eliminated from the frame, then frame error will result in survey result errors. This is an obvious danger for e-researchers, in that the entire general population does not currently have access to the Net. Thus for the foreseeable future there will always be elements of the whole population that are eliminated from a Net-based survey due to coverage error. However, there are a growing number of target populations to whom 100 percent or close to 100 percent of the members are online. This group would include employees of many companies and members of certain professions or social organizations. Coverage error has led some researchers to conclude that e-surveys are not useful (Dillman, 2000) for general population studies at this time. Although we agree that one cannot make inferences about the whole population based on the subset who use the Net, we contend that there is still a great deal of valuable information that can be obtained from sampling from the growing number of people who access the Net on a regular basis.

Measurement Error

Measurement error occurs when there is a variation between the information the researcher is looking for and that obtained from the research process. Measurement error can begin in the design process if the researcher is not clear what type of information is being sought. It is most commonly found in measurement bias within the survey itself, in the form of confusing, uninterpretable, or biased questions producing results that are inaccurate, uninterpretable, or both. Measurement error may also occur during completion of the survey if respondents make data entry errors when completing the survey. Finally, measurement error may result from error in data analysis. Careful wording of instructions and provision of examples are useful ways to reduce measurement error.

Nonresponse Error

Nonresponse error occurs when those who did not respond to the survey are in some ways different from those who did respond and that difference is relevant to the research study. An obvious example would be an e-survey to determine workload levels of school principals. The principals with the heaviest workloads may be the ones least likely to take the time to complete an e-survey and thus their critical information will be lost, resulting in considerable nonresponse error.

Response Bias

Response bias occurs when survey respondents deliberately or inadvertently falsify or misrepresent their answers. Respondents may falsify answers to give socially acceptable answers, to avoid potential embarrassment, or to conceal personal or confidential information. Misrepresentations occur when respondents provide incorrect responses to questions to which there is a correct answer.

ACHIEVING A HIGH RESPONSE RATE

Although there is no absolute minimum for an acceptable response rate, the higher the response rate, the more accurately the survey sample results will reflect the opinions of the target population. Researchers use theories to help explain and predict a variety of communication, interaction, and other human behaviors. For example, in the field of social sciences, social exchange theory has been usefully adapted to provide guidelines for the construction and administration of surveys (Dillman, 2000). Underlying this theory is the premise that human behavior occurs and is channeled by the rewards that result from these behaviors. If the behavior is to continue, the rewards to the individual must exceed the costs of engaging in the behavior. Further, since the rewards may be long term or delayed in arriving, the participant must have trust (in the researcher) that the benefits will outweigh the costs. In the following section, we describe the general means by which these three important variables—rewards, risks, and trust—can be used by the researcher to increase the response rates of e-surveys.

Rewards

There are a variety of techniques by which the e-researcher can enhance the respondents' perception of reward for participating in the e-survey. Most obviously, the e-researcher may wish to build in tangible incentives such as gift certificates, promises of cash, discounts, or prizes. Reward is also engendered by the respondents' perception that the survey is useful and worthwhile and that their participation in the survey is important. Efforts should also be made to validate the position of respondents by acknowledging their inclusion in the important group selected for this study. Engaging participants immediately in the text of a cover letter and in the first few questions is vitally important to this perception of reward. Engagement is facilitated by the use of personalized greetings and friendly language and by the appropriate use of humor.

Risk

Reducing risk is accomplished in e-surveys by outlining the ways in which privacy and confidentiality will be protected by the researcher. The respondent may also feel at risk because of the length of time required to complete the survey, and thus, an estimation of this commitment should be provided. Obviously, the researcher should insure that none of the questions or text of any introductory materials insult, embarrass, or denigrate respondents.

Trust

Trust can be established between the e-researcher and the participants by establishing both personal and institutional or organizational credibility. Provision of a hyperlink to the home page of the researcher, as well as to that of any sponsors or institutional affiliation, also serves to establish feelings of trust. Finally, trust is engendered by building on the commonality and the relationship between researcher and respondent. Identification of a common interest in the research questions and a common desire to increase professional competence are ways to build trust in many e-research contexts.

Theories of persuasion developed from marketing research can also be useful in devising ways in which survey response rates can be improved. In the February 2001 issue of *Scientific American*, Dr. Robert Cialdini distilled his thirty years of marketing research into six factors that influence a person's decision to respond to a request. These are reciprocation, consistency, social validation, liking, authoring, and scarcity. Reciprocation implies that if the requester offers a gift or some other form of inducement, the respondents will feel obliged to reciprocate by doing the task asked of them. Such inducements could be an offer of an online gift certificate, lottery ticket, or some other gift. Cialdini reports results of including a gift of mailing labels in a request for charity giving resulted in nearly doubling of successful solicitations. Consistency works by reminding the potential respondent of some behavior—or indication they have given—of having an interest in the survey (such as responding to an initial letter of invitation). To be self-consistent, the respondent then feels more obligated to complete the survey research process. Social validation refers to the subject wanting to be associated with groups of highly regarded persons. An e-researcher can use this persuasion rule in follow-up letters or emails by reporting to nonrespondents that a large group of influential and well-educated people (or other flattering adjectives) have already responded and you are anxious to include their response in this group. The fourth persuasive rule is liking, which can be induced by writing personally and including affective comments in any correspondence with potential respondents. Revealing personal details (e.g., I am very excited about the potential for this research and its impact on . . .) or otherwise creating an affable picture of the researcher in the mind of the respondent can create a sense of attractiveness and empathy. Fifth is authority, which can be built from any connection the research has with prestigious research organizations. Finally, scarcity, or a sense that the opportunity to participate is not available to just anyone, can be used by noting how the sample selection was done and how lucky the respondent is to have been chosen to participate. Of course, these rules can easily be overdone and the credibility of the researcher reduced to marketing hype. However, adapting these rules to the context and purpose of your research and noting how your approach to potential respondents adheres to or violates these rules can significantly affect the research results.

CREATING EFFECTIVE e-SURVEY ITEMS

Most of the techniques and tips for creating paper and pencil surveys are directly relevant to the creation of e-surveys. It is beyond the scope of this text to delve deeply into this subject, and the reader is encouraged to review books or articles specifically focused on survey design such as Dillman (2000) or Alreck and Settle (1985). However, there are a number of principles related to survey item construction that are especially relevant to e-surveys. These are:

- *Use as few items as possible.* Respondents are busy people; they will not spend long periods of time completing your survey.
- *Make sure that every question directly addresses a significant problem.* Try to imagine exactly how you will use the results of each question. A question that is of only marginal or of indirect use to your research may be the one that is perceived as "one question too many" by a potential respondent and could result in noncompletion of the whole survey.
- *Keep the items short.* Few people enjoy reading from a screen, therefore questions should be as short as practically possible.
- *Create simple and direct questions.* The less the item lends itself to divergent interpretations the more reliable the responses will be.
- *Insure that the items are single-faceted.* Often novice researchers attempt to reduce the number of questions by combining two questions in a single item. The result of such a mistake is an inability to determine which of the components (if either) the respondent is answering.
- *Insure all items are bias free.* The wording of an item can reflect the opinion or bias of the researcher and thus obscure the respondents' true feelings. For example, asking a question such as why male students use the Internet more then females communicates the researcher's bias by presenting an assumption that may or may not be true.
- *Use plain language.* The U.S. Government maintains a useful plain language guidance site at http://www.plainlanguage.gov/ that provides a tutorial, examples, and reference links to the techniques that help authors write for their intended audiences, use conversational language, and create visually appealing layouts.

- *Use appropriate vocabulary and grammar.* When creating survey items, try to put yourself in the mind-set of a projected respondent. Use vocabulary that is appropriate to the educational level and experience of your average respondent. Appropriate grammar relates to construction of items that are as simple as possible, with little opportunity for confusion by the respondent. For example, a poor question might use double negatives (forcing a respondent to say "yes," when they mean "no"). Survey scales should be equally balanced, with an undecided or not applicable response at the end of the list of options so as to distinguish it from a neutral answer.
- *Use meaningful, mutually exclusive descriptions for scales.* Response scales should be logically ordered and should account for at least 90 percent of survey items. If possible, avoid providing more than five to seven response choices. Although electronic space is far cheaper than paper, too many choices increases cognitive load, clutters the screen, and can result in too much vertical or horizontal scrolling. The practice of not defining a list of intermediate scale choices between two extremes is not recommended as reporting results is challenging and respondents are forced to guess the meaning of their choice.

CREATING AN EFFECTIVE COVER LETTER

The email or Web-based introduction to your survey is critical to achieving both high completion rates and quality responses. This communication between you and potential respondents must motivate the respondents to feel positively inclined to give you their time to complete the survey. It must also assure the respondents that the research is important and worthy and that they are not opening themselves to any form of risk by assisting you.

Remember that the Net is not only a distribution channel but it is also a community or, more accurately, thousands of communities. To induce strangers to help you, you must understand their community to the extent that you can appeal to their values and communicate to them in a way that inspires both cooperation and trust. Like all effective communication, knowing and talking directly to the intended audience is critical. The values and ways in which you communicate within your research community may be very inappropriate for communication with potential respondents. Pilot studies with subjects who closely match the demographics and worldview of the target audience are thus a critical means of assessing both the format and the content of this important first communication. E-researchers must also explicitly state (sometimes more than once) that they are neither selling anything, nor are they using the survey as a way to infiltrate the participant's community or wallet.

Finally, the increasing use, integration, and sophistication of Net-based tools are giving rise to appropriate concerns about privacy by potential participants. Your cover letter (see sample letter that follows) should be explicit about the ethical guidelines that define your research and about the steps that you will take to protect and maintain the privacy of your respondents.

Sample Invitation to Participate Letter

[Print on the letterhead of the institution that the researcher is affiliated with (if sent by mail or HTML formatted) or print name, address, and any other identification typed and centered on the first line.]

May 13, 2002

Dear Respondent: (personalized with respondent's first and last name if at all possible)

We are conducting an important study of parents' perception of the way their children use the Internet for school and leisure-related activities. This study will provide important clues as to ways in which educators can make most effective use of, and insure equitable access to, Internet-based information and communication tools.

The study consists of an email survey that can be completed via email or on the Web. The survey has eighteen questions and additional space is provided for your comments or concerns. Completing the survey should take no more than fifteen minutes.

This invitation is being sent to all parents of Mapleview Jr. High School. The results of your individual survey will be protected, and there will be no attempt to directly link your answers with you or your children. All individual data collected will be safeguarded and protected and will not be released to others. The results of the survey, however, will be made public in published reports and on our Web site at http://www.Mapleviewsurvey.edu.

I hope you will be able to assist us with this important survey by emailing me at Fred.Smith@mapleview.edu or by logging on to our Web site at http://www.Mapleviewsurvey.edu. I would be pleased to answer any additional questions you may have about the survey or any of the survey questions.

Once again, thank you for helping us and your children!

Sincerely,

Fred Smith, Ph.D.
Professor, Altima University

INSURING THE QUALITY OF E-SURVEYS

The most important finding from survey studies (Dillman, 2000) is that the wording of the question has profound effects on the results. It is prudent to develop a strategy for checking your survey before it is released to respondents. Three techniques are recommended to reduce the possibility that your questions, rather then the respondents' opinions, will influence the results.

Expert Review

Construction of a quality survey uses skills studied in anthropology, linguistics, psychology, psychometrics, and computer science, to name only the most prominent disciplines. Obviously, many e-researchers will lack most, if not all, of these skills. For this reason it is highly recommended that the survey be reviewed by experts in at least one of these fields and, as importantly, someone who has had practical experience doing survey research. Tools of the network facilitate this review. It is a relatively simple process to attach a draft survey to an email and to encourage the reviewer to use the reviewer tool sets found in modern word processing packages (in Microsoft Word it is called "track changes") to suggest corrections and add comments about the survey, then return it to the researcher. It is an easy task for the researcher to then accept or reject any changes and respond to or delete any comments left by the reviewer. If the survey is created online, then only the URL need be sent to the reviewer; however, the reviewer should be encouraged to download the document(s) to their machine so as to utilize the reviewer tool sets.

Pilot Testing

Pilot testing provides extremely valuable information. Make sure that you measure—or request that the participants measure—the length of time required to complete the survey. Surveys generally should not take more than ten to fifteen minutes. From this pilot information, you can gain a number to be used to inform participants of the approximate time commitment you are requesting of them.

Statistical Analysis of the Items

Analyzing the survey items provides statistical validation of the items selected and is especially valuable when items are to be combined to create larger-scale scores. Standard statistical packages provide tests of item reliability. More sophisticated analysis, such as differential item functioning (Johanson & Johanson, 1997), can be used when there are questions about the reliability of certain items with particular sets of respondents. These techniques are typically used after the full set of data has been collected but can also be used on data from pilot testing if the size of the pilot test sample is large enough.

TYPES OF e-SURVEYS

Ever-increasing bandwidth capacity coupled with improvements in the tools and techniques of Net-based software development has spawned a somewhat bewildering (and growing) set of options for conducting e-surveys. We briefly review the options in this section, knowing full well that variations and combinations of these techniques will likely be more available and affordable in the future.

Email Surveys

The original and still the least expensive method of e-surveying is the ubiquitous email delivery, with a reply going to the researcher's private email box. Email surveys have the advantage of looking similar to paper-based surveys, thus retaining the familiar respondent mind set acquired with pen-and-paper surveys. In fact, it is a relatively simple job to import a paper-based survey into email. The length of the survey and the instruction procedures for respondents are self-evident and respondents will likely have had previous experience completing this type of survey.

Email surveys are more flexible than paper-based equivalents. MacElroy (2000) notes that respondents can easily change their answers in email surveys if they wish to do so. Respondents can even go so far as to change the question if they feel it needs improvement! Such changes of course present challenges in tabulating results, but may provide valuable insights into the respondents' thoughts and provide suggestions for subsequent survey revision.

Email surveys are the preferred choice for many small-scale researchers working on a limited budget. This type of survey requires no special technical expertise, other than the capacity to format the questions for an email interface. However, because of the proliferation of email packages in use, even this task is surprisingly difficult. Careful piloting on a variety of email systems is therefore highly recommended. It is possible to include the survey as an attachment that opens in the respondent's word processor. This technique allows for more sophisticated and controlled formatting but is not recommended for two reasons. First, it increases the necessary effort on behalf of the respondent, because replying changes from a single keystroke to readdressing an email and attaching the completed survey. Second, respondents are rightfully concerned with macro viruses that may be hidden within an executable attachment, and therefore they are less likely to open any attachment received from a source that is not trusted and known.

Email surveys allow the user to respond in a variety of ways. Most will choose to respond directly on screen and immediately reply to the researcher. However, some respondents may wish to print the survey and respond via fax or postal mail services. Thus, required information for both fax and postal return should be provided in a covering letter.

Email is ubiquitous and allows for very easy forwarding and copying of the survey. If the research design allows, it may be possible to increase the response pool by encouraging respondents to forward the email to acquaintances or even relevant email groups. Alternatively, if the design calls for only particular respondents, instructions in a covering letter should direct respondents not to forward the survey to colleagues. The included return address on each completed survey is a simple and useful way to determine who has responded. However, this identification precludes anonymous responses. If anonymous responses are an important component of your email survey, utilizing the services of an anonymous forwarding system such as http://anonymizer.com may be necessary.

Sending surveys via email is fast, both because the time required for creation is limited and respondents can (and often do) respond immediately from reception in their email inbox. As with other forms of surveying, multiple reminders will improve response rate. It is easy and recommended to include an additional copy of the full survey when sending these reminders.

However, tabulating email survey results can be problematic. At its simplest level, the researcher may choose to print out all responses and then manually enter them into a spreadsheet or other analysis package. This method is time-consuming and introduces the possibility of data entry errors. Entering data directly from the screen view of the returned survey eliminates the cost of printing, but increases the possibility of transcription error as manual data entry requires attention to two computer programs at the same time (the email viewer and the analysis input program). It is possible to create customized programs that search through or *parse* the completed email survey and automatically tabulate results. This task however requires the skills of a programmer using tools such as Visual Basic or a sophisticated text-editing tool set. Alternatively, some of the professional email survey packages discussed in the next section offer such analysis services as a component of the package. Thus, the choice of method for tabulating email survey results depends on the number of surveys to be processed, the time available, and the budget of the researcher.

Obtaining Email Addresses. There are a number of approaches to obtaining email addresses of potential participants for your research study. The easiest method is to use the email list of an established group whose members will likely be supportive of your research. Examples of this type of sample are professional associations or employers, such as school boards or colleges. A list of email addresses may be obtained from the association, or, alternatively, the association may already maintain an active email list discussion group. Usually the members of this type of group will not have requested your research invitation, therefore your contact may be perceived as spam or bulk email. It is generally considered exploitative of the existing group for a researcher to join a group exclusively with the intent of posting a request or advertisement and then quitting the group. If you are in doubt as to the probable tolerance or acceptance of your project to the group, you should send a letter to the list owner with a copy of your proposed posting with a request for the owner's review and suggestion(s).

A second way to obtain email addresses is to intentionally solicit large numbers of participants through a tasteful and short information notice posted to a wide number of email lists, Usenet groups, and open discussion forums. Good netiquette calls for the sender to apologize for cross-posting (an annoyance to those who see the same message more than once). The invitation should focus on relevant details of interest to respondents: What is the purpose of the research? Why is the research important? How much time and effort is required to participate? Generally, it is not appropriate to post a full survey; rather, potential respondents should be presented with an active hyperlink that opens directly to the permission form and/or survey or a mailto link that sends a message to the researcher for follow-up email interaction.

Third, a researcher can purchase lists of email users. These lists are of two varieties—those gathered without the permission of the end user, and those known as *permission email lists* in which the list members have consented to allowing their email addresses to be made available for commercial, research, or other specific purposes. Obviously, permission email lists are more useful to the e-researcher, and research shows that higher response rates are obtained from lists in which members have explicitly provided their address for particular purposes (IMT Strategies, 2000). However, purchase of permission email lists is much more expensive than lists obtained in other ways. The most common ways of obtaining email lists without permission are to gather lists from Net-based white page services such as Internet address finder (http://www.iaf.net) or Yahoo! (www.yahoo.com) (Sheehan & Hoy, 1999) or to obtain email addresses gathered by so-called search spiders that scour the Net in search of posted emails. Finally, some commercial lists are obtained (in some cases without the consent of the email owners) from manufacturers or suppliers listings provided by purchasers or registrants at Web sites. The ethical researcher must be careful and prudent when purchasing lists of email addresses to be sure they were gathered in appropriate and ethical ways.

TIPS FOR EMAIL SURVEYS

- Make the line length short (no more than forty to fifty characters to reduce horizontal scrolling problems on narrowly formatted screens). The recent increase in WebTV use exacerbates this problem as WebTV screens accommodate a display width of only 544 pixels. It may make sense to create at least three versions of your survey: one for standard 640 × 800 (or higher resolution) screens; one for WebTV; and a third for Personal Digital Assistants (PDAs).
- Use underscores surrounded by square brackets [_] to indicate position for respondent entry. Provide an example of a completed question using the letter [X] to indicate correct choice. This procedure reduces respondent confusion as to response position and correct response behavior.
- Instruct respondents to turn off the insert function to retain screen formatting.
- Pilot test the survey as formatted by a variety of popular email systems (Netscape, Hotmail, Eudora, Outlook, etc.).
- The first question is important. It must engage the respondent, and should be easily answered by all respondents, as respondents are most likely to abandon the survey at or before answering this first question. If possible make the introduction short enough so that this first, captivating question appears, without scrolling, when the email is first opened.
- If you are requesting demographic data, do so at the end of the survey. Many people feel vulnerable providing personal data, but are more likely to do so when

they are at the end of the survey and understand the nature and value of that information in relation to the full survey.

- If at all possible, personalize the introduction letter with the respondent's name, using mail merge features, to build personal trust.
- Develop and implement a strategy to deal with nonrespondents (i.e., plan to send two to four follow-up letters including copies of the original survey to nonrespondents). The tone and content of subsequent invitational letters should change with each mail. A suggestion is to assume the respondent is busy and thus the second copy should acknowledge this. The third letter might give statistics as to how many others have completed the survey, thus encouraging the potential respondent to identify with and join this larger social group. The fourth and final letter should remind the respondent that their important viewpoint may be lost from the survey and provide a timeline by which their completed form must be returned if it is to be included.
- Consult with your Internet Service Provider (ISP) if you are about to send a very large number of emails. They may have concerns about volume.
- Hide or cloak the list of email addresses to which the survey is being sent to avoid violating the privacy of your respondents. An easy way to do this is to send the e-survey to potential respondents using the Blind Carbon Copy (BCC) field of the email form, rather than the usual TO field.
- Store a unique identifier in the subject line so that additional demographic data can be correlated with the response and so that you can track nonrespondents if the return address does not provide this information.
- Keep it short—ten to fifteen minutes, fifteen to thirty-five questions.
- Keep it simple. Generally multiple short sentences are easier to read and generate more accurate responses than fewer complex, multi-clause sentences.
- Start with broad questions and then get more detailed—a technique referred to as the funnel method.
- Build your survey questions in a logical progression. Questions read better and completion rates increase when respondents are able to recognize a logical progression of questions.
- Provide multiple response formats so that respondents who wish to print the email survey and reply by post or fax are able to do so.
- Include a cut-off response date to both motivate respondents and give yourself a date for analysis.
- An interesting technique recommended by Dillman (2000) is to send a preliminary email notifying respondents that an email with the survey will arrive in a few days. This both alerts respondents to expect the survey and provides opportunity to reply, indicating they do not wish to participate in the e-survey. This default participation technique may increase commitment to complete the survey and allows the researcher to immediately disregard names (and thus avoid multiple reminder notices) of those expressing overt unwillingness to participate.
- Email surveys can usually be formatted as text only or as HTML documents. HTML formatting allows the e-researcher to add special fonts, colors, and graphics to their surveys. Unlike a few years ago, it is likely that the vast majority

of respondents will be using mailers that support HTML and thus the enhanced formatting features will normally make this the solution of choice.

- Send long surveys in two to four parts with one part sent per week. Respondents are more likely to give four small pieces of their time rather than one long component. In addition, once a respondent has completed one component of the survey, they will likely feel more committed to seeing the task through and completing subsequent sections.

Web-Based Surveys

Web-based surveys have a number of advantages over email surveys. However the creation and administration of Web-based surveys are considerably more expensive and complex than email surveys. Web surveys are stored on an active Web server and thus are able to take advantage of the processing power of the server or the processing power of the respondent's machine to validate the survey while it is being completed. Validation is extremely useful as missed responses, outrageous responses, and inconsistencies can be analyzed instantly and the respondent can be asked to correct obvious errors. Without such correction, the researcher might be forced to discard the survey, thus reducing the effective return rate.

The processing power of the server can also be used to provide transparent branching, so that the answer from one question allows subsequent questions to be customized. Customization avoids the complexity and potential confusion of paper and email surveys that provide instructions such as: "If answer is yes, then go to question #10, else go to question #12." Web-based surveys can be created as a single page that scrolls to reveal the full survey. Alternatively, each question can be formatted as a separate Web page, with the response from each question triggering the delivery of subsequent questions. There seems to be no clear advantage to either approach, though each has advantages and disadvantages. Longer forms allow the respondent to gauge the number of questions in the full survey and permit scrolling backwards to review or even change previous answers. Error checking on long forms must be built using more complex client-side programming. Client-side programming may not be available in all versions of participant browsers and may be disabled by other participants. Short forms allow for branching and immediate server-side error checking but may be frustrating to participants if the connection speed to the server is slow. Thus, the degree of complexity of the form and the planned connection speed of typical respondents help determine how long to make individual components of a Web-based survey.

In an interesting overview of the mechanics (down to illustrations of actual coding) of client- and server-side processing of Web surveys, White, Carey, and Dailey (2001) illustrate actual code (http://fcit.coedu.usf.edu/surveydemo/) and discuss their use of a Web survey to determine students' potential for success in distance education courses. They found that coding for automatic tabulation of results was easier now than some years ago but still presents challenges for e-researchers who do not know how to program. Thus, their findings reinforce the efficacy of using commercial packages as described later in this chapter.

Since the Web-based survey is live on the Web, many of the more advanced graphical and annotation features of the Web can be used. Color and font size can be used to draw attention to an important component; however, the excessive use of either can be distracting. Any of the paper-based or online books on Web page and site design should be consulted to provide guidelines for e-researchers who are designing their own survey interface. The Yale style guide available at http://info.med.yale.edu/caim/manual/contents.html provides a free and very useful resource for Web page creators.

Very sophisticated multimedia surveys can also be created in Java and other Web-based programming languages. The developers of such surveys claim increased usage because of the attractiveness and instructiveness of the format, however we have not seen empirical evidence to back such claims. One commercial company, Survey-Said (http://www.surveysaid.com), provides examples of both Web-based and multimedia, Java-enabled surveys at http://www.surveysaid.com/marketing_masters/ssdocs/examples.htm.

Multipage surveys produced by the Web server can also be used to determine the length of time that a respondent spends on each page (or individual question) thus allowing the researcher greater insight into the respondent's behavior during the survey completion. Batagelgj and Vehovar (1998) found that completion rates for single (long) page Web-based surveys were not significantly different from multipage versions, although, again, multipage versions took longer to complete. Given the advantages of skipping, jumping, and time analysis provided by multipage surveys, it seems they are the preferred format except when connection speeds are known to be slow or problematic.

A good format consists of clear and brief instructions, transitional phrases, coherent groupings of items, appropriately used graphics, and an aesthetically pleasing arrangement of questions. The general principle to follow is to put the need of the respondent first. Put yourself in the respondent's place and you can come up with creative ways to make the questionnaire appealing to the eye and as easy as possible to answer.

TIPS FOR WEB-BASED SURVEYS

- Set metatags in your Web-based survey so that search engines can troll and properly index your site if you wish to attract as many participants as possible.
- Include a direct link to the Web-based survey in any invitational email.
- Include a cut-off date to both motivate respondents and give yourself a date for analysis.
- Provide clues as to the total length of the survey. This is especially important with multipart Web surveys since the respondent may not be able to quickly scan to the end of the survey to see how much more time is required. A graphical meter (like a gas gauge) indicating progress through the full survey works well for this purpose.
- Be thorough when debugging, pilot testing, and error checking to insure that respondents are not prohibited from completing the survey due to a misunderstanding or misreading of the survey.

- Use automated checking software to insure that all internal and external links are active and that the site is accessible to handicapped users. See http://www.help4web.net for links to testing sites and other Web creation resources.
- Concerns with multiple submissions by a single user can be reduced through strategies that make use of cookies or that assign unique passwords for each user. Cookies are code that is attached to the users' browser when they interact with a Web site. They can be used effectively to remember who the users are or to remember where the users were in the process of completing a Web survey. However, some users intentionally turn off the browser's capacity to store cookies, and thus cookie-based strategies may fail for certain respondents. Unique identifiers such as passwords may be included in the invitational email. This strategy can reduce anonymity and convenience but greatly enhances the respondents' flexibility in that answers can be reviewed or the survey completed over multiple sessions, because the Web server knows what particular information has been keyed by individual respondents.
- Do not attempt to force participants to respond to every question through use of server- or client-side validation routines. Participants may have moral or intellectual reasons for refusing to answer a question. Forcing an answer before displaying subsequent questions will only result in reluctant participants abandoning the survey. Therefore, for ethical and practical reasons participants should be allowed to indicate they have no answer to any particular question and be allowed to continue.

Overcoming Sample Bias in Web-Based Surveys

One of the inherent problems of Web-based surveys is the self-selection that occurs among respondents. As mentioned, a survey is designed to inform us about the full population, not just those who are inclined to complete surveys. This problem is especially challenging with Web-based surveys, as return rates can be very low, especially when the invitation to participate is provided only through a passive link on a Web page. Further, it is almost impossible to calculate the response rate from this form of invitation. Have all those who have seen the page actually made a decision to participate or not in the survey? Or have many merely skimmed over the link or banner as is customary with much Net advertising?

The Swedish researcher, Micael Dahlen, proposed a method of sampling for Web-based surveys that illustrates an innovative way to control the gathering of a Web sample (Dahlen, 1998). First, the researcher carefully defines the sample frame, often selecting those who frequent a particular site on the Web. Second, a random selection is made from this sample frame and a specific invitation is made to this sample. Dahlen experimented with a server-side javascript to create a popup window to issue the invitation, but there are a variety of alternative programming techniques available on most large-scale sites that can accomplish this task. The respondent is thus challenged to participate in the survey and the decision to participate or not allows for the calculation of response rate. Finally, Dahlen recommends a means to identify the respondents so that the invitation is not issued to return visitors to the site. Dahlen suggests the use of browser-stored cookies for this task; however, as discussed earlier, this solution may be problematic as some users do not allow external cookies to be stored on their machines. For these users, a choice of response indicating the user has already completed or refused to complete the survey may be useful to delete these users from response-rate calculations. Together these techniques allowed Dahlen to conduct a Web survey on a major Swedish site that collected over 2,600 responses in six days by issuing an invitation to a randomly selected sample of one in every 200 unique visitors to the site. The number of respondents who explicitly refused to participate was a low 12 percent. This example illustrates the ways in which enhanced Web technologies (e.g., server-side programs, cookies, etc.) can be used to overcome some of the challenges of sample selection that are associated with Web-based surveys. We can expect such programming enhancements to continue to create more powerful tools to aid the e-researcher.

Strategies for Attracting General Respondents to Your Web-Based Survey

In many types of survey research the target and sample populations are well known and personal communications are the most effective way of soliciting respondents. The hints provided earlier for obtaining email addresses or mailing postal invitations to participate in a Web survey apply when the sample audience is well known. Providing a hotlink within the invitational email is the most common way to solicit participation in Web-based surveys.

Some types of e-research design seek large numbers of respondents from more generalized populations, for example, parents, taxpayers, or other large groups of potential respondents. The Web provides means to reach very large numbers of potential respondents; and thus it is possible to get rather large numbers of respondents using these "broadcast" type appeals. It is tempting to think that these respondents, especially when they are numerous, are representative of a larger or the whole population. However, the cautious e-researcher knows that this population is self-selected, and, though their opinions may be interesting and useful, they are not representative of any particular population. To attract and induce these larger samples a variety of promotional and awareness tactics can be used. Following are a few tactics that the e-researcher can use.

Register with the Major Search Engines. A number of sites provide tutorials (i.e., http://www.citiescommerce.com/consult.htm) on ways to promote the site that contains your e-research survey and automated programs (i.e., http://selfpromotion.com/) that allow researchers to list their site with multiple search engines.

Obtain Links from Related Sites. Since e-researchers are often interested in a particular subset of the general population (e.g., English language teachers or disabled students), appropriate subjects can often be obtained by linking from major, well-trafficked Web sites that are frequented by members of the target population. The easiest way to obtain these links is to write a carefully crafted email to the site owner requesting that a link to your site be created. A small thumbnail icon for use as a link may be appreciated by the Web site owner. Often Web site owners are interested in supporting qualified research related to the focus of their site.

Paid Banner Advertisements. Banner ads are the most prevalent form of commercial promotion currently used on the Web. Such banners can be purchased by the e-researcher to promote the site and the Web-based survey. However, the economical researcher should first assert whether many potential and appropriate respondents regularly frequent the site. In addition, the researcher will want to negotiate the price for such services, as there seems to be no single means (number of viewings, number of click-throughs or individuals who actually use the Web banner to link to the target site, number of successfully completed referrals, etc.) nor a standardized price for maintenance of a Web banner on a commercial site. Interested e-researchers should refer to http://www.wilsonweb.com/webmarket/ad-pricing.htm for discussion and links to current pricing models.

Post to Appropriate Email Lists or Usenet Groups. Since many potential respondents will already be members of affiliated mailing lists, posting requests to participate in related email lists or Usenet groups is an obvious and very inexpensive means to attract e-survey respondents. However, e-researchers should be cognizant of both official policy and the unofficial culture of such groups in regard to unsolicited postings. Generally, solicitations for research of a noncommercial nature are an acceptable use of appropriate mailing lists and Usenet groups. Appropriate groups are those whose members are generally interested in the subject of the e-research. For example a survey seeking teacher respondents related to experiences of online collaborative writing projects is an appropriate posting in alt.education.alternative or to the list ECOMP-L College English Composition Discussion List, but would be inappropriate for posting to lists or newsgroups relating to dog breeding or e-commerce.

Provide Incentives. Perception of reward is a major factor in respondent completion of survey research. In the most up-front use of incentives, respondents are paid directly for completion of the survey (see http://momoneyclues.webhostme.com/surveys.htm for a listing of firms that pay online, mail, and telephone survey respondents). Research on paper-based incentives shows that immediate rewards are more effective than promised rewards in the future (Church, 1993). For example, including an electronic gift certificate for a popular online vendor is more effective than promising a check to be delivered by mail some months later. Nonmonetary incentives such as promises of recognition, copies of final e-research results, and e-lottery tickets may also increase participation rates. However there is little solid research confirming cost/benefit ratios of such incentives for either the researcher or the respondent.

Advertise in Traditional Media. Traditional media includes such communication formats as newspapers, posters, telephone, and the like. Placing ads in traditional media may be an appropriate way to reach potential respondents. The media used should be related to the interest of the target population to obtain good returns however the size of circulation and cost per insertion must also be considered when using traditional media to advertise e-research opportunities.

TABLE 10.1 Comparison of Email And Web-Based E-Surveys

EMAIL	SURVEYS	WEB-BASED SURVEYS
Advantages	Pushed to subject's private mailbox Ubiquity of email Guarantee of privacy Can be printed and returned via post, fax, or email	Easy error checking Instant results Monitoring of subject behavior while completing survey
Challenges	More difficult to error check Results must be parsed from returned email No anonymity unless returned by post or fax or a "stealth service"	Users need to be pulled to the site Constraints on anonymity

Finally, is email a better alternative than Web-based surveying? Table 11.1 illustrates a comparison of the advantages and challenges of email surveys versus Web-based surveys.

COMMERCIAL e-SURVEY PACKAGES

Like the creation of home pages, Net-based surveys can be created using the simplest of text editors. However, many people find that the purchase or rental of dedicated software makes the task easier and faster, while adding features that would require programming expertise beyond that of most e-researchers. Survey packages originated as ways to create, analyze, and organize paper-and-pencil surveys. Many packages are now Net enabled allowing for creation, distribution, and analysis of surveys via the Web, email, fax, or post. The development and increasing sophistication of these products will continue past the date of this text, so it is useful to check with current home-pages of the manufacturers and reviewing guides, such as those printed in *PCWorld* for the latest software developments. Next we discuss the features of the most popular e-survey software currently available.

FEATURES OF POPULAR SURVEY PACKAGES

Survey Creation

A good software package aids in the creation of surveys in a number of useful ways. Many packages provide "wizards" that present fill-in forms that the researcher completes and then the program automatically formats the survey data. Some packages provide examples of generic question types (multiple choice, matching, etc.) that provide structural and formatting guidance to the creator as he or she edits these questions to reflect his or her own content. Some packages also support database storage of questions, a feature of value to the researcher who plans to create many surveys and wishes to cut and paste items from previous surveys. Finally, most packages accept input in popular word processing formats such as Word and WordPerfect.

Survey Hosting Services

Most packages will format and administer Web-based surveys on their Web sites, while others support the creation of Web pages and scripts that can be run on your own server. Unless you are engaged in continuous survey development, the ease, convenience, and access to advanced services make running your survey on someone else's server a compelling reason to choose the hosted option. The task of installing the necessary scripts and permissions to administer a Web-based survey system on your own system is becoming easier. However, you will certainly need special permission and likely the assistance of the server's administrator to install your own Web-based survey.

Many Question Types

Most packages support a variety of item types, including multiple choice, fill in the blank, essay, matching, allocation (must total to a certain number), and ranking. Check to insure that the survey package you choose supports all the types of questions that you plan to use.

Question Validation

As discussed earlier, Web-based surveys can be validated to reduce intentional or accidental error. This can take place at the server after the parts of or the entire survey are completed and submitted. Alternatively, a more effective and convenient method is to have the respondent's computer verify each field as it is entered. Net-based computing languages such as Java script or Active X are specifically designed for this type of Net-based processing and so are the languages of choice for this application. Different packages provide a variety of validation functions, such as required answers to certain questions, forcing a different answer for each question for ranking items, specifying minimum or maximum values, specifying minimum or maximum number of words in essay answers, electing a minimum or maximum number of choices, and validating the format of specific content fields, such as those for email or Web addresses. Researchers should investigate the types of error checking provided by the service and note the type and configuration of client software needed to use the error-checking service.

Data Analysis Tools

Some survey developers are bundling a variety of analysis tools into the services they provide. This creates a one-stop service that will probably be adequate for calculation and display of results, using the common descriptive statistics. Researchers wishing to do more complex statistics will likely wish to import their results into dedicated statistics packages that run on their own machines.

Consulting Services

As a final step in providing a full service, some suppliers of Net-based survey systems will also provide advice, programming, or even formatting of your survey. Although these services may be useful, e-researchers will find that most expertise of these consultants is related to market and consumer analysis, and not orientated to the requirements of educational or social research.

WINNING COMMERCIAL e-SURVEY PRODUCTS

In its January 2001 review of survey products *PC Computing* (see http://www.zdnet.com/products/stories/reviews/0,4161,2417503,00.html) looked at twenty-five different products and extensively reviewed six. We will neither attempt to evaluate nor will we print a list of these products, but we will highlight a few of the winners in this last review to illustrate the variety of packages available.

- EZSurvey from Raosoft (www.raosoft.com/raosoft) is a stand-alone product that creates and serves surveys from your Web site or through a fairly extensive management of email lists.
- InsightExpress (http://www.insightexpress.com/) uses a custom template system to rapidly (estimated ten to thirty minutes) create a simple survey. InsightExpress also sells lists of email addresses based on qualifications requested by the researcher. This automated service guarantees that the survey will be online within four hours of being submitted (during office hours), and final results of the survey are emailed twelve to seventy-two hours after the site goes live. InsightExpress offers twenty-four-hour live help chat service and typical costs are $1,000 per survey project.
- Perseus's Survey Solutions for the Web (http://www.perseusdevelopment.com) was the Editor's Choice in the January 2001 *PC Computer* review. It scored particularly well on ease of use. Perseus also provides a useful tutorial on particular Web survey products at http://www.perseusdevelopment.com/customersupp/ssftw_v20_manual/index.htm.
- WebSurveyor (http://www.websurveyor.com/) offers both hosted and customer server installations of its software suite. In the hosted version, a free client program is distributed to the researcher to support survey creation and the resulting survey can be hosted for about three months for around $200.
- Net Creations (www.postmasterdirect.com) does not provide survey software; rather, it provides lists of qualified email addresses that can be used in a variety of e-research projects. These mailing lists are organized in a variety of topics that can be rented for one time or multiple use. Net Creations Opt-In system guarantees that every name on its lists belong to an Internet user who has come to its network of more than 350 partner sites and signed up to receive commercial email messages about topics of interest (Net Creations Web site December 13, 2000). The costs for use of these commercial lists range from $0.15–0.30 a name. Their

education options contain over 3,000,000 names divided into thirty-eight subgroups with specific groups such as "home schooling," "distance education," and "special education." Net Creations also handles the actual mailing of your email to client groups that you have rented—a useful service to you that also keeps control of the list names securely in the hands of the owners of the address list.

- Finally, we were impressed with the free trial services offered by Zoomerang (http://www.zoomerang.com) that allow any user to develop a survey (maximum of twenty questions) and have it mounted on Zoomerang servers for up to fifty responses. More serious users can upgrade to the pro version for $599 per year that allows more "branding" (or customization, to highlight or identify the form or source of the survey) of larger-sized surveys and more respondents. Both the pro and free survey versions can be created from scratch or by modifying one of over 100 templates designed for a variety of applications including educational use.

SUMMARY

We believe that the convenience and reduced cost of the e-survey, coupled with the increasing ubiquity and acceptance of email and Web access, will result in the continued growth in the number of tasks and populations for which e-surveys are the most effective data collection device. Further, the development of low-cost Internet appliances and the incorporation of Net access into television and mobile devices will make it easier to reach ever-expanding populations.

However, it is likely that the days of completely free access to the Net are limited. Jupiter Communications's research (2001) predicted that advertisers will send 268 billion email messages in 2005—twenty-two times the number of promotional marketing emails sent in 2000. This will result in more end-user resistance to unsolicited email and a growing sophistication of filtering devices that may automatically reject your survey invitation before it is even read by the potential respondent. Further, Jupiter predicts that routers will deliver mail differentially based on the priority paid for delivery by the sender. Thus, e-researchers may have to pay for instant delivery to private mailboxes. If they do not wish to pay this premium, then their survey may wait with other lower-tier mail to be sent if and when bandwidth becomes available to the sender's system. Despite these challenges, the advantages of email and Web-based surveys, in combination with increased resistance to telephone surveys and the increased cost of door-to-door surveying, hold promise for continued expansion of this efficient means to gather relevant data.

REFERENCES

Alreck, P., & Settle, R. (1985). *The survey research handbook.* Homewood, IL: Irwin.

Anderson, T., & Kanuka, H. (1997). On-line forums: New platforms for professional development and group collaboration. *Journal of Computer Mediated Conferencing, 3*(3). [Online]. Available: http://www.ascusc.org/jcmc/vol3/issue3/anderson.html.

Batagelgj, Z., & Vehovar, V. (1998). Technological and methodological issues in WWW surveys. Paper presented at AAPOR '98 Conference, St. Louis, MO, May, 1998. [Online]> Available: http://www.ris.org/ris98/stlouis/index.html.

Church, A. H. (1993). Estimating the effect of incentives on mail survey response rates: A meta-analysis. *Public Opinion Quarterly, 1*(57), 62–79.

Cialdini, R. B. (2001). The science of persuasion. *Scientific American*, (February) 76–81.

Dahlen, M. (1998). *Controlling the uncontrollable: Towards the perfect Web sample.* http://www.hhs.se/fdr/research/Internet/Uncontrol.pdf.

Dalkey, N. C. (1972). *Studies in the quality of life*. Lexington, MA: Lexington Press.

Dillman, D. (2000). *Mail and Internet surveys. The tailored design method* (2nd ed.). New York: Wiley.

Feenberg, A. (1989). The written world: On the theory and practice of computer conferencing. In R. Mason and A. Kaye (Eds.), *Mindweave: Communication, computers, and distance education* (pp. 22–39). Toronto: Pergamon Press.

Gilbert, S. (2001). AAHESGIT List AAHESGIT-77: E-mail survey results. [Online]. Available: http://www.cren.net/ftp/archives/aahesgit/log0101.

GuideStar Communications (1999a). Client and respondent views of e-surveys. [Online]. Available: http://www.guidestarco.com/e-survey-client-testimonials.html.

GuideStar Communications (1999b). E-survey features and benefits. [Online]. Available: http://www.guidestarco.com/e-Survey-Features-and-Benefits.htm.

IMT Strategies (2000). Permission Email: The future of direct marketing. [Online]. Available: http://www.imtstrategies.com/download/Permission_E-mail_white_paper.pdf.

Johanson, G., & Johanson, S. (1997). Differential item functioning in survey research. In American Education Research Association (Ed.), *American Education Research Association*. ERIC # ED399293.

Jupiter Communications (2001). Jupiter Media Matrix. [Online]. Available: http://www.jup.com/company/pressrelease.jsp?doc=pr010124.

Kerns, I. (2000, February). E-survey quality ranks higher than print. *American Society of Business Publication Editors Newsletter*. [Online]. Available: http://www.asbpe.org/archives/2000/02esurveys.htm.

Langford, H. W. (1972). *Technological forecasting methodologies: A synthesis*. New York: American Management Association.

MacElroy, B. (2000). Comparing seven forms of on-line surveys. [Online]. Available: http://www.modalis.com/english/news/7forms.html.

Martino, J. P. (1972). *Technological forecasting for decision making*. New York: American Elsevier.

Perseus Development Corporation. (2000). [Online]. Available: http://www.perseus.com/surveytips/Survey_101.htm.

Shearin Jr., E. T. (1995). *Development of a definition and competencies for network literacy: a Delphi study*. Unpublished doctoral dissertation. Raleigh, NC: North Carolina State University.

Sheehan, K., & Hoy, M. (1999). Using e-mail to survey Internet users in the United States: Methodology and assessment. *Journal of Computer Mediated Communication, 4*(3). [Online]. Available: http://www.ascusc.org/jcmc/vol4/issue3/sheehan.html.

Stone Fish, L. S., & Busby, D. M. (1996). The Delphi method. In D. H. Sprenkle and S. M. Spoon (Eds.), *Research methods in family therapy*. New York: Guilford Press.

Thibault, J. W., & Kelly, H. (1959). *The social psychology of groups*. New York: Wiley.

White, J., Carey, L., & Dailey, K. (2001). Web-based instrumentation in educational survey research. *WebNet Journal: Internet Technologies, Applications and Issues, 3*(1), 46–50. [Online]. Available: http://fcit.coedu.usf.edu/surveydemo/surveypaper.html.

Yun, G., & Trumbo, C. (2000). Comparative response to a survey executed by post, e-mail and web form. *Journal of Computer Mediated Communications, 6*(1). [Online]. Available: http://www.ascusc.org/jcmc/vol6/issue1/yun.html.

CHAPTER TWELVE

CONTENT ANALYSIS OF ONLINE DOCUMENTS

A word is not a crystal, transparent and unchanged, it is the skin of a living thought and may vary greatly in color and content according to the circumstances and the time in which it is used.

Oliver Wendell Holmes

Content analysis is conceptually a simple technique. Specific indicators are defined and searched for as they appear in the content being investigated. These indicators are then counted, classified, and interpreted as descriptive data by the e-researcher to create a deeper understanding of the content. In some studies, these variables are used as dependent variables to confirm or disprove a hypothesis in quantitative research. However, this conceptual simplicity often hides practical complexities related to the subjective interpretations necessary to qualify and quantify the content created in Net-based interactivity.

Content analysis is a research technique that does not easily fall into either the qualitative or quantitative classification schemas that researchers love to fight over. It is a crossover technique that requires critical qualitative skills to assign content to any number of variables. Later, quantitative techniques are used to display and calculate relationships between these variables. To further complicate the nomenclature, the term *content analysis* is used by different groups of researchers to describe different processes. In the best case scenario, the term is qualified by noting that the analysis either follows a qualitative or quantitative orientation.

Before discussing these two types of content analysis, we pause to look first at the nature of the online interaction that we are researching and how the form, the media, and the context of the application affects how best to analyze the content.

TYPES OF CONTENT TO BE ANALYZED

Content analysis can be used with any type of artifact of human discourse or activity. It is often associated with the analysis of text documents, and in e-research investigation these documents are often email, chat, or computer conferencing transcripts. However, content analysis tools and techniques can also be used to study video or audio transcripts (such as a video of a master teacher at work) or with written transcripts of oral conversation such as those that are created in voice interviews or focus groups.

Content analysis techniques can also be used on a wide range of communications or business artifacts including minutes of meetings, newspaper clippings, or the contents of mass media broadcasts. In addition to the use of the application, the media in which the transcript has been captured also impacts its study. We are not quite sure if Marshall McLuhan's famous quip that the medium changes the message" is completely true, but the medium certainly influences the message.

The content analysis of graphic, video, or sound content requires the use of quality editing tools, so that segments of the content that reveal instances of the concept being studied can easily be gathered together, classified, and interpreted. There is always the challenge of including enough background detail to reveal the concept in sufficient context to make it meaningful, without making the segments so long as to obscure the concept being studied. For this reason, tools that allow the researcher to view the content in its full context as well as in an extracted form are most useful for content analysis.

IDENTIFYING THE CONTENT OF INTEREST

Key to content analysis is clear identification of the object of the investigation. How will researchers know when they encounter an instance of the object? Since there are a wide variety of applications for content analysis it is no surprise to find distinct differences in the nature of the content being analyzed. The following is a discussion of the various types of content that can be the subject of content analysis.

Manifest Variables

The process of demarcating and labeling a variable in content analysis is often referred to as *coding*. The challenge for coders is to reliably and consistently identify and qualify each instance of the object or variable they are looking for in the content. In some cases, the coding task is relatively simple because the object is manifest and easily recognized and counted. For example the number of words in a posting or the number of times special punctuation marks are used are manifest variables.

The analysis of manifest variables provides us with a wide variety of descriptive information that helps us understand the nature and scope of the online activity. Analysis of manifest content helps us answer questions such as: How long is the average email message? How often are personal nouns used? What is the average number of responses to a request for help in a computer conference? These descriptive accounts help us to describe and quantify typical patterns of interaction, discourse, and participation—each useful in understanding the Net's use in education contexts. Since the identification and counting of manifest variables is done relatively easily, a growing number of manifest variables can be identified and tabulated automatically by computers, using various mechanical and artificial intelligent identification algorithms.

Latent Variables

Unfortunately, not all research questions, and especially many of the most interesting ones, can be answered by focusing on the manifest or surface content of the content. As Colford (1996) points out, "once we have written something down, it can remain there for others to see as a lasting record of our thoughts. But what also remains there for others to see is the person, the self, the interior being, responsible for our thoughts" (p. 40). Developing techniques to reveal this hidden "interior being" requires the content analysis of latent variables. Latent variables of interest to educational researchers, for example, include important concepts such as evidence of creative or critical thinking, the effect of teacher humor on student achievement, and the measurement of student motivation. Latent variables must be inferred from manifest content and this inferential procedure inevitably provides opportunities for inconsistency and error on the one hand and insight and interpretation on the other. The nature of the latent variable influences the manner in which it is identified and described.

Potter and Levine-Donnerstein (1999) make a distinction between two types of latent variables, both of which are useful in the content analysis of online transcripts. The first type of latent variable is latent "pattern variables." To identify these variables the "locus of meaning is in the content but must be inferred by recognizing a pattern across elements" (p. 261). This form of latent variable is relatively easy to code because the variables appear in the content within recognized and consistent patterns. An example of a pattern variable might be the manner in which an instructor closes messages to an online class. These latent pattern variables can be identified by focusing on the final words of the message, often preceding a signature. In this example the variable is not manifest in that there is an infinite set of closing statements and occasionally no ending at all appears or the ending is followed by a postscript, yet the pattern of its usage provides strong clues as to its identification and function.

The second and more challenging type of latent variable is called "latent projective variable." This variable is identified by judgments based on a "projection" of an abstract concept by the researcher. An educational example of a latent variable could be "showing respect for students" or "providing effective teacher interjection." Training for coders identifying the variables includes involved discussions and testing of instances and noninstances until a designed level of reliable identification of the variable results. Reliability for the variables will always be problematic and is exacerbated by social and cultural differences among coders. For this reason some researchers (especially those with a quantitative nature) steer away from projective variables, while others (from a qualitative bent) seek out projective variables as the most meaningful type of information found in the transcript. Having a clear understanding of the nature of the variables being investigated helps the e-researcher develop an appropriate strategy for selecting content analysis techniques, devising training procedures for coders, calculating acceptable reliability rates, and interpreting the results.

QUALITATIVE CONTENT ANALYSIS

Qualitative content analysis has a long tradition from analysis of texts (notably the Bible) and more recently mass and multimedia productions. This research is often interpretative in nature and is associated with critical, phenomenological, hermeneutic, semiotic, and other forms of qualitative research. Some of these techniques and the rich tradition that accompanies this form of research can be applied to Net-based interaction and publication (Bauer, 2000).

Qualitative content analysis is usually associated with research on latent variables. In one interpretive form, qualitative content analysis involves the unstructured reading and rereading of the text with the researcher developing a narrative or interpretation that eventually reveals the meanings within the text. A slightly more structured form of qualitative transcript analysis often uses the techniques known as grounded theory (Strauss & Corbin, 1990). A grounded theory-based content analysis involves the careful study of the artifacts of the investigation (often the transcripts of electronic exchange) and coding the content into categories. Grounded theory tends to concentrate on extracting the categories inductively as they emerge from the data (open coding). These categories are then refined, combined, or differentiated in a process known as *axial coding*. The categories are then related in some theoretical sense to generate hypotheses that can be tested and that provide deeper understandings and interpretations of the phenomena under investigation. Researchers often find it useful to create network views or other graphical models of the codes that indicate their relationships to each other (Kelle, 2000).

A final example of a more structured, but still qualitative, analysis might consist of identifying variables (especially latent variables) that are coded from the transcripts based on an existing theory originating from within another context. This type of research is often referred to as hypothetic-deductive and is most often associated with quantitative content analysis; however, we argue that a preconceived and formatted set of categories can be used to guide qualitative coding. Nevertheless, the nature of qualitative epistemology compels the researcher to be open to alterations or additions to this preconceived schema. For example, a researcher may seek to identify the different forms of group process in online groups using variables that describe predefined stages of group development identified in face-to-face groups.

Qualitative content analysis techniques are most useful when latent projection variables are the object of study. These variables are complex and not easily categorized or quantified. It allows for the emerging interpretation of the researcher to guide the analysis and gets above the bean-counting type of criticism associated with some forms of quantitative content analysis. In a sense, qualitative content analysis allows us to position, relate, and ultimately understand the abstractly inferred content from higher-level processing of the text and interaction that is not directly revealed by counting or categorizing of the content. Qualitative content analysis thereby allows us to work with the meanings that underlie the content rather than directly with the content we are studying. We are reminded of Karl Popper's comment that "science must begin with myths, and with the criticism of myths." Qualitative content analysis is a very useful tool in the task of identifying, understanding, and criticizing these myths. As mentioned, though, the disadvantage of qualitative analysis is its dependence on the interpretation of the researcher, thus there is no guarantee of replicability or reliability among multiple researchers. Although we recognize and appreciate the value of qualitative content analysis in e-research—especially at the exploratory stages of investigation—we focus the bulk of our discussion on the more quantitative application of content analysis.

QUANTITATIVE CONTENT ANALYSIS

Fifty years ago Berelson (1952) defined content analysis as "a research technique for the objective, systematic, quantitative description of the manifest content of communication" (p. 519). This definition is still relevant for much e-research activity. However, we emphasize the mention of quantitative description in Berelson's definition and remind the reader that his definition only applies to the type of research known as quantitative content analysis.

Berelson's definition of content analysis begins with the term *objective.* In the methodological context, we use this contentious term to refer only to the scientific practice of making verifiable observations of operationally defined constructs. The use of terms like *objectivity* seems somewhat anachronistic in the postmodern era of e-research that marks the early twenty-first century. We hasten to qualify our understanding of *objective* to imply only that subsequent researchers, with adequate amounts of training, will be capable of identifying the same units and categories of analysis as have been identified by earlier researchers. In other words, the primary test of objectivity is reliability. We do not believe that there is a single objectivity that resides outside of the interpretations of those who perceive it, but we do believe that human beings can and do learn to consistently describe and understand their external environment. Objectivity for us is reflected in the broader, more technical category of reliability.

Berelson then defines quantitative content analysis as being systematic. The term *systematic* has two denotations: orderly and systemic. Orderly refers to the organized and rational way in which effective e-researchers select and store the data that they are analyzing. Reber (1995) defines systemic as "a more or less well structured set of ideas, assumptions, concepts and interpretative tendencies, which serves to structure the data of an area" (p. 780). Thus, there should be a consistent selection of tools and techniques that resonate with the objects of study, the outlook of the researchers, and the goals of the investigation. As an example, in an earlier study of the use of computer conferencing by professional development groups, we (Kanuka & Anderson, 1998) recognized an association between the attributes of computer conferencing and the tenets of constructivism. We selected a transcript analysis instrument that views communicative behavior in terms of the active and collaborative construction of knowledge. We followed up with open-ended survey questions to further understand the ways in which the end users constructed their understanding and use of this new tool.

Quantitative content analysis usually deals with manifest variables, since they are the only ones to which very high levels of reliability can reasonably be expected among multiple coders. An excellent example of a large quantitative content analysis is Project H, an international research project that involved 107 researchers in some twenty different countries (Allbritton, 1996). Project H analyzed a large number of mostly manifest variables identified in over 100 Usenet and email list discussions. The complicated processes involved in coordinating such a large research team as well as excellent description of methodological and ethical issues involved in this exemplar content analysis project are provided in a 1996 article by the principal investigators of Project H, Sudweeks and Rafaeli. Their article is appropriately entitled "How do you get a hundred strangers to agree: Computer mediated communication and collaboration."

THE CODING PROCESS

Our discussion of quantitative content analysis illustrates the difference between qualitative and quantitative content analysis, yet there are also similarities. Despite our concern with differentiating between different methods that use the same terms, we are cognizant of the research axiom "there can be no quantification without qualification." This expression underlines the necessity of first being able to identify and categorize the variable before we can count, assign a category, or interpret the content. The challenge is twofold: first we must be able to find a commonly understood and easily distinguishable unit of analysis, and, second, we must be able to reliably and consistently classify each of these units.

DEFINING THE UNIT OF ANALYSIS

The following hypothetical example of an email extract among students in an e-learning context provides us with an example of the challenges that confront the e-researcher engaged in quantitative content analysis.

Hi folks,

I really hate the way we have to answer ALL THESE QUESTIONS before getting the data right—how about you? I have very little time this week for this assignment. The last time I tried this I got bogged down with chapter 3 do we really have to know about semiotics, I want to get onto the project analysis first then decide if we need all this theory how about I'll do the first question and you guys do the rest.

Your-confused-comrade-in-arms,

Terry

How many sentences are there in this extract? How many words? How many paragraphs? How many ideas? The difficulty of answering these questions illustrates a number of serious challenges in both qualitative and quantitative content analysis. The challenge of identifying the unit of analysis (or, as it is sometimes termed, *unitizing*) is critical to reliable content analysis (Rourke, Anderson, Garrison, & Archer, 2001).

The Sentence as Unit of Analysis

In text transcript analysis, a common method is to use a grammatically defined unit of analysis. Some e-researchers have used the sentence as the unit of analysis (Fahy, Crawford, Ally, Cookson, Keller, & Prosser, 1999; Hillman, 1999), however, as the sample email illustrates, online text dialogue often follows its own rules. These rules create a relaxed grammar that falls somewhere between text and voice communication. This often makes the identification of sentences problematic. The sentence as a unit of analysis is also challenging in that the number of sentences can be very large, making for a time-consuming process. In addition, it may also be difficult to identify a relevant variable in each and every sentence.

The Paragraph as Unit of Analysis

Other e-research content analysts (Hara, Bonk, & Angeli, 2000) have chosen the paragraph as the unit of analysis. This unit has an advantage in that it is larger, requiring fewer decisions of the researchers. In addition it should be "a distinct division of written or printed matter that begins on a new, usually indented, line, consists of one or more sentences, and typically deals with a single thought or topic or quotes one speaker's continuous words" (www.dictionary.com). However, our email example shows that often users do not write in clearly defined paragraphs, leaving an unfortunate amount of interpretation to the e-researcher. As the size of the unit expands, so does the likelihood that the unit will encompass multiple variables. Conversely, one variable may span multiple paragraphs. Our experience does not support Hara, Bonk, and Angeli's optimism that "college-level students should be able to break down the messages into paragraphs" (p. 9). Further, once the syntactical criteria are lost, the definition of the unit as a paragraph becomes meaningless, and what the coders are identifying are, in fact, arbitrary blocks of text. Hara, Bonk, and Angeli's ad hoc coding protocol reveals these problems: "when two continuous paragraphs dealt with the same ideas, they were each counted as a separate unit. And when one paragraph contained two ideas, it was counted as two separate units" (p. 9). Thus, the selection of the paragraph presents a very problematic unit of analysis.

The Message as Unit of Analysis

The full email or computer conferencing message has also been the unit of analysis (Ahern, Peck, & Laycock, 1992; Marttunen, 1997). This unit has important advantages. First, it is objectively identifiable. Unlike other units of analysis, multiple raters can agree perfectly on the total number of cases. Second, it produces a manageable set of cases. Marttunen and Ahern, Peck, and Laycock recorded a total of 545 and 185 messages respectively, a total that would have been considerably larger if the messages had been subdivided. Third, it is a unit whose parameters are clearly determined by the author of the message—they explicitly choose when to end the message. The major disadvantage of the message as the unit of analysis is that often more than a single idea of interest is expressed in a single message. We are familiar with email authors who can never seem to end their messages without "one final point," while others regularly author extremely sparse messages. Thus, defining the length of a message is as challenging as defining how long a piece of string is. These concerns with grammatically determined units of analysis have promoted some e-researchers to look for units that are defined, not by grammar or syntax, but by meaning.

The Meaning Unit as Unit of Analysis

Henri (1991) rejected the process of a priori and authoritatively fixing the size of the unit based on criteria that are not directly related to the construct under study. Instead, she proposes a thematic or meaning unit. Budd, Thorp, and Donohew (1967) define thematic units as "a single thought unit or idea unit that conveys a single item of information extracted from a segment of content" (p. 34). Quoting from Muchielli, Henri (1991) justifies this approach by arguing that "it is absolutely useless to wonder if it is the word, the proposition, the sentence or the paragraph which is the proper unit of meaning, for the unit of meaning is lodged in meaning" (p. 134). The task of explaining what this enigmatic statement meant to pragmatic researchers was taken up by Howell-Richardson and Mellar (1996). Drawing on speech-act theory, they explained that transcripts should be viewed with the following question in mind: What is the purpose of a particular utterance? A change in purpose sets the parameters for the unit. MacDonald (1998) provides a slightly expanded set of guidelines for identifying a speech segment as the unit of analysis. She observes the following:

> These authors also evaded some of the difficulties that Henri's scheme presents by sticking to manifest content such as the linguistic properties of the posting and the audience to whom it was directed. Coding a complex, latent construct such as "in-depth processing" with a volatile unit such as Henri's "meaning unit" creates large opportunity for subjective ratings and low reliability.

Our discussion of meaning units thus far illustrates that choosing the unit of analysis for a content analysis of a transcript from an online activity is not an easy task. Our advice is to try coding using a number of units, checking for ease of identification of the unit, ease of classification of the content, and finally, the reliability of both processes by multiple coders. The value of being systematic may also guide the selection of the unit of analysis, since some variables lend themselves to particular units. For example, if the study is looking at the level of argumentation shown by students, the whole message will most logically reveal this complex variable, whereas a study of frequency of postings may make the time stamp on each message the most logical unit of analysis.

SOFTWARE TOOLS TO AID IN CLASSIFICATION, ANALYSIS, AND THEORY BUILDING

Once the unit has been identified it is classified according to a preconceived classification scheme (deductive coding) or into classifications that emerge from the researchers reading (inductive coding). Usually this process involves considerable training and discussion if multiple coders are used. In a quantitative content analysis, the reliability of these multiple coders is critical and should be calculated and presented as an important component of any results.

We have found the use of qualitative analysis software packages such as Atlas Ti, Nudist, or HyperQual to be very useful in undertaking the coding process. At their most basic level these packages allow the text documents (or even multimedia content) to be imported and conceptually organized. Next, the researcher codes the content by highlighting exemplar quotes and assigning them to one or more categories or families of categories. These packages also support a variety of types of automatic coding, which can be used to quickly code and count some types of manifest variables. These packages are also useful during the interpretation phase when categories are combined or expanded and relationships between categories clarified. Finally, exemplar quotes illustrating the category can be quickly retrieved from the content and cut and pasted into publications or final reports. So-called next generation code and retrieve packages provide enhanced features that are useful for mapping, defining relationships between codes and categories, and generating theory that accounts for the grounded observations (Kelle, 1997).

The numerical results of quantitative content analysis can be analyzed using a wide variety of statistical techniques. Most often these techniques begin with descriptive presentations of the results, often displayed graphically to aid understanding and interpretation by both researcher and subsequent readers. Further analysis of those variables that are coded using interval scales can be done with parametric analysis techniques such as T-tests, correlation, ANOVA, and MANOVA analyses. For data that are ordinal in nature (not scored with an equal interval between scoring values) nonparametric statistical analysis of the relationships between the variables should be undertaken. Many researchers also use parametric analysis by making the assumption that they are extracting and coding interval variables from the content. Although this assumption of interval data is, strictly speaking, not appropriate with many extracted variables, the practice is quite common and can produce meaningful results. However, be prepared for criticism from informed statisticians if one makes this assumption during the analysis stage. The statistical software producer Statsoft provides a useful summary of this issue and suggested nonparametric analysis techniques at http://www.statsoftinc.com/textbook/stnonpar.html.

A variety of new and sophisticated analysis techniques are being applied to the quantitative results of content analysis. For example, Sudweeks and Simoff (1999) illustrate how messages that have been coded with forty-six binary variables (mostly manifest) can be subjected to neural network analysis to yield a description of each message in relation to any other variable. For example, messages that are coded as "humorous" can be compared to those that are not, in terms of length, position in a thread, gender of author, time of posting, and numerous other variables.

TIPS FOR CONTENT ANALYSIS

- Spend time carefully reading the content of your study *before* making irreversible methodology decisions.
- Clearly identify the type of analysis (quantitative or qualitative) that will best answer your research questions.
- Initially identify a unit of analysis and do pilot coding to see if the unit can be reliably identified and coded.
- Clearly identify the type of variables (manifest, latent projective, or latent pattern) that you will be looking for in the data.
- Document through memos to yourself the processes involved in the selection of the unit and coding so that you will be able to train others in the technique to provide for reliability calculations.
- Identify exemplars of the concept and discuss these with any other coders.
- Use a qualitative analysis package to automate identification of some manifest variables and to aid in recall and organization of coded transcripts.
- Use appropriate analysis techniques, often nonparametric tests, when analyzing quantitative content analysis results.

SUMMARY

In this chapter, we have attempted to overview the promise and the perils of content analysis. We strongly believe that there is much to be learned by actually studying, classifying, and interpreting the behavior that occurs online. Content analysis provides us with a set of tools to undertake this challenge. Unlike the subjective opinions provided by participants in focus groups or interviews, or the often artificial behaviors observed in experimental labs, content analysis looks at the "real thing" and thus provides an empirical grounding for further investigation techniques. However, the task can be daunting. Over a three-year period, a team led by one of the authors (Anderson) undertook a major project to identify and quantify instances of cognitive, social, and teaching presence in educational conferences. The results of our work and the first generation of these instruments can be found at the project Web site at http://www.atl.ualberta.ca. We hope this work will be picked up and improved on by future e-researchers.

REFERENCES

Ahern, T., Peck, K., & Laycock, M. (1992). The effects of teacher discourse in computer-mediated discussion. *Journal of Educational Computing Research*, *8*(3), 291–309.

Allbritton, B. (1996). *Collaborative communication among researchers using computer-mediated communication: A study of Project H.* Unpublished doctoral dissertation, University of Albuquerque, New Mexico. [Online]. Available: http://www.arch.usyd.edu.au/~fay/netplay/marcel/.

Bauer, M. (2000). Classical content analysis: A review. In M. Bauer and G. Gaskell (Eds.), *Qualitative researching with text, image and sound.* London: Sage.

Berelson, B. (1952). *Content analysis in communication research.* Clenco, IL: Free Press.

Budd, R., Thorp, R., & Donohew, L. (1967). *Content analysis of communications.* NY: Macmillan Company.

Colford, I. H. (1996). Writing in the electronic environment: Electronic text and the future of creativity and knowledge. *Occasional Papers Series Dalhousie University.*

Fahy, P., Crawford, G., Ally, M., Cookson, P., Keller, V., & Prosser, F. (1999). The development and testing of a computer conferencing transcript analysis tool. *Alberta Journal of Education Research, 46*(2), 85–88.

Hara, N., Bonk, C., & Angeli, C. (2000). Content analysis of on-line discussion in an applied education psychology course. *Instructional Science, 28*(2), 115–152.

Henri, F. (1991). Computer conferencing and content analysis. In A. Kaye (Ed.), *Collaborative learning through computer conferencing* (pp. 117–136). London: Springer-Verlag.

Hillman, D. (1999). A new method for analyzing patterns of interaction. *The American Journal of Distance Education, 13*(2), 37–47.

Howell-Richardson, C., & Mellar, H. (1996). A methodology for the analysis of patterns of participation within computer mediated communication courses. *Instructional Science, 24*, 47–69.

Kanuka, H., & Anderson, T. (1998). On-line social interchange, discord and knowledge construction. *Journal of Distance Education, 13*(1), 57–74. [Online]. Available: cade.athabascau.ca/vol13.1/kanuka.html.

Kelle, U. (1997). Theory building in qualitative research and computer programs for the management of textual data. *Sociological Research Online 2*(2).[Online}. Available: www.socresonline.org.uk.

Kelle, U. (2000). Classical content analysis: A review. In M. Bauer & G. Gaskell (Eds.), *Computer assisted analysis: Coding and indexing* (pp. 282–298). London: Sage.

Marttunen, M. (1997). Electronic mail as pedagogical delivery system: An analysis of the learning argumentation. *Research in Higher Education, 38*(3), 345–363.

McDonald, J. (1998). Interpersonal group dynamics and development in computer conferencing: The rest of the story. In Wisconsin Distance Education Proceedings. [Online]. Available: http://www.mrc.gc.ca/publicaitons.html.

Potter, W., & Levine-Donnerstein, D. (1999). Rethinking validity and reliability in content analysis. *Journal of Applied Communication Research, 27*(3), 258–284.

Reber, A. (1995). *Dictionary of psychology.* Toronto: Penguin Books.

Rourke, L., Anderson, T., Garrison, D. R., & Archer, W. (2001). Methodological issues in the content analysis of computer conference transcripts. *International Journal of Artificial Intelligence in Education, 12*(1), 8–22.

Strauss, A. L., & Corbin, J. (1990). In *Basics of qualitative research. Grounded theory procedures and techniques.* Newbury Park, CA: Sage.

Sudweeks, F., & Rafaeli, S. (1996). How do you get a hundred strangers to agree: Computer mediated communication and collaboration. In T. M. Harrison and T. D. Stephen (Eds.), *Computer networking and scholarship in the 21st century university* (pp. 115–136). Albany, NY: SUNY Press.

Sudweeks, F., & Simoff, S. (1999) Complimentary explorative data analysis. In S. Jones (Ed.). *Doing Internet research.* Thousand Oaks, CA: Sage.

CHAPTER THIRTEEN

NET-BASED DISSEMINATION OF e-RESEARCH RESULTS

No publications, no funds; no funds, no job.
Jeremy Flower-Ellis, 2001

The dissemination phase of e-research is the climax of the research cycle, and it occurs when researchers share the results of their important research studies with the world. Unfortunately, it is this stage that is fraught with indecision and unhealthy bouts of procrastination. In some cases, the funders of the e-research set deadlines that serve to motivate and pace the researcher through this final sprint. However, all-too-often in academic research, the dissemination phase comes after the defense of a formal thesis or major project, when the grant money has been spent, and in both cases, energy may be low. The result is that too often the outcomes of significant research studies remain hidden in a bound thesis resting on a dusty library shelf or filed as a completed research report in a bureaucrat's office.

We begin this chapter with an overview of the reasons why the dissemination process is important and worth putting forth the extra energy that is involved. We then provide an overview on the selection of the networked tools best suited for this task and end with tips for effectively and efficiently disseminating the findings of a research project.

WHY PUBLISH YOUR RESULTS?

In academic circles it is easy to answer the question of why publish—it relates directly to success, as aptly characterized in the familiar ultimatum to "publish or perish." However, the greatest and most compelling reason to publish is that you have something worth saying and your research efforts will make a contribution (however major or minor) to improving education and opportunities for learning. There are also more mundane and practical reasons for disseminating the results of your e-research work. The Literati Club (www.literaticlub.co.uk), a support site for authors sponsored by MCB University Press, provides a listing of four compelling reasons to publish.

Because I Have To

Being a professor (or undertaking any of the roles associated in the long apprenticeship trail from graduate student through assistant and associate professor) means that one is obliged to profess. *Webster's Revised Unabridged Dictionary* (1998) defines *profess* as "to make open declaration of, as of one's knowledge, belief, action." Thus, you are asked, as a member of the research community, to publicly declare what you know and what your research has revealed. This declaration is a form of accountability in which you show that the time and effort spent on your study is justified and worthy of your personal as well as societal support.

Disseminating your materials also repays your debt to those whose ideas and efforts have assisted the work. The research process that you are now completing has been aided by many other professors who have publicly given their insights into related problems, methodologies, and solutions. Publishing also helps repay those participants who have given their time and insights to you throughout the research process. It is now your turn to repay this social debt and add to the accumulated public knowledge and wisdom. This is not only a great responsibility, but it is also a great honor. The dissemination process, like all components of the e-research cycle, is marked by hard work and attention to detail. However, it is also nearest to the pay-off stage and thus can be the most rewarding component of the e-research process.

Because I Want to Get Ahead

Public dissemination of results often results in a flurry of contacts and connections with other researchers. Gaining a reputation as a competent researcher who creates valuable knowledge and who knows how to communicate these results provides a focus to which additional opportunities gravitate. These may include offers to collaborate on future work, invitations to speak at conferences or other gatherings, invitations to travel and visit with other researchers, requests for advice or offers of further research or related employment. In academic circles, publishing, especially in peer-reviewed journal articles and books, is one of the few quantifiable contributions to scholarly life and thus the count of publications often takes inordinate importance in promotion, tenure, and salary decisions. Graduate students who have the beginnings of a publishing record on their resumes are inevitably more sought after than those who can show competence only through successful completion of courses. There are a variety of personal and institutional ego-related reasons for disseminating as well. In sum there are many compelling reasons why dissemination of results is a very reliable indicator of future success.

Because I Need to Learn from Others

The public nature of dissemination means that others will critically read and reflect on your work. This review may be highly formalized and undertaken by peers whose identities are hidden from you. Alternatively, the review may take the form of a thorough proofreading by a skilled editor. Ultimately, countless members of the general public review your results. Each of these reviewers will have suggestions, concerns, and even major problems with your research. Rather than viewing this feedback as deterrents to dissemination, these reviews provide opportunity to hone the results and present them in ways that clearly and succinctly reveal the knowledge that you have created. Good research is a dialogue between the researcher and the many potential consumers of the results. This dialogue often continues with ideas you choose to pursue, identification of new insights, and applications of the results—as well as opportunities for building on your prior research by identifying new questions and new opportunities to pursue these questions.

Because I Need to Clarify My Own Thoughts

The final reason provided by the Literati Club is to meet the specific needs of many different audiences. E-researchers, as authors, need to focus on particular audiences as they present the results of their work. By asking themselves what these results mean to different groups of knowledge consumers, additional clarity and insight often arises. This insight is then honed through successive rewrites and presentation formats until the research is packaged in such a way that the results are perceived as both accessible and of value to the intended audience(s). Normally this revision and focusing exercise brings additional insights into the work that enhance its usefulness, not only to the audience but even more so to the researcher.

Because It Can Be Satisfying

We add a fifth reason to publish, which may not always be attested to by struggling e-researchers. The dissemination stage is one of expansion. The development and testing of ideas is often a shrinking and focusing activity in which meaning is created by tightly focusing research tools on carefully defined and circumscribed events, ideas, or activities. In the dissemination phase, researchers are able to expand their thinking by creating and sharing not only the direct results but also the implications for practice and for further research. This opportunity to reveal the significance of your research is often the most satisfying component of the research process.

The dissemination process can provide entertaining, creative, and interactive learning experiences when you publish your results using the multimedia capacity of the Net. The development of engaging Web sites that use the Web's multimedia capacities can facilitate new learning as one masters graphics, Web creation, discussion forums, and other interactive tools. This learning and playing with the presentation of your results is usually enjoyable work and can be a most satisfying component of the e-research process.

CREATING QUALITY CONTENT

There are many guides to academic writing that describe the process and format of disseminating your findings. Rather than focus on these more generic skills, we look at the diverse ways in which writing for the Net is unique and the multitude of ways in which the Net can be used to disseminate the results of your work.

Research has shown that we process information from the screen in ways that are different from the way we read texts or paper content (Kanuka & Szabo, 1999). Net readers are more likely to skim rather than read meticulously through screen-presented content. Thus, e-researchers should use the techniques of the newspaper editor, rather than the novelist to present their findings in a Web document. For example, the style of screen formatted materials should make extensive use of headings, bolding, numbered and bulleted lists, keywords, and highlighting, and effective use of white space. These formatting techniques allow the reader to focus on items of particular interest and skim through that which is not of interest. For these same reasons, the content should be concise and to the point.

Some experts suggest using the inverted pyramid style of presentation that was developed by newspaper editors and reporters. Unlike traditional research papers that begin with an unresolved problem, then present all the relevant past research and methodology, and finally conclude with results and applications, an inverted pyramid style begins with the most important and relevant content. Less relevant and more detailed content is placed at, or near, the end of the article. Incidentally, this style not only allows busy readers the capacity to stop reading at any time knowing they have already covered the most relevant material, but it also provides the writer or editor the capacity to omit content from the end of the article when space problems arise. While the space element does not apply to the Web (with the exception of server space), the psychological benefits of brevity remain as relevant as ever.

Readers of Web documents are also less impressed with superfluous, hyper-marketing text common in television ads, posters, and flyers. Web readers want the facts and want to believe that you are telling them the unbiased results of your research. In an empirical study of these techniques, Morkes and Nielsen (1998) found significant improvements in time to read, errors in recall, and overall satisfaction between content formatted for the Web versus a technical report formatted for paper presentation.

Despite the large number of prescriptive guidelines and articles for Web writing (for example see Introduction to Hypertext Writing Style at http://www.bu.edu/cdaly/hyper.html), we are also aware that the nature of the Web, and readers' approach to screen reading, is changing. New technologies (including electronic paper and very high resolution screens) as well as evidence of successful Net publication using a variety of writing formats and styles, remind us that the Net thrives on diversity and that there is no single formula for all forms of effective research results dissemination (Bresler, 2000).

The e-researcher's goal is to work the content into a form that is clearly and easily understood by the intended audience. This will include detailing the purpose of the study and for whom the results will be of interest. It should also provide enough background and/or contact information for the interested researcher to build on the work in their own research. In our exploration of the Net, we discovered a site designed to assist researchers in publishing their results. The Literati Club site provides a host of hints, guidelines, and resources in addition to discussion lists and email notifications for prospective publishers. As an example of the type of resources available at the site, Robert Brown suggests an "action learning" approach to creating dissemination materials, especially peer-reviewed articles (Brown, 1995). He suggests that aspiring authors organize a "learning set" ideally composed of five experienced researchers. These researchers read the proposed dissemination articles(s) and meet face-to-face to review the author's answers to the following questions:

1. Who are the intended readers? (list three to five of them by name)
2. What did you do? (limit fifty words)
3. Why did you do it? (limit fifty words)
4. What happened? (limit fifty words)
5. What do the results mean in theory? (limit fifty words)
6. What do the results mean in practice? (limit fifty words)
7. What is the key benefit for your readers? (limit twenty-five words)
8. What remains unresolved? (limit fifty words)

Regardless of the actual use of a collaborative "learning set," the e-researcher should be able to answer all of these questions clearly and concisely. The answers become the framework on which the dissemination article is built. Brown notes that beginning authors tend to focus on the second and fourth questions and tend to de-emphasize those components that are of interest to most potential readers—the third, sixth, and seventh questions.

Creating clear and meaningful results is to some degree independent of the medium used to disseminate these results. However, as Marshall McLuhan reminded us, the "medium is the message," and thus we focus on the new media provided by the Net for the dissemination of results.

ADVANTAGES OF DISSEMINATING YOUR RESULTS VIA THE NET

The Net provides additional venues for disseminating results in addition to the pre-Net era's focus on paper and print production of articles and press releases. The Net offers obvious cost savings for dissemination in that printing and postage costs are eliminated. Production costs associated with design and formatting are, however, equal or even greater for Net-distributed material than those associated with paper-based dissemination. In addition, the capacity to add multimedia tends to set an expectation for the addition of this type of graphic, animated, or audiovisual enhancement. Multimedia production costs can be very high and the budget conscious researcher will plan carefully and manage such expenditures judiciously.

DISSEMINATION THROUGH PEER-REVIEWED ARTICLES

The peer-reviewed article has, for over 300 years, been the mark of quality, credence, and acceptability for the academic researcher. This exalted status has arisen not because the process is perfect, but, like democracy, because it may be the best alternative from a set of even less attractive options. But before we discuss these advantages, we briefly describe the main components of the peer-review process. An understanding of the steps of this rather convoluted process may help e-researchers determine if this means of dissemination is the most appropriate vehicle for their results.

The editor of the selected peer-review journal acts as an important first filter for all article submissions. This person, or a very small committee, generally reviews articles submitted and makes a critically important initial decision. If the article is deemed relevant to the journal's readership and is at least of minimal legibility and comprehensibility and not repetitive of previously published articles, then the editor usually makes a decision to proceed with a full peer review. Often as many as 50 percent of the articles submitted are rejected by the editor at this first point in the review process. The editor then decides on the most qualified persons to review the articles that pass this first hurdle. These persons are usually active researchers who have considerable publishing experience and often serve as members of the journal's editorial review committee. The article is then sent for external review to two to three reviewers, theoretically chosen by the editor for the extent of their expert knowledge that is directly related to the content of the article. In fact, the pool of prospective reviewers is often limited to those known to the editor and those having a track record of timely return of reviews and whose feedback is not likely to be in radical opposition to the other reviews, which would create more work for the editor. Usually a review assessment form, sent with the article, is used by the reviewers to make their publishing recommendation and provides a space for suggestions and ideas for improvement. The process is double blind in the sense that any references that could identify the author are removed and the reviewers themselves do not identify themselves or the organization with which they are affiliated. Only in rare circumstances are articles accepted without attention to the concerns and suggestions of the reviewers. Normally, based on the reviewers' comments and suggestions, the article is either rejected outright or returned to the author for edits and revisions . The author is expected to address each of these concerns (or defend why they need not be addressed) and return the revised article. In some cases the revisions called for are so extensive as to require a second round of peer review. Otherwise, the revised article is usually reviewed by the editor and then sent for formatting and printing or publication via the networks.

The peer-review process is cumbersome and can be very lengthy. Peer-reviewed journal publication has also been criticized as being narrow (only two to three reviewers see the work), secretive (only the editor knows all the actors), arbitrary (the editor may only have a limited number of reviewers to choose from, none of whom may have the necessary knowledge or time to produce a quality review), expensive (the rising cost of academic journals tends to restrict access to only those affiliated with the largest research universities), and slow (even after the lengthy review process, long waits may result as the editor weaves the disparate articles into a theme issue or waits until the right-sized opening appears in the production cycle). Of even greater concern is the inherent conservatism of the process that has been shown to accept refinements of ordinary science and to reject research that is more revolutionary or explores a new paradigm. Readings (1994) rather caustically describes the reviewer's task as follows: "Normally, those who review essays for inclusion in scholarly journals know what they are supposed to do. Their function is to take exciting, innovative, and challenging work by younger scholars and find reasons to reject it."

Until relatively recently, the paper-based peer-reviewed journal was the only venue that researchers had for scholarly publishing. Of course, academics who were early adopters of the Net quickly recognized that the Net could provide a new venue for scholarly publications. Today the Net provides a variety of means to improve the production and dissemination of peer-reviewed research results. As the early pioneer editor of psychology content online, Stephen Harnard (1996) notes:

> The scholarly communicative potential of electronic networks is revolutionary. There is only one sector in which the Net will have to be traditional, and that is in the validation of scholarly ideas and findings by peer review. Refereeing can be implemented much more rapidly, equitably, and efficiently on the Net, but it cannot be dispensed with. (p.109)

Although not all researchers agree that the peer-review process is the penultimate achievement in dissemination, it is a safe bet that without peer review, electronic publications would not be accepted for hiring, tenure, and/or promotion within academia. Electronic publication without peer review may, however, provide many other benefits to society and individual researchers. These advantages are discussed in the following sections related to personal Web sites and popular press dissemination.

The principle advantages of electronic publishing of peer-reviewed articles include:

- increased accessibility;
- improved capacity for search and retrieval;
- capacity to link to additional content including source data;
- capacity to publish whenever the review is finished, rather than waiting for a publication date;
- increased speed of distribution; and
- the ability to insert hyperlinks and multimedia into the publication.

These reasons seem to us to create important advantages over paper-based publications that will eventually lead to the migration of most scholarly journals to an online format. Most obviously, e-journals have the proven capacity to significantly reduce the time for dissemination. For example the Royal Society of Chemistry reduced the time of production from 100 days to 40 days using electronic publications (Wilkenson, 2000). A more esoteric advantage of Net publications in hypertext format is the capacity to question the epistemological assumptions of scholarly communication.

McKerrow, Wood, and Smith (1995) point out that "this opening of the text represents an opportunity to reassert that sense of scholarship being a collegial exchange, rather than received knowledge from expert opinion." Finally, a number of Net-based systems have been developed to improve the peer review process, most notably by speeding up the process, tracking the movement of the article through the review stages, automating key functions and providing increased opportunity for review and comment. For example, Yu and Schmid (1999) describe a system of intelligent publishing "agents" that assists editors, reviewers, and authors in tasks such as exchanging information, reminding of deadlines, and selecting appropriate resources.

An example of a traditional educational journal that disseminates exclusively via the Net is the *International Review of Research in Open and Distance Learning* (see http://www.irrodl.org/). This journal conducts all its reviewing processes online and produces the final reviewed articles on the Web free of charge to all users. The review process is rather traditional, only using the Net for circulation of drafts to blind reviewers and to distribute the final publication.

A much more radical example of the capacity of the Net to expand the review process is provided by the *Journal of Interactive Media in Education* (*JIME*) (http://www.jime.open.ac.uk). *JIME* uses an open review process designed to make the review process more responsive and dynamic. Specifically, the *JIME* process acknowledges that

- authors have the right of reply;
- reviewers are named and accountable for their comments, and their contributions are acknowledged; and
- the wider research community has the chance to shape a submission before publication (via the *JIME* Web site).

These principles create a review process that includes opportunity for both expert and public review and alterations by authors before final publication. The process is illustrated in Figure 13.1.

Unfortunately, the increase in access to peer-reviewed articles at no charge via the Net does not always meet the commercial needs of the publishers. Thus, there are a variety of means by which access is restricted to those who compensate the publishers in some way. The most common means is to provide access to the online version of a journal only to those subscribers who already subscribe to the paper version of the journal, who pay a personal subscription fee for online access directly to the publisher, or who are affiliated with an organization that pays a site-license subscription fee. Often users from these organizations are forced to log on through their institution's computer system or through a proxy service that has authenticated their identity before being allowed access to the full text of these journals. There are also commercial service libraries, such as CARL (http://www.carl.org), that provide access to particular articles or faxed copies on a fee-for-service basis. CARL charges $10.00 plus the fee from the copyright owner (varies by article) plus the fax costs if the article is not available in electronic format. CARL currently indexes over 18,000 periodicals (both paper and Net-based) amounting to over 440 new citations being added to their database of available articles per day.

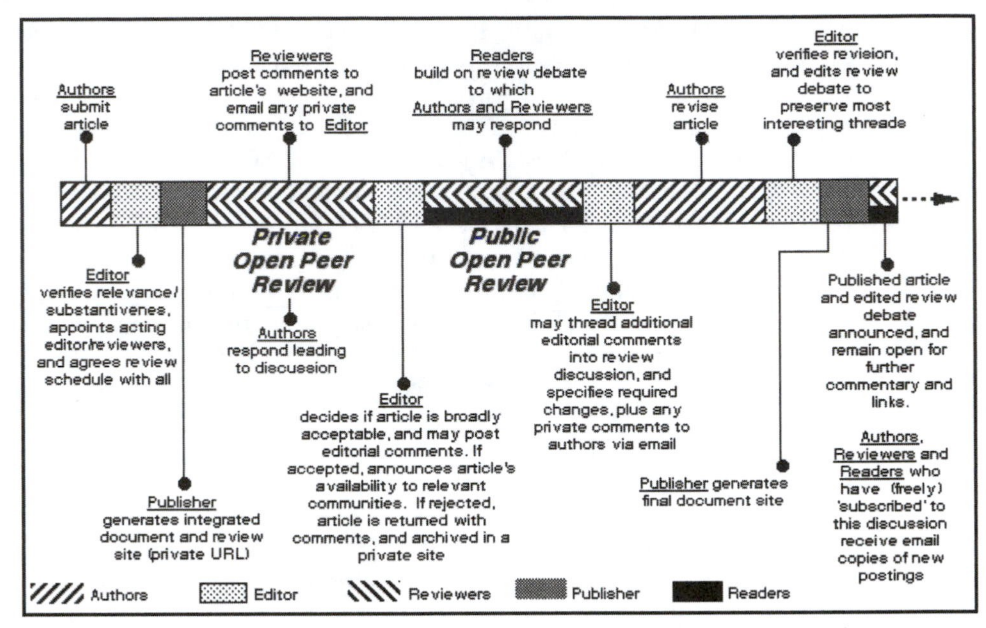

FIGURE 13.1 Nontraditional Review Process at the *Journal of Interactive Media in Education* (http://www-jime.open.ac.uk/resources/icons/lifecycle.gif)

There is a serious debate among academic researchers as to the value of publishing in online journals. A significant group of authors contend that e-journals do not offer the permanence nor the prestige of traditional paper journals. There is also disagreement among faculty related to the thoroughness of review for online publications (Sweeney, 2000). It is true that we feel something quite comforting about being able to hold a paper copy of one of our traditionally published works. However, we believe that this pleasure is due more to familiarity and sentimentality than to real value. Unlike a good novel, most consumers of educational research do not wish to curl up in bed with the latest edition. Since Net-distributed papers can usually be printed if desired, we can anticipate continued evolution from paper to electronic publication.

Many periodicals are now publishing both paper and electronic versions, thus providing the benefits of both media. We have published in both electronic and paper journals and find that there is currently not a great deal of difference in interest nor resulting reward or prestige between the two modes. However, we find it is very useful to be able to respond to inquiries by providing a hyperlink URL rather than taking the trouble and expense of photocopying and mailing copies of our work.

Determining which format and which particular journal to submit your results to is often a challenging task. Our advice to the prospective author is to review the e-journals available in your discipline and judge for yourself their quality and the compatibility (in terms of style, methodology, typical subject topics, etc.) between your results and that presented in previous articles. You will also likely want to consult with colleagues to judge the bias for and against e-journals in your affiliated institution. Finally, bear in mind that the enhanced accessibility of electronic distribution will send a signal to readers that you are willing and able to take an academic chance and strike one small blow for accessibility by publishing electronically.

How Does One Locate Prospective e-Journals?

E-journals can be located using the large subject directories such as Yahoo! or Lycos. A January, 2002 search of Yahoo! provides links to 205 electronic journals in all subject areas. Stanford University library (http://www-sul.stanford.edu/collect/ejourns.html#subj) provides a specialized listing and access to many of the most popular e-journals that are distributed either from the Web or via email. We think you will be delightfully surprised by the quality of many of these e-journals and will likely seriously consider sending your work for dissemination via this means.

DISSEMINATION THROUGH THE POPULAR PRESS

Similar to peer reviewed publications, many opportunities exist for publishing in the popular press in both paper and online formats. Publishing in the non-peer-reviewed popular press does not have the academic prestige of a peer-reviewed publication, but may, in the long run, be more effective at disseminating the results of your e-research. Publishing in the popular press has a number of advantages over scholarly peer-reviewed journals. First, the review process is generally much faster and often consists of only proofreading for grammatical errors by an editor. Second, your production may get much wider distribution than the often-limited circulation lists of many academic publications. This wider distribution of your research outcomes may result in more tangible connections and opportunities across a wider set of readers. Third, you may be paid for your efforts!

The list of online publications is long and continually expanding. Unfortunately many Net-based publications are experimental, and too many are short-lived. A search of popular directories such as Yahoo! reveals a host of online publications, usually catalogued under each of the major subject categories. Many of these sites attempt to provide a two-way communication flow between authors and readers—or even go so far as to attempt to create a virtual community based on the published articles. For example eserver (http://eserver.org/) provides access to literary, artistic, and rhetorical works from over 200 scholars organized into forty-two collections. As a cooperative of producers, eserver "provides a forum where your project can receive feedback and assistance from our members—and when you're ready, working with one of our collection editors, you can publish to a worldwide audience" (eserver.org homepage, 2001).

It is often desirable for an e-researcher to publish at least two versions of their results: one for the specific target audience who paid for or inspired the research (often contract, employment, or educational obligation) and a second, more popular, version that is designed for a more general audience. The Net provides ideal venues for this later publication.

Dissemination through a Web Site

Creating an e-researcher Web site is likely the most cost-effective means to distribute the results of your research. Finding a server and developing and maintaining Web sites is covered in more detail on this book's accompanying Web site where we discuss ways in which a Web site can be used for promotion, gathering data, and other tasks besides dissemination of results. We do however, wish to highlight one critical issue related to dissemination through a public Web site. Are e-researchers able to disseminate their own articles via their own Web site? The answer to this question may seem blatantly obvious: of course. Or is it an obvious answer? In fact, when e-researchers do develop their own Web sites, many encounter a major problem if they have previously published the results in other academic journals. Often, as a condition of publication, authors are requested to relinquish their copyright ownership of the article to the publisher of the scholarly journal, edited book, or other format of publication. Once authors relinquish this right, they are not entitled to further disseminate their work—even on their own Web site. This may seem unfair and an example of excessive control on the part of the publishers. However, publishers have to protect their readership and if the information is freely available on the author's Web site, they may not sell as many subscriptions to their journals. They also note that they have real costs associated not only with publication and distribution, but also those associated the with editing and the peer-review process. Of course, at a certain point in time sales of the particular issue of the journal come to an end. At this point promotion of the journal, through noting the source of the article's original publication, becomes more likely than loss of sales, so publishers eventually either support or conveniently turn a blind eye to copies of articles to which they own copyright appearing on authors' dissemination sites. The prestigious American Psychology Association (APA) recently formalized their policy in regard to self-dissemination of authors' work as follows:

> Authors of articles appearing in APA copyrighted journals may put up—on their personal Web sites—the final draft copies of their manuscripts three years after publication. Please consult other publishers and the publishers of APA division publications for their policies (http://www.apa.org/journals/posting.html).

In our experience, we have sought and usually receive permission from publishers to place copies of our articles on our Web sites long before the three year limit set by the APA. However, this issue reinforces the value of publishing in online journals, so that a direct link can be created from any Web site, providing full access to the complete article.

The screen shot in Figure 13.2 is an example of the dissemination site created by a research team led by one of the authors (Anderson) of this book for dissemination of results. We have tried to keep the main page rather free of clutter, but emphasize our affiliation (via the logo at bottom left) with a well known university. We are dissemi-

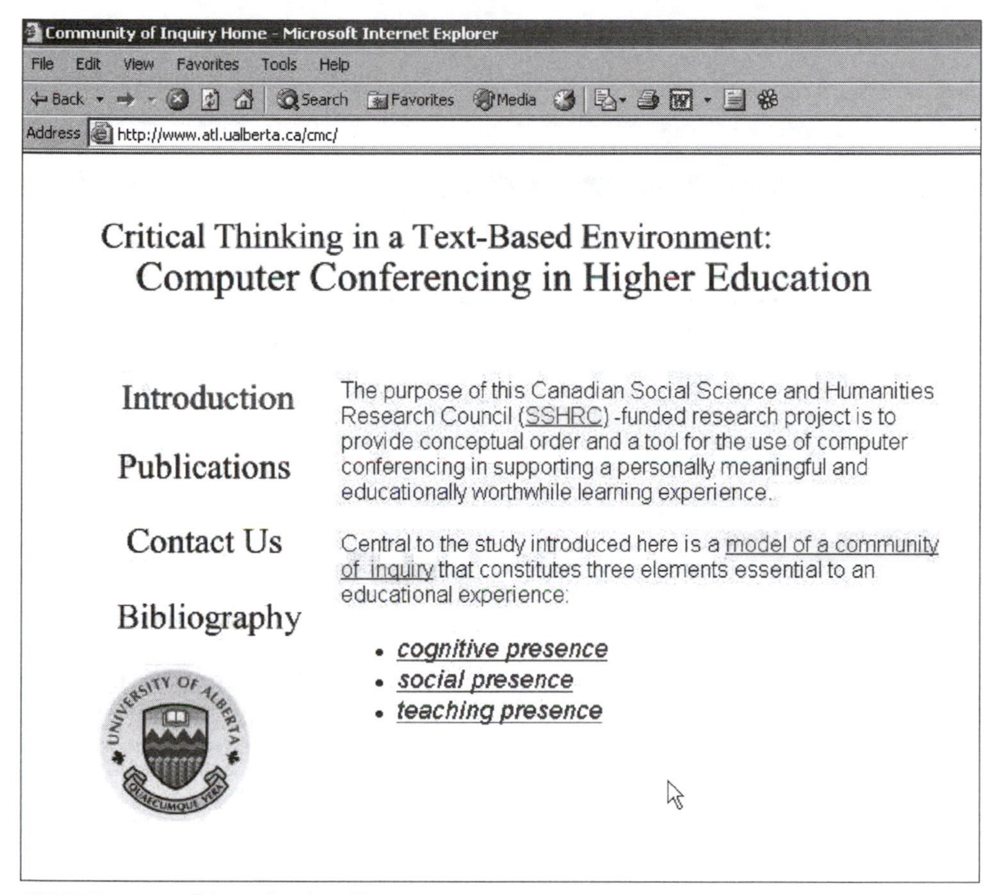

FIGURE 13.2 Dissemination Site

nating most of the publications from this project after obtaining permission from the journal publications in which they originally appeared. We provide abstracts in HTML format with the complete articles available for download in PDF format.

Laura LaMonica's Web site (see Figure 13.3) is an attractive homepage that distributes information about her as well as the results of her latest research. The site thus serves to promote her, acquaint the interested reader further as to her varied interests and experiences, and promote an important research project.

DISSEMINATION THROUGH EMAIL LISTS OR USENET GROUPS

Topic-specific mailing lists and Usenet groups are often excellent avenues by which you may alert many potential consumers of your research. However, there are a variety of

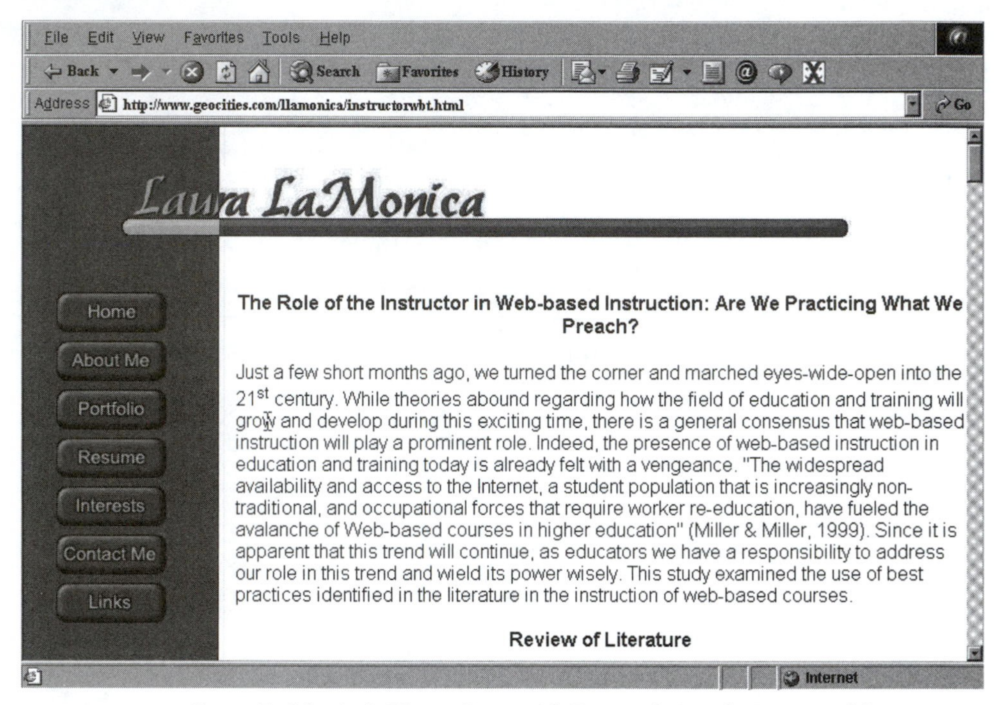

FIGURE 13.3 Laura LaMonica's Home Page with Research Article Presented for Dissemination. See http://www.geocities.com/llamonica/instructorwbt.html.

cultural norms that dictate the way in which these distribution channels may be appropriately used for dissemination purposes. Of prime concern to both list owners and subscribers is the quantity and quality of material that appears in their private email boxes or their newsreaders. In some locations, readers pay by the byte or the time to download for reception of these emails. Thus, they are very protective of proper use. Generally, it is not appropriate to post long articles and especially word processed or other applications as attachments to these lists (such files may harbor viruses). Such attachments are generally very large, and some readers will not be able to open the attachment, thus the email may be expensive, irrelevant, or both and perceived as spam by the recipients.

The most effective dissemination messages consist of a short abstract (two to three paragraphs) of your results and at least one method to obtain further information. A Web link or a site for anonymous FTP retrieval of more detailed results as well as an email address for communication with yourself are the most useful and convenient means of providing this additional information for the interested recipient.

The volume of email arriving in most consumers' mailboxes and Usenet lists forces the e-researcher to carefully package the message, so that it will be read by busy subscribers. The first and most important filter readers use is the subject line. The subject often provides the only opportunity you may have to communicate with potential readers. Thus, it must be short (long subject lines are usually truncated by the email reader), and as importantly the subject line must grab the attention of potential readers. We are most responsive to headers that indicate that the message relates to research results—not disguised forms of advertising. Thus a subject heading such as "Research on teacher attitudes" will grab our attention while a subject such as "What do teachers think?" tells us very little, and its accompanying message is readily deleted.

Dissemination through a Virtual Conference

The final means of Net-based dissemination we review is the virtual conference. Surman and Wershler-Henry (2001), in their book on using the "commonspace" of the Net, argue that the best way to encourage the rapid spread of your ideas is to "work to create an amenable environment for people to form their own opinions and allow them to talk to each other" (p. 255). We believe that the virtual conference offers the best means of engaging others in in-depth discussion of your ideas. In addition, virtual conferences offer a very cost-effective way to disseminate the results of any e-research project. If the results available are large and multifaceted, you may wish to host an entire conference dedicated to your results. Alternatively, you may offer to be a presenter in a virtual conference organized by another organization or institution.

A virtual conference is a professional development activity, often modeled on a face-to-face conference, which is facilitated over the Net. One of the authors of this book organized the first virtual conference ever held online in 1992 (Anderson & Mason, 1993). This event used the early Internet as well as precursor networks including BitNet, NetNorth, FidoNet, and Usenet to disseminate a series of email presentations and subsequent discussion over a two-week period. Since that time there have been hundreds of virtual conferences organized, many enhancing presentations with video and audio, as these technologies have evolved. An indication of the popularity of the virtual conference was the return of over 21,000 hits to a recent Google search on the phrase "virtual conference."

The Virtual Conference is characterized by the following.

- *Availability: anytime, anyplace, or both.* Most virtual conferences are conducted asynchronously, meaning that the presentations and interaction take place over a period of days or weeks and that it is not necessary for participants to be online at any particular time. This is especially important when participants are located across many time zones. Asynchronicity also allows participants to reflect on their responses before posting them to defend their comments with references or links to additional content and to participate without fear of being stigmatized for shyness, gender, race, or other prejudices. Recently there has been a trend towards starting the virtual conference with a synchronous event, such as a webcast of a keynote speech. This synchronous event signals the commencement of the conference and allows for a limited amount of spontaneous and fast-paced real-time interaction (using either audio, video webcasting, conferencing, or text chat). However, the virtual conference usually extends beyond this initial activity through asynchronous interaction. This interaction need not necessarily be limited to text interaction. Newer systems such as Wimba (www.wimba.com) support threaded voice conferencing and many systems allow voice or video attachments to email messaging.

- *Interactive.* Unlike a one-way presentation or webcast, a virtual conference provides for interaction between and amongst speakers and participants. Often in this exchange the e-researcher gains insight into the applications or the potential problems that consumers of the research find with the results.

- *Structured.* A virtual conference is not a free-flow chat session. Usually a moderator introduces the session and the speaker(s) are introduced and acknowledged by the conference organizers. The event is promoted by a variety of means most of which are online, such as posting to relevant email lists; but they also can be promoted through more traditional paper-based publications. Some virtual conferences charge participants a registration fee. In these cases, the presentations and discussions are usually restricted by passwords. There are both advantages and disadvantages (see Anderson, 1996) to using either push-type technologies, such as email, and pull-type technologies, such as conferencing systems, or streamed media to support the virtual conference. Push technologies regularly remind participants of the conference activity by their appearance in the participants' email box. Pull technologies provide better archiving, retrieval, and organization, but may be ignored by busy participants.

- *Limited in time.* Virtual conferences are dissimilar to ongoing mailing list discussions or Web conferences in that they have a scheduled starting and finish time. This creates a degree of timeliness and serves to induce participants to pay active attention because they know that the attention requirement is limited.

Virtual conferences have a number of qualities that make them more advantageous than their face-to-face equivalents. Virtual conferences are

- *Cost saving.* Obviously, virtual conferences save both the time and the money that is associated with the travel required for face-to-face conferences. In addition, the sometimes significant expense of renting conference facilities is eliminated. The first virtual conference held on the Internet and mentioned earlier in this chapter was funded for a total cost of less than $50.00 and had many hundreds of participants. The conference that it mirrored took place in Southeast Asia and had a registration fee of over $400 per person. As we can see from these examples, virtual conferences are extremely cost-effective to organize and to participate in.

- *More accessible.* The capacity for participants to time shift their participation allows for much more flexibility and accessibility. In addition, virtual conferences can be delivered anywhere that the Internet reaches, which today means to every corner of the earth.

- *Self-documenting.* Unlike face-to-face conferences, virtual conferences are normally recorded and archived. Thus, presentations or interactions can be searched and retrieved by interested participants long after the conference is finished.

- *Networked.* Like most other communications that are based on the network, virtual conference presenters are able to create and maintain hyperlinks to further documentation, applications, simulations, or animations, thus providing a variety of multimedia presentation options that often are not available in face-to-face presentations.

Virtual conferences are not, however, without their disadvantages. Ironically, the features that participants find most attractive about virtual conferences—the ability to remain at the workplace and to save money—are directly related to the factor that participants list as the major detractor. The major detractor has been identified as professional isolation related to not being able to gather physically in a location that is removed from the distractions of the workplace (Wilkenson, 2000). Like other applications of virtuality, virtual conferences have inherent disadvantages over both formal and informal face-to-face interaction. No mediated interaction yet allows for the rich, familiar interaction supported by face-to-face contact. However, we continue to believe that the advantages in terms of cost and accessibility will cause virtual conferences to be an important means for researchers to disseminate the results of their research. Figure 13.4 provides a screenshot from the 1998 Australian Computer in Education Virtual Conference Web site. Notice how the site provides links to detailed instructions for participants as well as schedules and listings of activities that will take place during the conference.

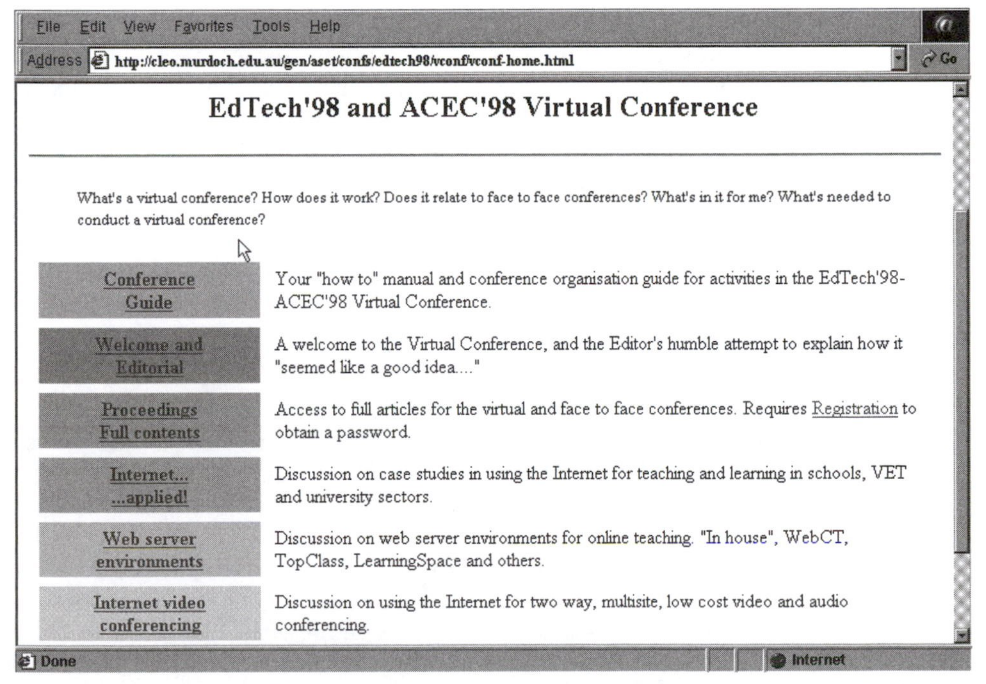

FIGURE 13.4 Screen Shot of 1998 Australian Computer in Education Virtual Conference Welcome Page

TABLE 13.1 Activities for Presenters at the Seventh Annual Teaching in the Community Colleges Online Conference

MAY 21–23, 2002

Theme: THE NEXT LEAP FOR INTERNET-MEDIATED LEARNING

ACTIVITIES FOR PRESENTERS

* All presentations will be posted on the conference Web page two weeks prior to the start of the conference.
* All presenters will be expected to respond to email questions and comments from conference participants.
* All presenters and participants will be included in the conference discussion list.
* All presenters will be expected to submit a photo and brief professional bio for the conference Web site.
* All presenters will be scheduled for a one-hour informal chat session on one of the conference days to meet with participants.

Table 13.1 illustrates the activities proscribed for presenters at the annual Teaching in the Community Colleges Online Conference. This conference is distributed on a number of moderated, email list forums established specifically for the virtual conference. It also features a synchronous text chat session with each presenter at a scheduled time during the three-day conference. Faculty members Jim Shimabukuro and Bert Kimura from the University of Hawaii provide a nice review of the organizational issues and the technologies they have used while facilitating this conference over the past six years at http://leahi.kcc.hawaii.edu/org/tcon2002/whatis.html.

TIPS FOR DISSEMINATION

- Package your ideas in more than one of the formats described in this chapter. Different audiences will be attracted to different formats, and the results of your e-research should probably be conveyed to all.
- Post short announcements detailing the availability of your results on appropriate mail lists, newsgroups, and conference sites.
- Label announcements of your results with short, catchy subject lines.
- Participate and/or present in a few virtual conferences before attempting to host your own. When advertising for upcoming virtual conferences, announcements are often carried on subject-related Web sites and email discussion lists.

SUMMARY

In this chapter we have attempted to provide suggestions and hints for ensuring that a maximum number of researchers, educators, and the general public has the greatest access to the results of your e-research. As Jake Kirchner, editor of *PC Magazine* aptly stated: "It is better to light an e-candle than to curse the darkness."

REFERENCES

Anderson, T. (1996). The virtual conference: Extending professional education in cyberspace. *International Journal of Educational Telecommunications*, *2*(2/3), 121–135.

Anderson, T., & Mason, R. (1993). The Bangkok Project: New tool for professional development. *American Journal of Distance Education*, *7*(2), 5–18.

Bresler, K. (2000). Myths and takes on writing Web content. [Online]. Available: http://www.clearwriting.net/webwriting.htm.

Brown, R. (1995). Write right first time. [Online]. Available: http://www.literaticlub.co.uk/writing/articles/write.html.

Harnard, S. (1996). Implementing peer review on the net: Scientific quality control in scholarly electronic journals. In R. Peek and Newby G. (Eds.), *Scholarly confronts academia: The agenda for the year 2000* (pp. 103–118). Cambridge, MA: MIT Press.

Kanuka, H., & Szabo, M. (1999). Conducting research on visual design and learning: Pitfalls and promises. *Canadian Journal of Educational Communication*, *27*(2), 39–57.

McKerrow, R., Wood A., & Smith, M. (1995). Publishing on-line: Challenging standards of hiring, promotion, and tenure. *American Communication Journal*, *1*(3) [Online]. Available: http://acjournal.org/holdings/vol1/iss3/curtain3.html.

Morkes J., & Nielsen, J. (1998). *Applying writing guidelines to webpages*. [Online]. Available: http://www.useit.com/papers/webwriting/rewriting.html.

Readings, B. (1994). Caught in the Net: Notes from the electronic underground. *Surfaces*, *4*(104). [Online]. Available: http://www.pum.umontreal.ca/revues/surfaces/vol4/readings.html.

Surman, M., & Wershler-Henry, D. (2001). Commonspace: Beyond virtual community. Toronto: FT.com. [Online]. Available: http://www.ft.com/home/ww/.

Sweeney, A. (2000). Tenure and promotion: Should you publish in electronic journals? *Journal of Electronic Publishing*, *6*(2). [Online]. Available: http://www.press.umich.edu/jep/06-02/sweeney.html.

Wilkenson, S. (2000). Electronic journals gain ground. *Chemical & Engineering News*, *78*(33), 33–38. [Online]. Available: http://pubs.acs.org/hotartcl/cenear/000821/7833scit1a.html.

Yu, L., & Schmid, B. (1999). *Managing Internet peer review process in a multi-agent framework*. [Online]. Available: http://www.knowledgemedia.org/netacademy/publications.nsf/all_pk/1321.

CHAPTER FOURTEEN

THE FUTURE OF e-RESEARCH

A real understanding of Quality captures the System, tames it, and puts it to work for one's own personal use, while leaving one completely free to fulfill his inner destiny.

Robert Pirsig—Zen and the Art of Motorcycle Maintenance

As human beings, we have always been unsatisfied with the basic gifts provided by Mother Nature; thus, we have spent a great deal of time and energy devising means to enhance and augment our natural, albeit limited, physical attributes. This has motivated the development of machines and tools that allow us to extend our voices across distance and time; to lift and manipulate the heaviest and the tiniest of masses; to travel through water, air, and space; to alter our environment through music, perfumes, visual and performance art; and to alter our perception through meditation, drugs, and education. In the domain of formal education we have developed tools (from chalk slates to computers) and techniques (from phonics instruction to Web safaris), to expand our intellectual capacity and to master new information and skills more quickly and effectively. Research has been a pivotal means by which we have advanced our understandings in order to evolve and grow, and to stretch our natural human capabilities.

Much hyperbolic writing has celebrated the Internet's capacity to change just about everything. These superlative claims have often been accompanied by illusions to past mega ideas that have led to profound societal change, such as the advancement of agriculture, the invention of the printing press, and the industrial revolution. These examples give us a sense of the magnitude and capacity of the Internet to capture the imagination of everyone from scientists and artists to teachers and reporters. In an illuminating text that identifies the Net community itself as the real "killer application" (or "killer app"), Surman and Wershler-Henry (2001) declare that "we are creating a digital gestalt—a new, more complex version of ourselves. We are growing a collective mind between the bits. And that is changing everything."

We conclude this book by examining features of the Net and the components that are driving significant change. Through this examination of the driving components, we hope to illuminate a future path for e-researchers that will help in the selection of the best Net-based tools and in applying them to significant issues worthy of research. Because the Net has acquired a reputation of proving wrong those who proclaim to have discovered or invented the "next big thing," we hope this chapter will at least insure that e-researchers are there to assess, chronicle, and improve the next "killer application"—whenever it arrives!

Drivers of change on the Net have been described by AT&T Lab researcher Dana Moore (http://www.computer.org/internet/v4n1/moore.htm) as residing in three dimensions, referred to as the "three Vs" of the Internet Age (Moore, 2000). He argues that each of these dimensions is expanding daily, explaining the speed and growing importance of the Net in many aspects of our social and economic interest. These three Vs are Volume, Velocity, and Variety. Within this ever-expanding landscape, we struggle continuously to find an all-important "fourth V"—Value.

Throughout this book, we have attempted to describe and summarize the way the Net impacts directly on the processes and products of research. The effect of the Net on educational and social sciences research is more pronounced than in many other fields because the four Vs of the Net age are having a profound impact and sometimes very disruptive effect on the process, institutions, and participants in formal education itself and our society as a whole. These changes come in addition to the effect of these four factors on the practice of all research.

FUTURE OF THE NET: VOLUME, VELOCITY, VARIETY, AND VALUE

Volume

Beginning with the first of the four Vs framework, we note that the volume of activity on the Net continues to increase. The rate of adoption of the Internet is eclipsing that of all other technologies preceding it. In its first four years of availability to the public, fifty million people logged on to the Internet worldwide. It took thirty-eight years for radio and thirteen years for television to achieve this level of acceptance (U.S. Department of Commerce, 1998). The number of new users in North America has slowed from the 100 percent per year rate of the 1990s, but still growth, beyond the current 50 percent of citizens and 80 percent of households who use some aspect of Net services, continues unabated. The volume of applications also continues to expand and diversify. Despite the meltdown that consumer-products-based dot com businesses experienced in this new millennium, there is still continued growth and expansion in Net-based applications, at a more manageable and hype-free speed. We are just beginning to see the disappearance of the Net as a stand-alone device and its reemergence as an integral and integrated component of many commercial and consumer devices (Denning, 2001). Examples of this deep integration of the Net into ordinary devices include automobiles connecting to the Net through a host of sensors, logs, and communications devices; homes wired to the Net to provide security, energy management, heating and ventilation control; desktop computers functioning as telephones, video conferencing studios, movie editing suites, and home entertainment centers. Soon most consumer and industrial devices will have the capacity to be controlled and monitored either remotely or automatically by other Net-connected devices.

Volume also accelerates as the Net grows beyond its largely Western birthplace and begins utilizing the talent and creative energy of businesses, institutions, and individuals located throughout the world. While still dominated by major world language applications (in particular English) and technologically advanced societies, the rapid diversification of new users is creating suburbs of most languages commonly spoken. The renowned Welsh linguist David Crystal estimated in 2001 that there are over 1,500 languages on the Net and that 35 percent of content is in non-English languages. Crystal also notes that this percentage of non-English content continues to increase each year (Crystal, 2001).

As the number of users on the Net increases, so does the value of the Net to each of us. Robert Metcalfe (the inventor of Ethernet) formulated this idea as Metcalfe's Law over twenty-five years ago. Metcalfe's original articulation of the law states that:

> The value of the network increases as the square of the number of users connected. This exponential growth results in more truly useful applications of the Net every month. In turn, as the Net becomes more useful, it inspires more users creating a self energizing development environment.

We believe this critical mass and exponential growth has resulted in the creation of a resource that will be a major evolutionary force on human development for the foreseeable future.

Velocity

The raw speed and throughput capacity of the Net also increases annually with deployment of multifrequency fibre carriers and faster switching devices that direct these streams of data. These higher speeds are the basis for new varieties of networked products—many based on transmission of multimedia and especially one- and two-way video. Although there is no doubt that Digital Subscriber Line (DSL) and cable speed for home Web surfing is a real added value compared to dialup speeds, it is less clear what the killer application will be for very high-speed networks. Many of the experimental research networks that we have used, including Canada's CANARIE Network and the U.S. Internet 2 network, are having problems finding real applications that consume the amount of bandwidth that they can supply. In a speech by the director of Canada's high-speed network in 1999, for example, there was a prediction made that distance education would be the killer application that would best consume the high bandwidth that his network supplied. Three years later, it would appear that distance educators have not been as enthusiastic about high-speed networking as some predicted. Currently, most high-bandwidth educational applications are based on video conferencing for interactive classroom lectures, a model that neither students nor faculty find particularly valuable or convenient. Nevertheless, based on past experience, we can predict that useful applications in education and other fields will arise that more than consume all available bandwidth.

Variety

Much of the e-research today is focused on analysis of text interchange between and among people and researchers. In the very near future researchers will be provided with the opportunity to decide which communication format best meets their application needs, rather than which is most readily available. They will select from video, audio, animated and text-based interaction. These interactions will shift between real-time exchanges and time-shifted, asynchronous interaction. The Net will also migrate into a variety of smart, networked machines that were originally developed as manually controlled, stand-alone entities, but that are now automated and controlled by Net-enabled agents. For example, cameras will send their images automatically to owners and large energy-consuming devices, such as dishwashers, will patiently suspend operations until the power grid is least used and consumer energy prices are lowest.

We are also experiencing tremendous increases in the variety of ways in which information can be retrieved from the Net. Mobile devices have spawned an interest in m-learning—the intersection of mobile computing and e-learning. M-learning promises an "always on/always available" capacity to retrieve information, compute, and communicate and, thereby, be involved in learning activities "anytime/anywhere." These services will be especially useful for the mobile worker, the commuter, or anyone who operates from more than a single workplace.

This variety with which Net-based information and learning resources are accessed and displayed will be of benefit to those with particular learning styles and especially those with sensory disabilities. Information and displays will be customizable, dependent on the need of both the user and the application. In sum, these developments foreshadow a blossoming of the Net beyond its birth as a text-only environment into one that supports kinetic movement as well as sound, video, and even smell!

Value

Value is directly related to quality and unfortunately both are defined socially by individuals, groups, and societies, and they are not amenable to thorough objective measurement. In his seminal 1974 book *Zen and the Art of Motorcycle Maintenance*, Robert Pirsig insightfully noted the problem that decries all of us (at least the square component of us all) when we try too hard to define quality and value empirically. He wrote:

> Squareness may be succinctly and yet thoroughly defined as an inability to see quality before it's been intellectually defined, that is, before it gets all chopped up into words . . . . We have proved that quality, though undefined, exists. Its existence can be seen empirically in the classroom, and can be demonstrated logically by showing that a world without it cannot exist as we know it. What remains to be seen, the thing to be analyzed, is not quality, but those peculiar habits of thought called 'squareness' that sometimes prevent us from seeing it. (p. 196)

Although it seems very "seventies" to even think about "squareness" as a personal attribute in the twenty-first century, we think that those of us interested in e-research and new ways to define and invent our world need to practice suspending our judgmental and natural conservatism when attesting value to Net-based innovation. While we need to retain a critical perspective as competent researchers and scholars, we also need to remember that the Net has created educational, economic, and social opportunities, and contexts more diverse and unpredictable than any we have dealt with in the past. It will be many years before we will develop theory and applications that adequately explain and define this new environment.

One of the most intractable problems of the Net is the chaotic organization of content. The Net will not gain its true value as an educational or information retrieval device until the structural and relationship problems between diverse pots of information is resolved. The solution, when it arises, will produce two fundamental advantages. First, the Net will be navigable and understandable by a host of nonhuman servants, or bots, who will be assigned a very wide range of tasks to perform on behalf of their human creators. Second, humans will be abetted in the process of finding and evaluating content in formats and packages that are accessible and understandable. In short, we will be able to throttle down the fire hose that we are currently forced to drink from and have our information served as and where we like it, in a conveniently sized container.

The solution to this organizational problem is of course not trivial. The best effort to date to bring about this evolution is being led by the primary governing body (if such an entity exists) of the Web—the World Wide Web Consortium (W3 Consortium). The W3 is currently led by the original designer of the WWW, Tim Berners-Lee. He coined this effort to design and build a smart, user-friendly, and intelligent Web, the Semantic Web Project (Berners-Lee, 1999).

The *American Heritage Dictionary of the English Language* defines the term *semantic* as "relating to meaning." The original WWW was created to allow human beings to navigate and search between content stored on multiple machines and linked through hyperlinks. Thus, it is primarily a display system that allows human beings to select and search their way through content. Machines have been developed to read this content, but time spent on any of the major search engines illustrates the limitations of brute force and best-guess indexing that characterizes these current indexes of Web content. For example, typing the term *smoke* retrieves sites related to burning tobacco, a treatment to preserve meat, a slang term for a murder, a suspension of solid particles in a gas, a euphemism for a cigarette, or the act of uncovering something hidden. Without a larger sense of the semantics or as Berners-Lee says, the "ontology of the term," it is difficult for a human, and nearly impossible for a machine, to automatically navigate and manipulate terms that are endowed with so many diverse meanings. A key feature of the Semantic Web is the organization of information into multiple ontologies that show the relationship between data items (Berners-Lee, Hendler, & Lassila, 2001). For example, each of our names is associated with a street address and telephone number. Each of these items in turn is associated with other related items—for example, an address is associated geographically with that of the neighbors. In theory, the Semantic Web will be able to follow these ontological relationships, based on personal requests. These requests are normally executed by personal autonomous agents who are sent to retrieve information on request or at scheduled times. The future Web will be permeated by logic systems and ontologies that describe the relationship between the information contained on a particular page or even the capacity stored within a networked machine (such as a cell phone or a home heating system). Agents will be constructed to navigate this Web of information, querying databases, attesting to information veracity, monitoring sensory devices, and negotiating with other agents to a variety of existing and new services for their owners.

Perhaps an example of an educational application to the Semantic Web will illustrate how much value this will add to the Net:

> The Semantic Web will be capable of supporting a teacher-commissioned agent assigned the task of searching the entire public Web for a simulation of a particular chemistry experiment that is written in English that costs less than 50 cents to rent and that has been positively reviewed by experts from at least two well-known universities. A second agent will take this content and integrate it as an assignment into the teacher's course delivery system and have the integrated assessment activity automatically calculated into the course grade schema. A third agent will alert all current students to this new addition to the course. A fourth will monitor activity, sending reminder notes to students who have not logged on and sending individual and summary statistics of students' use and outcomes to the teacher. Obviously such systems will add great value to the existing Web, and, of course, research opportunities related to the efficacy and efficiency of such agent enhanced teaching and learning will abound.

The second way in which value for e-researchers is enhanced by Web technologies is the increased communications capacity of the Net. E-researchers may now expand the scope and the frequency of their contacts with both collaborators and subjects. E-research teams can now work effectively, though separated by distances and time zones.

Communications between researchers and participants in the research are also enhanced through capacity to quickly and cheaply exchange drafts, error check and return surveys, and perform member checks with participants to ensure the researcher has accurately captured the participants' comments and opinions. Finally their quality is enhanced by the capacity to disseminate results much more quickly and economically than in pre-Net eras.

Each of these four Vs contributes enhancements to the Net, making it more reliable and useful for the e-researcher. However, the Net is not only expanding in its usefulness as a research tool; the Net is also expanding the quality and scope of most social, political, and economic institutions.

CONCLUSION

The mindful integration of new technologies and new forms of research promises a golden age for Net-based research. In this chapter we have tried to assist researchers in identifying the most likely aspects of the Net that add the greatest velocity, variety, volume, and most importantly, value, to e-research. These emerging tools will be propelled by a demand that will grow in a world dedicated to lifelong learning. New tools in conjunction with large and growing demands inevitably fuel high levels of innovative research. However, successful innovation relies on high-quality research. Thus, as e-researchers we have a tremendous opportunity to make a profound difference in the rapid evolution of network-enhanced research.

Our goal in writing this book has been to share our knowledge and experiences in ways that will benefit current and future e-researchers. We hope that this book has provided at least one good idea that makes your research easier, more productive, and more rewarding. We invite you to share your experiences, questions, and concerns about e-research on our Web site at http://www.e-research.ca.

REFERENCES

Berners-Lee, T., Hendler, J., & Lassila, O. (2001). The semantic web. *Scientific American*, (May). [Online]. Available: http://www.sciam.com/2001/0501issue/0501berners-lee.html.

Crystal, D. (February 26, 2001). *A chat with David Crystal*. [Online]. Available: http://www.word-smith.org/chat/dc.html.

Denning, P. (Ed.) (2001). *The invisible future: The seamless integration of technology into everyday life*. New York: McGraw-Hill.

Moore, D. (2000). The changing face of the infosphere. *Internet Computing, 4*(1). [Online]. Available: http://www.computer.org/internet/v4n1/moore.htm.

Surman, M., & Wershler-Henry, D. (2000). *Commonspace: Beyond virtual community*. Toronto: FT.com.

Pirsig, R. (1974). *Zen and the art of motorcycle maintenance*. London: William Morrow.

U.S. Department of Commerce (1998). The emerging digital economy. [Online]. Available: http://www.ecommerce.gov.

BIBLIOGRAPHY

Abrams, M., & Williams, S. (1996). Complementing surveying and demographics with automated network monitoring. *Web Journal, 1*(3). [Online]. Available: http://www.w3j.com/3/s3.abrams.html.

Ahern, T., Peck, K., & Laycock, M. (1992). The effects of teacher discourse in computer-mediated discussion. *Journal of Educational Computing Research, 8*(3), 291–309.

Allan, C. (1996). What's wrong with the "Golden Rule"? Conundrums of conducting ethical research in cyberspace. *Information Society, 12*(2), 175–187.

Allbritton, B. (1996). *Collaborative communication among researchers using computer-mediated communication: A Study of Project H.* Unpublished doctoral dissertation, Albuquerque, University of New Mexico. [Online]. Available: http://www.arch.usyd.edu.au/~fay/netplay/marcel/.

Allen, T. H. (1978). *New methods in social science.* New York: Praeger.

Alreck, P., & Settle, R. (1985). *The survey research handbook.* Homewood, IL: Irwin.

Anderson, T. (1996). The virtual conference: Extending professional education in cyberspace. *International Journal of Educational Telecommunications, 2*(2/3), 121–135.

Anderson, T., & Kanuka, H. (1997). On-line forums: New platforms for professional development and group collaboration. *Journal of Computer Mediated Conferencing, 3*(3). [Online]. Available: http://www.ascusc.org/jcmc/vol3/issue3/anderson.html.

Anderson, T., & Mason, R. (1993). The Bangkok Project: New tools for professional development. *American Journal of Distance Education,* 7(2), 5–18.

Bandura, A. (1977). Self-efficacy: Toward a unifying theory of behavioral change. *Psychological Review, 84*(2), 191–215.

Bauer, M. (2000). Classical content analysis: A review. In M. Bauer and G. Gaskell (Eds.), *Qualitative researching with text, image and sound.* London: Sage.

Baym, N. (1995). The performance of humor in computer-mediated communication. *Journal of Computer Mediated Communications, 1*(2). [Online]. Available: http://www.ascusc.org/jcmc/vol1/issue2/baym.html.

Benedikt, M. (1991). Cyberspace: Some proposals. In M. Benedikt (Ed.), *Cyberspace: First steps* (pp. 119–224). Cambridge: MIT Press.

Berelson, B. (Ed.). (1952). *Content analysis in communication research.* Clenco, IL: Free Press.

Berners-Lee, T. (1999). *Weaving the Web: The original design and ultimate destiny of the World Wide Web by its inventor.* San Francisco: Harper Collins.

Berners-Lee, T., Hendler, J., & Lassila, O. (2001). The semantic web. *Scientific American,* (May). [Online]. Available: http://www.sciam.com/2001/0501issue/0501berners-lee.html.

Bickman, L., & Rog, D. J. (Eds). (1998). *Handbook of applied social research methods.* Thousand Oaks, CA: Sage.

Bogdan, R., & Biklen, S. K. (1992). *Qualitative research for education: An introduction to theory and methods.* Boston: Allyn & Bacon.

Borg, W. R., & Gall, M. D. (1989). *Educational research. An introduction* (5th ed.). White Plains, NY: Longman.

Bradley, J. (2000, January). Online business still needs the basics. *Washington CEO.* [Online]. Available: http://www.washingtonceo.com/archive/jan00/0100-E-Com.html.

Bresler, K. (2000). Myths and takes on writing Web content. [Online]. Available: http://www.clearwriting.net/webwriting.htm.

Brookfield, S. (1987). *Developing critical thinkers*. San Francisco: Jossey-Bass Publishers.

Brown, R. (1995). Write right first time. [Online]. Available: http://www.literaticlub.co.uk/writing/articles/write.html.

Budd, R., Thorp, R., & Donohew, L. (1967). *Content analysis of communications*. New York: MacMillan.

Center for Applied Special Technology (2001). [Online]. Available: http://www.cast.org/bobby/.

Center for International Higher Education (2000). Measuring quality in Internet based higher education: Benchmarks for success. [Online]. Available: http://www.bc.edu/bc_org/avp/soe/cihe/newsletter/News20/text1.html.

Choo C., Detlor, B., & Turnbull, D. (1998). A behavioral model of information seeking on the Web—Preliminary results of a study of how managers and IT specialists use the Web. [Online]. Available: http://choo.fis.utoronto.ca/FIS/ResPub/asis98/default.html.

Church, A. H. (1993). Estimating the effect of incentives on mail survey response rates: A meta-analysis. *Public Opinion Quarterly, 1*(57), 62–79.

Cicourel, A. V. (1964). *Method and measurement in sociology*. New York: Free Press.

Clark, R. (1994). Media will never influence learning. *Educational Technology Research & Development, 42*(2), 21–29.

Clark, R. (2000). Evaluating distance education: Strategies and cautions. *Quarterly Review of Distance Education, 1*(1), 3–16.

Clarke, R. (2000). Information wants to be free. [Online]. Available: http://www.anu.edu.au/people/Roger.Clarke/II/IWtbF.html.

Cohen, L., & Manion, L. (1994). Research methods in education (4th ed.). New York: Routhledge.

Colford, I. (1996). Writing in the electronic environment: Electronic text and the future of creativity and knowledge. *Occasional Papers Series Dalhousie University*.

Creswell, J. W. (1994). *Research design. Qualitative and quantitative approaches*. London: Sage.

Dahlen, M. (1998). Controlling the uncontrollable: Towards the perfect web sample. [Online]. Available: http://www.hhs.se/fdr/research/Internet/Uncontrol.pdf.

Dalkey, N. C. (1972). *Studies in the quality of life*. Lexington, MA: Lexington Press.

December, J. (1994). Challenges for a webbed society. *Computer-Mediated Communication Magazine, 1*(8). [Online]. Available: http://www.december.com/cmc/mag/1994/nov/websoc.html.

Diamond, E., & Bates, S. (1995). The ancient history of the Internet. *American Heritage*, (October), 34–45.

Dillman, D. (2000). *Mail and Internet surveys: The tailored design method* (2nd ed.). New York: Wiley.

Downs, S. (2000). Learning objects. [Online]. Available: http://www.atl.ualberta.ca/downes/naweb/column000523.htm.

Eastin M., & LaRose, R. (2000). Internet self-efficacy and the psychology of the digital divide. *Journal of Computer Mediated Communications, 6*(1). [Online]. Available: http://www.ascusc.org/jcmc/vol6/issue1/eastin.html.

Eisner, E. (1981). On the differences between scientific and artistic approaches to qualitative research. *Educational Researcher, 10*(4), 5–9.

Electronic Networking Association. (1991). *NetWeaver*, 7(3).

Fahy, P., Crawford, G., Ally, M., Cookson, P., Keller, V., & Prosser, F. (1999). The development and testing of a computer conferencing transcript analysis tool. *Alberta Journal of Education Research, 46*(2), 85–88.

Feenberg, A. (1989). The written world: On the theory and practice of computer conferencing. In R. Mason and A. Kaye (Eds.), *Mindweave: Communication, computers, and distance education* (pp. 22–39). Toronto: Pergamon.

Firestone, W. A. (1987). Meaning in method: The rhetoric of quantitative and qualitative research. *Educational Researcher, 16*(7), 16–21.

Fontana, A., & Frey, J. H. (1994). Interviewing: The art of science. In N. K. Denzin and Y. S. Lincoln (Eds.), *Handbook of qualitative research* (pp. 361–376). Thousand Oaks, CA: Sage.

Fowler, F. J. (1995). *Improving survey questions. Design and evaluation.* London: Sage.

Fraenkel, J. R., & Wallen, N. E. (2000). *How to design and evaluate research in education* (4th ed.). New York: McGraw-Hill.

Fullan, R. (1999). Time tracking. [Online]. Available: http://www.bellanet.org/advisor/index.cfm?Fuseaction=view_article&TheArticle=30.

Gilbert, S. (2001). AAHESGIT List AAHESGIT-77: E-mail survey results. [Online]. Available: http://www.cren.net/ftp/archives/aahesgit/log0101.

Glesne, C., & Peshkin, A. (1992). *Becoming qualitative researchers. An introduction.* White Plains, NY: Longman.

Guba, E. G. (1981). Criteria for assessing the trustworthiness for naturalistic inquiries. *ERIC/ECTJ Annual Review Paper, 29*(2), 75–91.

GuideStar Communications (1999a). Client and respondent views of e-surveys. [Online]. Available: http://www.guidestarco.com/e-survey-client-testimonials.html.

GuideStar Communications (1999b). E-survey features and benefits. [Online]. Available: http://www.guidestarco.com/e-Survey-Features-and-Benefits.htm.

Hall, B. (2001). E-Learning: A strategic imperative for succeeding in business. *Fortune*, (May 14).

Hara, N., Bonk, C., & Angeli, C. (2000). Content analysis of on-line discussion in an applied education psychology course. *Instructional Science, 28*(2), 115–152.

Harnard, S. (1996). Implementing peer review on the net: Scientific quality control in scholarly electronic journals. In R. Peek and Newby G. (Eds.), *Scholarly publicating: The electronic frontier* (pp. 103–108). Cambridge, MA: MIT Press.

Harris, R. (1997). *Evaluating Internet research sources.* [Online]. Available: http://www.sccu.edu/faculty/R_Harris/evalu8it.htm.

Hart, R. (1997). Information gathering among the faculty of a comprehensive college: Formality and globality. *Journal of Academic Librarianship, 23*(1), 21–27.

Henri, F. (1991). Computer conferencing and content analysis. In A. Kaye (Ed.), *Collaborative learning through computer conferencing* (pp. 117–136). London: Springer-Verlag.

Herring, S. (1996). Critical analysis of language use in computer-mediated contexts. *Information Society, 12*(2), 153–168.

Hillman, D. (1999). A new method for analyzing patterns of interaction. *The American Journal of Distance Education, 13*(2), 37–47.

Holmberg, B. (1989). *Theory and practice of distance education*. London: Routledge.

Howell-Richardson, C., & Mellar, H. (1996). A methodology for the analysis of patterns of participation within computer mediated communication courses. *Instructional Science, 24*, 47–69.

IMT Strategies (2000). *Permission email: The future of direct marketing.* [Online]. Available: http://www.imtstrategies.com/download/Permission_E-mail_white_paper.pdf.

Jackson, M. (1997). Assessing the structure of communication on the World Wide Web. *Journal of Computer Mediated Communication, 3*(1). [Online]. Available: http://www.ascusc.org/jcmc/vol3/issue1/jackson.html.

Jacobson, P. (1997). On-line focus groups: Four approaches that work. *Quirk's Marketing Research Review*, Article Number 0245.

Jenkins, S. (2000). Internet glossary. [Online]. Available: http://www.unisa.edu.au/itsuhelpdesk/faqs/glossary.htm.

Johanson, G., & Johanson, S. (1997). Differential item functioning in survey research. In American Education Research Association (Ed.), *American Education Research Association*. ERIC # ED399293.

Jonassen, D. H. (1991). Evaluating constructivistic learning. *Educational Technology, 31*(10), 28–33.

Journal of Interactive Media in Education. (2001). JIME Articles. [Online]. Available: http://www-jime.open.ac.uk/.

Jupiter Communications (2001). *Jupiter identifies new revenue opportunity for portals, ISPs and Web mail providers*. [Online]. Available: http://www.jup.com/company/pressrelease.jsp?doc=pr010124.

Kanuka, H., & Anderson, T. (1998). On-line social interchange, discord and knowledge construction. *Journal of Distance Education, 13*(1), 57–74. [Online]. Available: cade.athabascau.ca/vol13.1/kanuka.html.

Kanuka, H., & Szabo, M. (1999). Conducting research on visual design and learning: Pitfalls and promises. *Canadian Journal of Educational Communication, 27*(2), 39–57.

Kennedy, K. A. (2002). *IT and the Internet on higher education institutions. 2005–2015 A Delphi forecast.* Unpublished doctoral dissertation. Vancouver, British Columbia: University of British Columbia.

Kerns, I. (2000, February). E-survey quality ranks higher than print. *American Society of Business Publication Editors Newsletter*. [Online]. Available: http://www.asbpe.org/archives/2000/02esurveys.htm.

Kibirige, H., & Depalo, L. (2000). The Internet as a source of academic research information: Findings of two pilot studies. *Information Technology and Libraries, 19*(1). [Online]. Available: http://www.lita.org/ital/1901_kibirige.html.

King, S. (1996). Researching Internet communities: Proposed ethical guidelines for the reporting of results. *Information Society, 12*(2), 119–127.

Kozma, R. (1994). Will media influence learning? Reframing the debate. *Educational Technology Research & Development, 42*(2), 7–19.

Kvale, S. (1996). *InterViews: An introduction to qualitative research interviewing*. London: Sage.

Langford, H. W. (1972). *Technological forecasting methodologies: A synthesis.* New York: American Management Association.

Laurillard, D. (1997). *Rethinking university teaching: A framework for the effective use of educational technology*. London: Routledge.

Lincoln, Y. S., & Guba, E. G. (1985). *Naturalistic inquiry*. Beverly Hills, CA: Sage.

Lincoln, Y. S., & Guba, E. G. (1988). Do inquiry paradigms imply inquiry methodologies? In D. M. Fetterman (Ed.), *Qualitative approaches to evaluation in education* (pp. 89–115). New York: Praeger.

Lofland, J. (1971). Analyzing social settings: A guide to qualitative observation and analysis.

MacElroy, B. (2000). Comparing seven forms of on-line surveys. [Online]. Available: http://www.modalis.com/english/news/7forms.html.

Marchionini, G. (1988). Hypermedia and learning: Freedom and chaos. *Educational Technology, 28*(11), 8–12.

Martino, J. P. (1972). *Technological forecasting for decision making*. New York: American Elsevier.

Marttunen, M. (1997). Electronic mail as pedagogical delivery system: An analysis of the learning argumentation. *Research in Higher Education, 38*(3), 345–363.

McCracken, G. (1988). *The long interview*. Newbury Park, CA: Sage.

McDonald, J. (1998). Interpersonal group dynamics and development in computer conferencing: The rest of the story. In Wisconsin Distance Education Proceedings. [Online]. Available: http://www.mrc.gc.ca/publications.html.

McKerrow, R., Wood A., & Smith, M. (1995). Publishing on-line: Challenging standards of hiring, promotion, and tenure. *American Communication Journal, 1*(3) [Online]. Available: http://acjournal.org/holdings/vol1/iss3/curtain3.html.

McLuhan, M. (1964). *Understanding media: The extensions of man.* Toronto: McGraw-Hill.

Merrill, M. D. (1991). Constructivism and instructional design. *Educational Technology, 31*(5), 45–53.

Miles, M. B., & Huberman, A. M. (1984). *Qualitative data analysis: A sourcebook of new methods.* Beverly Hills, CA: Sage.

Milgram, S. (1963). Behavioral study of obedience. *Journal of Abnormal and Social Psychology, 67,* 371–378.

Moore, D. (2000). The changing face of the infosphere. *Internet Computing, 4*(1). [Online]. Available: http://www.computer.org/internet/v4n1/moore.htm.

Morkes J., and Nielsen, J. (1998). Applying writing guidelines to webpages. [Online]. Available: http://www.useit.com/papers/webwriting/rewriting.html.

Nelson, T. H. (1967). Getting it out of our system. In G. Schechter (Ed.), *Information retrieval: A critical review* (pp. 191–210). Washington, DC: Thompson.

Neuman, W. L. (2000). *Social research methods. Qualitative and quantitative approaches* (4th ed.). Toronto, ON: Allyn & Bacon.

Patton, M. Q. (1981). *Practical evaluation.* Newbury Park, CA: Sage.

Patton, M. Q. (1987). *How to use qualitative methods in evaluation.* London: Sage.

Patton, M. Q. (1988). Paradigms and pragmatism. In D. M. Fetterman (Ed.), *Qualitative approaches to evaluation in education* (pp. 89–115). New York: Praeger.

Patton, M. Q. (1990). *Qualitative evaluation and research methods* (2nd ed.). London: Sage.

Perseus Development Corporation. (2000). [Online]. Available: http://www.perseus.com/surveytips/Survey_101.htm.

Potter, W., & Levine-Donnerstein, D. (1999). Rethinking validity and reliability in content analysis. *Journal of Applied Communication Research, 27*(3), 258–284.

Readings, B. (1994). Caught in the Net: Notes from the electronic underground. *Surfaces, 4*(104). [Online]. Available: http://www.pum.umontreal.ca/revues/surfaces/vol4/readings.html.

Reber, A. (1995). *Dictionary of psychology.* Toronto: Penguin.

Roberts, P. (2000a). Ethical dilemmas in researching online communities: "Bottom-up" ethical wisdom for computer-mediated social research. [Online]. Available: http://www.com.unisa.edu.au/cccc/papers/refereed/paper40/Paper40-1.htm.

Roberts, P. (2000b). Protecting the participant in the contested private/public terrain of Internet research: Can computer ethics make a difference? [Online]. Available: http://www.aice.swin.edu.au/events/AICE2000/papers/rob.pdf.

Rourke, L., Anderson, T., Garrison, R., & Archer, W. (2000). Methodological issues in the content analysis of computer conference transcripts. *International Journal of Artificial Intelligence in Education, 11*(3). [Online]. Available: http://www.atl.ualberta.ca/CMC/publications.html.

Schrum, L. (1995). Framing the debate: Ethical research in the information age. *Qualitative Inquiry, 1*(3), 311–326.

Schwandt, T. (1989). Solutions to the paradigm conflict: Coping with uncertainty. *Journal of Contemporary Ethnography, 17*(4), 379–407.

Sharf, B. (1999). Beyond Netiquette: The ethics of doing naturalistic discourse research on the Internet. In S. Jones (Ed.), *Doing Internet research* (pp. 243–256). Thousand Oaks, CA: Sage.

Shearin Jr., E. T. (1995). *Development of a definition and competencies for network literacy: A Delphi study.* Unpublished doctoral dissertation. Raleigh, NC: North Carolina State University.

Sheehan, K., & Hoy, M. (1999). Using E-mail to survey Internet users in the United States: Methodology and assessment. *Journal of Computer Mediated Communication, 4*(3). [Online]. Available: http://www.ascusc.org/jcmc/vol4/issue3/sheehan.html.

Silverman, G. (2000). How to get beneath the surface in focus groups. *Market Navigation, Inc.* [Online]. Available: http://www.mnav.com/bensurf.htm.

Silverman, G., & Zukergood, E. (2000). Everything in moderation. *Market Navigation, Inc.* [Online]. Available: http://www.mnav.com/evmod.htm.

Smith, A. (1997). Testing the surf: Criteria for evaluating Internet information resources. *Public-Access Computer Systems, 8*(3). [Online]. Available: http://info.lib.uh.edu/pr/v8/smit8n3.html.

Snyder, S. U. (1992). Interviewing college students about their constructions of love. In J. F. Gilgun, K. Daly, & G. Handel (Eds.), *Qualitative methods in family research* (pp. 43–65). Newbury Park, CA: Sage.

Spink, A., & Xu, J. (2000). Selected results from a large study of Web searching: The Excite study. *Information Research, 6*(1). [Online]. Available: http://informationr.net/ir/6-1/paper90.html.

Stefik, M. (1996). *Internet dreams: Archetypes, myths, and metaphors.* Cambridge, MA: MIT Press.

Sterling, B. (1993, February). A short history of the Internet. *The Magazine of Fantasy and Science Fiction.* [Online]. Available: http://w3.aces.uiuc.edu/AIM/scale/nethistory.html.

Stewart, D. W., & Shamdasani, P. N. (1998). Focus group research: Exploration and discovery. In L. Bickman & D. J. Rog (Eds.), *Handbook of applied social research methods* (pp. 505–526). London: Sage.

Stone Fish, L. S., & Busby, D. M. (1996). The Delphi method. In D. H. Sprenkle and S. M. Spoon (Eds.), *Research methods in family therapy.* New York: Guilford Press.

Strauss, A. L., & Corbin, J. (1990b). *Basics of qualitative research: Grounded theory procedures and techniques.* Newbury Park, CA: Sage.

Sudweeks, F., & Rafaeli, S. (1996). How do you get a hundred strangers to agree: Computer mediated communication and collaboration. In T. M. Harrison, & T. D. Stephen (Eds.), *Computer networking and scholarship in the 21st century university* (pp. 115–136). Albany, NY: SUNY Press.

Surman, M., & Wershler-Henry, D. (2001). *Commonspace: Beyond virtual community.* Toronto: FT.com. [Online]. Available: http://www.ft.com/home/ww/.

Sweeney, A. (2000). Tenure and promotion: Should you publish in electronic journals? *Journal of Electronic Publishing, 6*(2). [Online]. Available: http://www.press.umich.edu/jep/06-02/sweeney.html.

Thibault, J. W., & Kelly, H. (1959). *The social psychology of groups.* New York: Wiley.

Thomas, J. (1996). When cyberresearch goes awry: The ethics of the Rimm 'Cyberporn' study. *The Information Society, 12*(2). [Online]. Available: http://venus.soci.niu.edu/~jthomas/ethics/tis/go.jt.

Thomas, J. (1999). Balancing the ethical antinomies of Net research. *Iowa Journal of Communication, 31*(2), 8–20. [Online]. Available: http://venus.soci.niu.edu/~jthomas/ethics/iowa.html.

Tillman, H. N. (1998). *Evaluating quality on the net.* [Online]. Available: http://www.tiac.net/users/hoe/findqual.html.

Turkle, S. (1995). *Life on the screen. Identity in the age of the Internet*. New York: Touchstone.

Two Crows Corporation (1999). Data mining glossary. [Online]. Available: http://www.twocrows.com/glossary.htm.

Underwired. (1997). History of the Internet. [Online]. Available: http://www.underwired.com/report/uw.css.

U.S. Department of Commerce (1998). The emerging digital economy. [Online]. Available: http://www.ecommerce.gov.

Van Nuys, D. (1999, November). Online focus groups save time, money. *Silicon Valley / San Jose Business Journal*. [Online]. Available: http://sanjose.bcentral.com/sanjose/stories/1999/11/29/smallb4.html.

Vehovar, V., & Batagelgj, B. (1996). The methodological issues in WWW surveys. In CASIC 96 (Ed.), *CASIC*. [Online]. Available: http: www.ris.org/casic96/.

Vierra, A., Pollock, J., & Golez, F. (1998). *Reaching educational research* (3rd ed.). Upper Saddle River, NJ: Prentice Hall.

Vygotsky, L. (1978). *Mind in society: The development of higher psychological processes*. Cambridge, MA: Harvard University Press.

Waskul, D., & Douglass, M. (1996). Considering the electronic participant: Some polemical observations on the ethics of on-line research. *The Information Society*, *12*(2), 129–139.

Weber, S. J. (1986). The nature of interviewing. *Phenomenology and Pedagogy*, *4*(2), 65–72.

Werner, O., & Schoepfle, G. (1987). *Systematic fieldwork: Vol. 1, Foundations of ethnography and interviewing, 1*. Newbury Park, CA: Sage.

Wilkenson, S. (2000). Electronic journals gain ground. *Chemical & Engineering News*, *78*(33), 33–38. [Online]. Available: http://pubs.acs.org/hotartcl/cenear/000821/7833scit1a.html.

Witmer, D. F. (1998). Practicing safe computing: Why people engage in risky computer-mediated communication. In F. Sudweeks, S. Rafaeli, & M. McLaughlin (Eds.), *Network and Netplay: Virtual Groups on the Internet* (pp. 127–146). Menlo Park, CA: AAAI/MIT Press. [Online]. Available: http://commfaculty.fullerton.edu/dwitmer/vita.html.

Yu, L., & Schmid, B. (1999). Managing Internet peer review process in a multi-agent framework. [Online]. Available: http://www.knowledgemedia.org/netacademy/publications.nsf/all_pk/1321.

Yun, G., & Trumbo, C. (2000). Comparative response to a survey executed by post, e-mail and web form. *Journal of Computer Mediated Communications*, *6*(1). [Online]. Available: http://www.ascusc.org/jcmc/vol6/issue1/yun.html.

Zaiane, O. (2001). Web site mining for better web-based learning environments. In T. Calvert & T. Keenan (Eds.), *Computers and advanced technology in education* (pp. 60–64). Calgary, AB: ACTA Press.

INDEX